THE AUTHOR

Edward Frederic Benson was born at Wellington College, Berkshire in 1867. He was one of an extraordinary family. His father Edward White Benson – first headmaster of Wellington – later became Chancellor of Lincoln Cathedral, Bishop of Truro, and Archbishop of Canterbury. His mother, Mary Sidgwick, was described by Gladstone as 'the cleverest woman in Europe'. Two children died young but the other four, bachelors all, achieved distinction: Arthur Christopher as Master of Magdalene College, Cambridge and a prolific author; Maggie as an amateur egyptologist; Robert Hugh as a Catholic priest and propagandist novelist; and Fred.

Like his brothers and sisters, Fred was a precocious scribbler. He was still a student at Cambridge when he published his first book, *Sketches from Marlborough*. His first novel *Dodo* was published in 1893 to great success. Thereafter Benson devoted himself to writing, playing sports, watching birds, and gadding about. He mixed with the best and brightest of his day: Margot Asquith, Marie Corelli, his mother's friend Ethel Smyth and many other notables found their eccentricities exposed in the shrewd, hilarious world of his fiction.

Around 1918, E.F. Benson moved to Rye, Sussex. He was inaugurated mayor of the town in 1934. There in his garden room, the collie Taffy beside him, Benson wrote many of his comical novels, his sentimental fiction, ghost stories, informal biographies, and reminiscences like *As We Were* (1930) – almost one hundred books in all. Ten days before his death on 29 February 1940, E.F. Benson delivered to his publisher a last autobiography, *Final Edition*.

The Hogarth Press also publishes *Mrs Ames, Paying Guests, Secret Lives* and *As We Were*.

AS WE ARE

A Modern Revue

E.F. Benson

New Introduction by
T.J. Binyon

THE HOGARTH PRESS
LONDON

Published in 1985 by
The Hogarth Press
40 William IV Street, London WC2N 4DF

First published in Great Britain by Longmans, Green & Co 1932
Hogarth edition offset from original British edition
Copyright the Executors of the Estate of the Revd K.S.P. McDowall
Introduction copyright © T.J. Binyon 1985

Second impression 1986
Third impression 1989

British Library Cataloguing in Publication Data

Benson, E.F.
As we are: a modern revue.
I. Title
823'.8[F]   PR6003.E66

ISBN 0 7012 0587 3

Printed in Great Britain by
Cox & Wyman Ltd
Reading, Berkshire

INTRODUCTION

In 1932, when he published *As We Are*, E.F. Benson was living in Lamb House, Rye; sixty-five and crippled with arthritis in both hips, Fred was the last survivor, lonely and embittered, of the six brilliant Benson children: the last of the line as well, for not one of the six had married, not one had left a descendant. The Benson family had formed a close, almost claustrophobically closed unit. Caught between two overpowering personalities – an extraordinarily energetic, authoritarian and awe-inspiring father, whose harsh faith was buttressed by strict religious observance, and an equally energetic mother with a creed based on emotional mysticism, whose maternal love was all-pervading, even at times intrusive – the children were forced into variations on the same basic psychological pattern. 'I suppose we all have a touch of something morbid and not quite controlled . . . which Papa had, but coupled in him with great physical strength. There is a touch of diseased self-consciousness about us all, I think,' wrote Arthur, one of the sons. Yet their childhood, as numerous memoirs and reminiscences make clear, remained always a golden age in their memory.

Of all the children, Fred escaped most lightly. The enormous success of his first novel, *Dodo* (1893), gave him independence. He led an immensely active social life, spent much of the year abroad – in Greece, on the Riviera, on Capri – at the same times producing books – novels, biographies, memoirs and others – with amazing rapidity.

Their father, Edward White Benson, the Archbishop of Canterbury, died in 1896 while kneeling next to Mrs Gladstone in Hawarden church. His widow, Minnie, moved to Winchester together with her daughter Maggie and Lucy Tait, from whom she had been inseparable for several years. 'My mother's intimacies and emotional friendships had always been with women . . . and this long love between her and Lucy was the greatest of all these attachments; it is impossible to think of them apart,' Fred wrote. A little later they moved again: to Tremans, a house in the country near Horsted Keynes in Sussex, which became the centre of the family until Minnie's death in 1918.

She had six children. Martin, the eldest, died of meningitis while still at school, six months before his eighteenth birthday. Intellectually he had promised much. His death hit his father hard; among the Archbishop's papers was discovered a poem to Martin's memory:

> The Martins are back to cornice and eaves
>   Fresh from the glassy sea.
> The Martin of Martins my soul bereaves
>   Flying no more to me . . .

Poor poetry perhaps, but the pathos is unmistakable and genuine.

Nellie, the eldest girl, was, after Fred, least touched by the Benson 'diseased self-conciousness'. She had 'annexed every distinction that could be annexed at the Truro High School', did very well at Lady Margaret Hall, became an extremely close friend of Ethel Smyth, the composer and feminist, and died of diphtheria in 1890, at the age of twenty-seven.

The youngest of the family, Hugh – he was born in 1871 – followed his father into the Church, but then converted to Roman Catholicism and was ordained as a priest in 1903: when he took great delight in setting up – having obtained a licence from the Pope – a private oratory in the attic at Tremans. His sermons were famous, and he also dashed off a number of propagandist novels, such as *Come Rack! Come Rope!*, devoted to the Roman cause. He died in October 1914 while on a preaching mission in Salford.

The second daughter, Maggie, followed her sister to Truro High School and Lady Margaret Hall, where she took a First in philosophy. Two years older than Fred, she was the closest to him in the family. Together they collaborated on a story which Fred later turned into his first novel, *Dodo*. She wrote too: children's stories and treatises in a philosophical-religious vein. Maggie was perhaps the only one of the family (except for her father) to be attracted to the opposite sex. She went, it seems, through some kind of emotional crisis in the early 1890s over one of the Archbishop's chaplains; this might have prompted her to write a very odd letter to her mother asking – inasmuch as it's possible to interpret her embarrassed circum-locutions – for a tactful hint or two about some of the basic facts of life. Since she had to spend two winters in Egypt for reasons of health, she took up archaeology and excavated a temple at Karnak. But the morbid, black depression of the Bensons was stronger in her than in any of the others. Without any real occupation she was restless and bored at Tremans, and jealous too of Lucy's relationship with her mother (now no longer called Minnie, but Ben, Lucy's pet name for her). One evening in the spring of 1907 she suddenly became homicidally violent, though whom she attacked, or with what, is unknown. She spent the rest of her life in a home for the insane, visited with religious regularity by Fred until her death in 1916.

Arthur, the second son, had become a popular and success-ful housemaster at Eton. But then he accepted an offer to edit Queen Victoria's letters, moved to Cambridge, became a fellow of Magdalene and was elected Master in 1915. He wrote even faster and with even more fluency than Fred, producing a life of Hugh in ten weeks after his brother's death, and leaving a four-million-word diary, together with the manuscripts of four unpublished novels and a host of short stories. His uplifting, reflective volumes, with titles such as *The Thread of Gold* (1905) or *Thy Rod and Staff* (1915), which combined essay, homily and narrative to draw an optimistic strand from the tangled web of life, were immensely popular. Indeed, one devout reader, a Swiss lady of American birth, was so impress-ed as to shower, through Arthur, a series of rich benefactions on Magdalene. He shared all the Benson psychological traits. Of him Fred wrote: 'He had many intimate friends, but with the exception of his mother, they were all of his own sex, and he never wanted any other companionship. He distrusted women'; and Arthur himself noted: 'My own failing is that I have never been in vital touch with anyone – never either fought anyone or kissed anyone!' His attacks of depression were almost as severe as Maggie's; he went through two especially bleak periods, spending much of the time in a nursing home, before his death in 1925, at the age of sixty-three.

After his mother's death Fred had had to sort and dispose of the vast collection of family papers and possessions at Tremans. Now he had to deal with the almost vaster accumulation which Arthur had piled up round himself in the lodgings at Magdalene – including 'a packet of letters of very dangerous stuff, and one to be burnt unopened'. When this had been done, the last link with the family was broken. About the same time another fragment of the past vanished. Before the war Fred had been accustomed to spend two or three months each summer on Capri, living with John Ellingham Brooks, a man of 'handsome but sinister' appearance, whose life was devoted to one object: the production of a perfect English translation of Hérédia's sonnets. He returned several times after the war, but the relationship gradually deteriorated, and Brooks died early in the 1920s.

There were, too, causes for melancholy in his own life. Arthritis kept him more and more confined to Rye, and though life there was fascinating (as the Mapp and Lucia books demonstrate), it didn't have the social glitter to which he'd been accustomed and which he had loved. He could no longer stroll – admittedly by mistake – into a party, find it composed solely of royalty, and yet be acquainted with all of those present. And he had just taken stock of his achievement as a novelist. 'I observed with a certain acuteness, but not with insight,' he writes. 'I made my people bustle about, indulge in what might be called "stock" experiences, talk with a rather brilliant plausibility, but, as a depressed perusal of some of my own volumes convinced me, they lacked the red corpuscle.' Finally, he found many aspects of the post-war age deeply displeasing: he disliked modern values, modern manners and modern art. It was from a combination of these feelings that *As We Are* was born.

He had expressed some of his views on the contemporary scene earlier. In *Mother* (1925) he describes pre-war society as having 'a stateliness, a breeding, a certain code of manners . . . Women did not dine at restaurants, and waggle their hands to friends at neighbouring tables, and wonder who was she with pearls by the window, and send a note to an acquaintance to find out . . . and most emphatically they did not, for value received, launch the unknown rich, crockery-kings, and silver-kings and railway-kings, in Society.' In *As We Were* (1930), the first half of a diptych concluded by *As We Are*, the contrast is repeated:

Autumns in London, lip-sticking in public, winters on the Riviera, the kippering of her arms and legs, bosom and back on the sands of the Lido, and inability to remain in one place for more than a week, were not habits of the great lady. Above all, she was possessed of that queer old quality called dignity . . . she did not permit, still less encourage, the public press to regale its readers with chatty paragraphs about the decoration of her 'boudoir', the tiles in her bathroom and the diet of her dogs, nor did she order her dressmaker to show the author of the column signed 'Jezebel' or 'Hermione' the dresses she intended to wear at Ascot.

And in *Travail of Gold* (1933), one of the few late novels, he paints a wonderfully horrific picture of the smart set on the Riviera: a collection of shady company promoters, society climbers, *rastaquouère* financiers, indigent and untalented artists, show-girls and foreign noblemen whose pedigree is not to be found in the *Almanach de Gotha*.

As We Are goes further: it is not just descriptive, but analytic. The fictional history of the decline of the Buryan family counterpoints and echoes the author's explanation of the social changes that have taken place. As social history, however, there are some oddities about it. The four personalities who are taken as subjects for pen portraits – Fred's forte, and here he excels himself – all really belong to the pre-war era. Only Archbishop Davidson, who resigned as Primate in 1928, is a contemporary figure. Parenthetically, it might be noted that there was almost a family relationship between Davidson and the Bensons, in that he had married Edith Tait, Lucy's elder sister. It seems perverse of the author not to mention the General Strike. He does not shine as an economic analyst: his account of the financial consequences of the war is simplistic and naive. He is wrong in maintaining that women kept jobs in preference to demobilized men: in 1921 the proportion of women in paid employment was smaller than before the war. And Lord Buryan probably shouldn't have been too distressed when a Labour candidate got in for the local constituency in 1924 (Fred must actually be referring to the election of 6 December 1923, which resulted in the formation by Ramsay MacDonald of Britain's first Labour government in January 1924): he probably lost his seat at the next election ten months later when the Conservatives regained power.

It could be said that the author is too close to the era to see it clearly; that, in addition, he does not pretend to be an accurate historian; his aim, as it was in *As We Were*, is to create rather the mood and the atmosphere of the period. Certainly the two books resemble each other very closely in method. In each the history of a family – the Bensons in *As We Were*, the Buryans in *As We Are* – fleshes out the history of the epoch. But the superficial similarities conceal an essential difference. *As We Were* refracts an age through the personality of the author, Fred Benson. In *As We Are* the opposite is true – the personality of the author is refracted through the history of an age. *As We Were* is about Victorian England; *As We Are* is about Fred Benson. Whereas in the earlier book he appears everywhere in the narrative, in the second he emerges only in the episode that is its emotional core: the dinner given to the three young ex-officers – two crippled, one unhappily married – which culminates in the riotous mock made of Laurence Binyon's 'For the Fallen', and ends with the remark of another ex-officer: 'Sometimes I wonder whether any of us are quite sane.'

Did Fred feel a nagging residue of guilt at not having taken part in the war? In *Up and Down* (1918), a novel told in the first person with obvious autobiographical elements, he contrasts his own easy civilian life with that of his friend – with whom he has been sharing a villa on Capri – who enlists in the ranks, is awarded a V.C., and finally dies of cancer. Fred was forty-seven in 1914, too old to enlist, but too young to be a member of the generation held responsible for the war. It is not at all clear, in fact, how he spent the war years. He seems to have written reports on Turkey and Poland for the Foreign Office. But the work cannot have been arduous, for he was able to go to Capri to finish one report.

As We Are ends with Fred expressing some muted hope for the future as a result of the formation of the National government – a coalition of Labour, Conservative and Liberal parties – in August 1931. But his hopes were not really for the future but for the past. He wanted not a National, but a national government, one which would heal the rifts in society and lead the country back to the illusory unity of pre-war England; and subconsciously he hoped that it would heal the rift in his own life, that he would be able to rediscover the idyllic family unity he had known in Wellington, in Lincoln and in Truro.

T.J. Binyon, Oxford 1985

AS WE ARE

CHAPTER I

THE PARABLE HOUSE

ACROSS the chasm which, in 1914, split time in two, making for the space of a generation at least a new era, A. B. or Anno Belli, from which to date our chronicles, little glimpses of a world, very distinct, but immensely remote, as if seen through the wrong end of a telescope, occasionally flit across the field of memory. It is not only the sundering years of the War which make them so distant, but chiefly the accomplished transition from the days when so much was taken for granted as being part of a secure and immutable order to the days when nothing seems secure, and when only the most reckless gambler would take the longest odds that he would live to see the discovery of a working hypothesis on which a return of national prosperity could be framed. Ever higher in the waste-paper basket for useless formulæ grows the debris of scrapped suggestions, and more frequent the collapse of Utopian palaces which idealists aspired to build in a world which the War, so they declared, had delivered from the possibility of its recurrence.

These glimpses are often evoked by the sight of some object once familiar, but long lost sight of: many middle-aged people, for instance, dreamed dreams and saw visions when in the recent rage to take advantage of the price of gold they discovered a sovereign or two in a derelict purse.   My case was similar: last autumn I happened to visit a friend who occupied a flat scooped out in one of those vast cliffs of dwellings which have reared themselves on the sites of impoverished great houses in London, and which are themselves so striking a monument of Anno Belli.   This flat had been lately decorated, and the walls of the drawing-room were covered in faded Spanish silk, still magnificent.   On one there was a square of more vivid colour as if a picture had once hung there.   That set some luggage-train of associations shunting about in my mind: I knew that I had seen just such Spanish silk before and that pictures then hung on it.   Then suddenly the scattered trucks linked up, and I asked whether it had not come from a sale, four years ago, at Hakluyt Park.   It was so, and now the recollections poured in thick and fast.   Rummaging among them I found that with a little selection and arrangement I could extract from them just such a sort of continuous living picture as I had long been trying to put together, in order to illustrate by contrast some of the changes which the War had brought about.   These sections of my book are told, in the hope of capturing a certain vividness, which disquisitions lack, in the form of a fictional narrative.   The discerning reader will possibly think he detects realities underlying it, and he may conceivably be right in his conjectures.

THE express had been stopped by signal on Saturday afternoon at a small wayside station on whose lamp-globes was painted the information that this was Hak-luyt, and all down the train indignant heads were thrust out of windows to ascertain the cause of this unusual halt. Already some forty folk had got out, and from the van came forth a swift vomit of copious portman-teaux and dress-baskets. Nearly half of this company, clean-shaven valets and cloak-laden ladies'-maids looked after these: the rest greeted each other and strolled away with hat-raisings and hand-shakes, talking together, to the exit from the station. A detachment of motor-cars waiting outside gobbled them up, and there were left behind a couple of omnibuses and a luggage cart for their properties.

The village stretched along some half-mile of high-road fringed by a broad riband of grass. On each side were neat two-storied cottages mostly built in pairs. Some were of brick, some of rough-cast, and over their doors was inserted a limestone slab, bearing an Earl's coronet carved thereon above the initial "B." Each had its garden in front of it, gay with the flowers of early summer; there were borders of forget-me-not, clumps of wallflowers, beds of violas, and up the cottage-walls climbed honeysuckle and budding roses. Each of these plots had its brightly painted fence and its tiled path. Beyond the village lay open country: cows cropped the rich pasturage of meadows through which flowed a clear chalk-stream fringed with loose-strife and meadow-sweet, and higher up on the slopes of the valley were fields of arable land on which the young corn was green.

Then came the lodge-gates of the Park: the lodge-keeper's wife, young and buxom, stood by them, and she curtsied as each motor passed through. Fresh-foliaged woods of milky-green beech and of oak still in tawny leaf bordered the road on either side: here in an open glade was a wired enclosure dotted with hen-coops for the rearing of pheasants, then came broad expanses of short-turfed grass where the fallow-deer were beginning to feed again in the cool hour and rabbits scuttled back into cover as the motors approached. Soon on the right rose the long red walls of the kitchen-garden topped by the glittering roofs of hot-houses within: stable-buildings built round a big square succeeded, and presently a small church of Early English architecture. Beyond that was an acre of velvet-napped lawn and, skirting round this, the road swept up to the front of a great red-brick house with the flag flying from the staff on the turret above the door.

The arrivals were taken through the marble-paved and panelled hall into the long gallery-shaped room on the garden side of the house. Here on the walls was an odd variety of pictures. There was a fine Bellini, a Botticelli and a Titian: these were the acquisitions of the first Earl of Buryan when, in the middle of the eighteenth century he made the Grand Tour: the Spanish silk on which they were hung was put up by his son.   His grandson was responsible for a couple of Landseers, and the signed engraving of Queen Victoria in deepest weeds gazing at a bust of the Prince Consort, and his great-grandson for a Leighton, a Rossetti, and a huge Edwin Long.   Another taste was manifest in the immense Aubusson carpet, another in the two Adam mantelpieces, and yet another in some monstrous pieces of heavy early Victorian furniture, which contrasted strangely with a set of French chairs and settee covered with *petit-point* needlework. Morris curtains draped the six windows.

It was precisely these violent incongruities that gave the room its authenticity as a document.   Each stratum of taste had been deposited there as by a natural and geological process.   No impatient iconoclast, however enlightened, had quarried away or sold a previous deposit: each owner had added to the room, now much overcrowded, some furnishing or decoration which was currently esteemed to be the best of its day.   Thus it was that an inherent underlying fitness rather than the violent superficial incongruities struck any fairly intelligent beholder.   The room was the creation of its successive owners; a long established home was evident in it, and though it bore the impression of incongruous, and sometimes terrible tastes, a historical and collective individuality had ordained it.

No doubt, had other Italian pictures been brought in

from other rooms in the house, had the dozen tall bro-
caded Venetian chairs been collected from the dining-
room, and the long Italian table and painted cassone from
the hall, this room might have been made into a period
room. The smaller drawing-room next door would
have given up a great gilded and carved mirror and, receiving in exchange the Aubusson carpet and the French
furniture, have become a period room also. The Victorian mahogany and rose-wood tables, the Landseers and
the Leighton could have joined their contemporaries in
the library and formed a very harmonious and appalling
whole. But though, æsthetically, much might have thus
been gained, much would also have been lost, for this
magnificent muddle, as a document, would have been
tampered with. Better as it was.

THE house had a tradition of stateliness which, even in
the years just before the War, many of the guests, who
were invited there in the summer for week-end parties
and in the autumn and winter for the shooting, found
somewhat oppressive. But both Lord Buryan and his
wife were of the stately and traditional school, and they
had no intention of changing their ways: it was open to
those who did not like their ways to refuse any further
invitation. And there was something compelling and
massive about the place, the authority of it was on their
guests, not a rigid handcuffing as of steel shackles, but a
firm and kindly and automatic pressure that was just as

binding. These parties were not confined to elderly persons: the friends of Lady Buryan's two married daughters and her only son were welcome there; so, too, were prominent folk, writers, artists or politicians, for Lady Buryan acknowledged the claims of distinction as well as those of birth, and though rooted in the past liked to feel that she kept abreast of the movements of the world. Granted that a man's or a woman's life was, as far as she knew, absolutely respectable, she would ask anyone in whose achievements she felt she should be interested. But she never asked a husband without his wife, nor a wife without her husband, and for such there were double beds in the bedrooms as well as a supplementary couch in the dressing-room. She addressed her husband as "Buryan," and spoke of him thus to her friends.

On Sunday morning attendance at church was taken for granted. Guests were not told to go to church any more than they were told to dress for dinner. There had been sporadic rebels, but never a concerted movement. On one occasion a misunderstanding arose. A friend of mine, one of those people common now, but then thought cranky, was not accustomed to eat any breakfast, for he thought it digestively advantageous to remain rather hungry all morning and then indulge without restraint at lunch. He endorsed this un-English conduct by not going to church: it was his first visit to Hakluyt, and his ignorance was pardonable. Coming in ravenous to lunch, he found that his place was next

Lady Buryan, who had observed his abstinence at breakfast and his absence at church. The footman left him
out in taking round the first dish, and he was about to
ask his hostess if he might partake of that appetizing
lobster-soufflé, when an elegant little bowl of soup, with
thin slices of toast was put in front of him. She whispered to him "Some chicken broth: I'm sure that can't
hurt you" . . . I am convinced there was nothing
ironical about this little attention: Lady Buryan had
acted from the most kindly and considerate motives, and
she never could have contemplated "scoring off" a guest.
Simply she had put on his odd conduct the only explanation of which it seemed capable.

But she could discourage with magnificent urbanity,
when she disapproved. Well I remember how the wife
of a distinguished diplomat, youthful but no longer
young, offered (and proceeded) to dance a *pas seul* after
dinner to the strains of a gramophone. Lady Buryan
felt it would not be polite to her guest to refuse this unusual treat; so two powdered footmen turned back the
Aubusson carpet and set chairs for the party, who, under
the spell of the place, obediently took their seats in a
circle round the arena. Then followed some very vigorous antics with high kickings and a bountiful display of
leg. At the conclusion of the first dance, Lady Buryan
led the orderly applause and was most complimentary.
"Such a pleasure !" she said. "You must rest after that.
How I enjoyed it !"

There was no more dancing.

To-night the party was, as usual, very notable, though no list of the guests would ever appear in the fashionable columns of the press. There were six married couples of the "class" to which their host and hostess belonged, people with broad lands and exalted titles, who in their hearts knew that God was the real head of the Tory party, though that did not prevent them from being most polite to the Secretary for Foreign Affairs in the Liberal Government then in office: there was the French Ambassador and the Danish Minister, there was the President of the Royal Academy, and the keeper of the Manuscript room at the British Museum, there was the Bishop of the Diocese (unmarried), there was the author of a recent "Life of Lord Palmerston," which lay, fully cut, on a table in the gallery, there were Members of Parliament and a Field Marshal whose passion was Oriental china, but to-day only a few younger folk, for neither of Lord Buryan's married daughters was present, and Henry, Lord St. Erth, his youngest child and only son, now in his third year at Cambridge, had preferred to stop there for the May-week festivities. All assembled in the gallery for dinner with strict punctuality, and the women wore their smartest gowns, their tiaras and their pearls. They went formally into the dining-room, men offering their arms to support the frail footsteps of their partners, and Lord Buryan asked the Bishop to say grace, for when there was a clergyman present, this was only proper. It took some of the party by surprise, but they hastily stood up again.

The light of the bouquets of candles that illuminated the table was not softer than the murmur of quiet voices that were never raised in excitement or loud mirth. Each man talked to the woman on his right whom he had taken in, for the space of soup and fish, and then, as if a change of wind had reversed the weather-cock of conversation, all heads hitherto turned to the right swung across to the left, and all heads turned to the left swung to the right: this smooth manœuvre took but a few moments. Lady Buryan, of course, had provided that on the other side of the French Ambassador there was a woman who spoke his language fluently, for His Excellency would use no other tongue, though he knew English perfectly, and all the new conversations were at once under way. Then again the wind veered, and all the original dialogues were resumed. Silver plates were used throughout dinner, and the table gleamed with ancient cups and tankards. The footmen all wore white gloves, lest they should make criminal finger-prints on the resplendent surfaces.

Then when the savoury, which concluded the meal, was finished, the Bishop was again invited to say grace: for dessert, for some recondite reason, was not accounted a matter for public thanksgiving even though, as on this occasion, it consisted of wondrous peaches and nectarines and of grapes, rivalling the spoils of Eshcol, from the acre of glass-houses along the walls of the kitchen-garden. Then Lady Buryan caught the Ambassadress's eye, the ladies withdrew to take their coffee apart, and

Lord Buryan moved round to his wife's place next the Ambassador. He could not talk French at all, and so spoke loudly and distinctly to His Excellency in English, as if to a drowsy or defective person. When a port of noble vintage had gone round twice, he rang for coffee: with coffee cigarettes were at last permissible.

Further down the table the Liberal Secretary for Foreign Affairs was engaged in a political discussion with two members of the opposition. They were polite but worrying, and he raised his voice to reply to one of them. At that precise moment a hush, not uncommon at Hakluyt, fell on other conversations, and his words were universally audible.

"I can't share your sense of security," he said. "I don't see any reason at all why a European war is impossible. As for the other matter, I hold it to be equally possible that we may all live to see a Labour Government in power at Westminster."

Never before had such sentiments been expressed in this Sanctuary of Toryism, and in the awkward silence that succeeded them Lord Buryan rose. It was time, in any case, to join the ladies, which was lucky.

THERE was a card-table ready in the library, said Lady Buryan, if anyone would care for a game of Bridge. A four was made up, and they agreed to play this newer variety of the game called Auction. The Ambassador was enchanted to hear there was a billiard-table: he much enjoyed a game of billiards, but he returned immediately, appalled at the boundless sward of the English table with those holes at the corners, and a small focus of the best French conversationalists was arranged for him.   The author of the "Life of Palmerston" talked to an appreciative circle: the President of the Royal Academy congratulated Lord Buryan on his ownership of that marvellous Leighton and the equally beautiful Landseers.   This modern slovenly stuff, he assured him, this French impressionism, was but a fashionable fad of the moment: it would soon be obsolete, and artists would return to the fine drawing, the fine colouring and above all, to that careful finish which distinguished the art of an earlier day.   Lord Buryan quite agreed, and he particularly admired the President's picture "Tea under the Cedar" which he considered the gem of the present exhibition at Burlington House.   The Bishop, in another group, spoke of the increasing influence which the Church of England was establishing over the minds and souls of the people.   Urban dwellers after six days in stuffy offices were quite right in wanting to spend Sunday mostly out of doors, but now bicyclists flocked to church-services, and parsons should certainly allow them to put their machines in the vestry or the belfry. Lady Buryan asked him what he thought about the sad antagonism between Science and revealed Religion, but he felt quite comfortable about that.   Earnest thinkers, and there were many of them, were beginning to see that Science was the handmaid of Religion: both, though from opposite directions, drew nearer to the one divine event: God fulfilled Himself, as Tennyson so aptly said, in many ways. Another group discussed the plays of Mr. G. B. Shaw which they were unanimous in finding most amusing. You could not take him seriously, of course, he was just a naughty but entertaining child who made fun of such stereotyped ideas as mothers being tenderly devoted to their daughters, whereas they were foul-minded old women who hated them. Similarly with girls: they were not, said Mr. Shaw, coy, virginal fairies, who were ardently wooed by chivalrous young men, but hypocrites and liars as able to take good care of themselves as ironclads and, under the urge of the life-force, relentlessly pursuing like weasels their squealing and paralysed victims. So droll ! But it was misunderstanding him altogether to consider him a thinker, he was only pulling our legs, and sometimes his own; as for his socialistic notions, which some people thought dangerous, he was a rich man, and a rich socialist was as harmless as a dove. . . All these interesting talks had for their leader a man; the women conscious of their own inferiority in intellectual grasp, sat and were strengthened.

Presently the groups coalesced, and the inevitable topic of female suffrage came up. All decent women, like those assembled here, deplored the outrages that were being committed: quite lately the portrait of Henry James in the Academy had been slashed by these hooligan enthusiasts. Then there had been that horrid incident outside the Houses of Parliament: the misguided creatures had tried to force their way into the sacred precincts in order to present a petition to the Speaker. A gloomy look-out for the country if the wives and mothers of England were to behave like that. There was pensiveness in the group discussing this melancholy incident, and the Secretary for Foreign Affairs tried to disperse it.

"There was an amusing story about that," he said, "which gives a lighter side to it. As you remember, the police had to intervene, and the ringleaders were arrested and charged with disorderly conduct at the Westminster Police-station. Among them was a particularly strapping and active young woman, who dodged in and out of the crowd, and eventually a handsome young Hercules of a constable picked her up and carried her. When he dumped her down in the police-station, she said: 'Well, I 'ave 'ad a noice ride !' and he replied: 'Come again soon, ducky !' "

There was laughter, but the after-taste was not quite agreeable. It was amusing, no doubt, but the whole subject, thought Lady Buryan, was not one for jests, and there was just a shade of coarseness about it: it implied a loose familiarity between the sexes, and she did not like having to translate the Cockneyism for the benefit of the French Ambassador. But there was no real harm in it, though perhaps it was more suited for the smoking-room. She remembered, however, that Mr.

Harman was a Liberal, and of very humble origin: his father, she had been told, was a baker in Northampton. All the more credit to him then, that he had made his way to the post he now occupied.

No smoking had taken place during the hour of these talks: that was one of the austerities of this luxurious abode. Lady Buryan would have acknowledged that she was a little old-fashioned there, for she did not like to see women smoking in mixed assemblies, it struck her as unfeminine: as for the men they had already had their indulgence in the dining-room, and would have more, if they chose, later. But it was now close on eleven o'clock, and she was sure the ladies would be wanting to go to their rooms. Breakfast, she said, as good-nights were exchanged, would be at nine, if no-one minded so early an hour, so as to enable the servants to get to church at eleven. She did not go upstairs herself, for she waited till the Ambassadress had finished her Bridge. Most of the men changed their evening coats for smoking jackets, though one or two did not bother to do this, but went as they were into the smoking-room, where presently the others joined them, wearing their braided and frogged habiliments. Lord Buryan made a more complete change and appeared in a suit of ruby-coloured velvet.

THE whole party appeared at breakfast. This was a very informal meal, for only a couple of footmen were in waiting, and nobody said grace. Men stood about eating porridge, and then inspected the dishes on the side-board.   There were dishes of kedgeree, poached eggs and bacon, mushrooms from a forcing house, grilled chicken and cold ham and tongue.   They then sat down where they pleased to consume their selections: no fixed places.   Lord Buryan did not approve of Sunday papers, so there were no fresh topics, but plans for the day were outlined.   For the morning, of course, there was church, but for the afternoon there were many secular diversions.   Some might like to play golf on the nine-hole course in the Park, some might like to see the farm, where the famous herd of Jersey cows was milked by machinery, or the stud where Lord Buryan bred shire-horses, and Lady Buryan had promised her mother, now ninety-one years of age to take over for tea anyone who cared to accompany her.   If her guests would decide now, she would telephone to her mother how many to expect.   Her house was only twenty miles off, and was interesting, for it had a moat and George II had stayed there. . . Everybody — such was the spell of the place — felt obliged to select one of these diversions.   What would have happened if they hadn't ? Impossible to say: but such contingencies did not arise.

The morning was sunny, giving promise of a brilliant day, and as the church was only five minutes' walk distant, all the ladies, hospitably catechized in turn, said that they would prefer to walk and thus there would be no need for conveyances.   The French Ambassador and his wife, however, were Roman Catholics, and as the nearest church of their denomination was half-an-hour's drive away, their motor would be at the door a few minutes before half-past ten, for Lady Buryan had ascertained that Mass was at eleven. Neither of their Excellencies had really intended to go, but with diplomatic tact they said it was too kind, and went, for the spell was on them.

The orthodox church-party accordingly assembled in the hall at ten minutes to eleven, and as this numerous company rustled richly into church, all the village folk stood up. They disposed themselves round the sides of an immense square family pew furnished with red cushions; on a table in the centre was a library of Bibles, hymn-books and prayer-books. The latter were of early Victorian date and included petitions for the welfare of Queen Adelaide. Today this loose-box would not hold them all, and two additional pews were cleared for the overflow. Lady Buryan left them there to preside at the organ, on which she immediately began to play by heart "O Rest in the Lord" (*vox humana* solo) as a voluntary. Her husband read the lessons, the Bishop preached for forty minutes and gave the Blessing. The March of the Priests from Mendelssohn's "Athalie," made a joyful recessional for the clergy.

A stroll through the garden and the tropical heat of the green-houses filled up the hour before lunch, and afterwards the guests dispersed to their appointed diversions. The contingents were about equal: a third of them drove twenty miles to have tea with Lady Buryan's

mother, a third to see farm and stables with Lord Buryan, a third to play golf in the Park. The fairway of
this course was a riband of mown turf lying between
tussocky grass on either side: trees and tufts of gorse
formed the bunkers, and there were no caddies. A few
miles off only there was an admirable links, but though
Lord Buryan was broad-minded enough to see no harm
in playing golf on Sunday afternoon, he felt very
strongly about not making extra work that day, and this
golf-club was taboo, since it entailed so much employment.

The party that assembled for tea was jaded: eyelids
were a little weary and spirits were faint, for they had
seen so many cows milked, felt so many fetlocks, or
they had lost so many balls in the finely timbered Park.
It was interesting, of course, to know that those two
oaks which stood near the seventh green were considered by arboreal experts to be the finest specimens of
Cromwellian trees in England, but it did not really con-
sole those whose approach shots had tapped sharply
against the trunks of those magnificent vegetables, and
had been thence deflected into impenetrable brambles,
nor did the fact that the rabbit-warren, which must be
crossed on the way to the ninth hole, furnished such
wonderful ferreting, render less bitter the thought of
the golf-balls that had gone to earth there. Golfers
felt they would have done better to see the moat round
the house where George II had stayed. Again, when
Lord Buryan produced, for the further instruction of

those who had visited the stud-farm, the pedigree of that fine stallion King Pippin and traced his authentic descent through Marble White, Magellan, Madagascar, Dodo, Orange Blossom, Sirius and Aphrodite, back it would seem to Noah's Ark, they wished they had played golf instead.

Gradually they ebbed away to their bedrooms for a period of recuperative solitude, and Mr. Harman, prey to the most virulent exhaustion, mental and physical, rang his bell and asked for a whisky and soda. A footman already plush-breeched and powdered for dinner brought up on a handsome silver salver a tantalus, a syphon, some chopped ice and a tumbler of Waterford glass.

Several neighbours came to dinner: among them was a Russian Grand Duke before whom everyone bowed or curtsied, and the parson of the parish who always dined on Sunday evening when Lord Buryan was in residence. The Grand Duke refused to take any interest in the subjects with which his hostess and the French Ambassadress plied him, he left most of his food uneaten, and smoked cigarettes between the courses. As soon as Lord Buryan perceived this he did the same, though never before in his life had he smoked during dinner. Elsewhere round the table the hum of conversation suffered slight intermittences. Shire horses and golf, moats and George II, the team of Australian cricketers, the nature of the beverage with which Mr. Gladstone used to refresh himself during his Budget statements were like seeds sown on stony ground; they sprang up and swiftly withered again.   The neighbours of the author of the "Life of Lord Palmerston" asked him whom he was "doing" next, the Bishop spoke of a piece of Roman tessellated pavement that he had found in his garden, the parson of his bees which had swarmed today during church-time and were lost.   There was a sense of strain, a feeling that a particular tone had to be kept up; brains, rapidly boiling down into an inert glue, had to be liquefied and made to froth.   The younger members of the party felt this most, and a deadly weariness of the spirit took hold of them.   They were well brought up young people; none yawned or attempted to be natural, but indeed these were waters of Babylon, and their harps were mute.   The stretched moral fibres longed to relax, hysterical desires awoke to say "Damn" and see what happened, to throw one of the famous peaches at the Grand Duke, to pinch the footman's calves as he handed them: anything to break this spell of splendour and high-breeding.   Then suddenly a complete silence fell which lasted so long that Mr. Harman wondered if it ever would be broken again, or if they would all sit there dumb, for ever and ever, looking at the peach-stones on their plates.

LADY BURYAN caught the Ambassadress's eye and rose. The Grand Duke got up also and, in foreign fashion, offered Lady Buryan his arm.   She realised the situation

and though the custom of the men sitting over their
wine for half-an-hour was of Median and Persian authority, the whole party went out in procession into the
gallery, and had their coffee there. When that was
done the Grand Duke said to her:

"I should like a game of Britch."

She did not hesitate, for now there was a matter of
principle at stake, which overrode all else.

"I am so very sorry, sir," she said. "But we do not
play cards on Sunday in my house."

"So ! Then I will have my car, please. I thank you
for a most pleasant evening. Pray do not trouble to
see me off."

He went the round of bows and curtseys, and Lady
Buryan sat down next the parson.

"I haven't had a word with you, Mr. Thorndyke," she
said. "How very tiresome about your bees. A clergyman's bees ought to be better Sabbatarians than that."

And not a word was said about His Royal Highness's
displeasure and departure. When people — whoever
they happened to be — were rude it was more becoming
to say nothing whatever about it. Neither host nor
hostess were the least perturbed: rather sorry for him
perhaps, but nothing more. Not quite a gentleman:
not to be asked again.

The post-prandial hour was unusually long tonight,
as there had been no sitting over the wine, but eleven
o'clock struck at last, and there was the business of find-

ing out what trains the guests desired to catch in the
morning.   The up-express from Bournemouth though
rather early, five minutes to ten, was the fastest, though
there was a slower one at twelve.   Everybody chose the
earlier, and so breakfast would be at a quarter to nine.
Then came the ritual of name-signing in the visitors'
book: Lady Buryan had a wonderful visitors' book full
of treasures.   Queen Victoria had signed it on a page
kept sacredly blank: the Empress Frederick, as Crown
Princess who had stayed here for three days in 1887 had
contributed a short poem in mixed German and English,
of which the last two lines ran:

> Your marvellous food will not make me lanker,
> Liebe Lady Buryan, danke, danke !

Then came the frolicsome age of the nineties when
those amusing games with pencil and paper afforded
sport after dinner.   Lord Salisbury had drawn a pig
with his eyes shut: it looked like a map of South America, and he had signed it "Salisbury fecit."   This was
pasted in, so too were specimens of that popular game
"Heads, bodies and legs."   One person drew a head on
a slip of paper, and, turning it down, so that only the
juncture of the neck was visible, passed it to his neigh-
bour who drew a body: a third, without seeing either,
added legs.   Lady Buryan's most distinguished specimen
was one in which Mr. A. J. Balfour had drawn a golf-
ball for a head, Mr. Henry Chaplin (it was Christmas)
had drawn a plum-pudding for a body, and Sir Henry

Stanley, the African explorer, had completed it with a pair of naked legs and a palm-tree in the background. So characteristic of them all. Today the President of the Royal Academy offered a charming little pencil drawing of the church-tower among the trees, which Lady Buryan would paste into the book tomorrow. Then the men went to the smoking-room and the ladies upstairs.

By half-past nine therefore in the morning all the guests had gone, and Lord and Lady Buryan were left to their magnificent solitude. The party had gone off very well, but for that one untoward incident, to which neither of them alluded, for there was nothing to say about it. He spent the morning with his agent, going into the cost of renewing nearly a mile of the wooden palings of the Park. Expensive work, and repairs were incessant: it might be cheaper in the end to replace the whole by a brick-wall. That must be done in sections, for there were six miles of it: it had better be spread over three years. Then he inspected the plans for a village club that he was proposing to build. It was to have a bar run on temperance lines, a big recreation room with bagatelle boards and draughts and chess, and a reading-room with a decent library of books and a plentiful supply of magazines, where the young men of the village could resort when the day's work was over. Otherwise, during the long winter evenings they were cooped up in their houses, and it was little wonder that

they frequented the public house. The plans for that
had better be put in hand at once.

The agent stopped to lunch, and afterwards Lady
Buryan went into the village to see the parson's wife.
She had been ailing, and a fortnight in nice lodgings by
the sea would do her good. She must be sure to make
herself comfortable, and she must take her little daughter with her: the entire charges from door to door, were,
of course, Lady Buryan's affair. Was there a touch of
condescension about this generous and thoughtful
scheme ? It was scarcely noticeable, for so much genuine kindness accompanied it. Possibly the pleasure of
enabling "such a good little woman" to get her health
back was combined with the sense of duty, but duty,
after all, was a pleasure to the right-minded. Countless
benefits of this sort (witness the village club) were constantly showered on the domain by its sovereigns, for
indeed they were no less. The cynical may suggest
that these generosities cost them nothing, in the sense
that they deprived themselves of nothing they really
wanted in order to make them. But it was the duty
of great landowners in those days to look after their
tenants, and they did it very conscientiously: among
their other duties also was that of being magnificent.
Tradition.

Lord Buryan meantime went to inspect the pheasants
that were being reared for the shooting in the autumn.
He was raising more than usual this year, and they
were a wonderful healthy lot of young birds. After

dinner he sat in his wife's sitting-room and read the *Field* while she played one or two of Mendelssohn's "Songs without Words," and knitted a woollen bedspread for a village sale.   Tomorrow, with regret, they had to go up to London, for there was a gala-night at the Opera and friends were coming to their box. Next week was Ascot and they were bidden to Windsor.

CHAPTER II

YOUNG MEN AND MAIDENS

I

IT WAS just two years after that a prominent announcement appeared in the papers of the engagement of Lord St. Erth, only son of the Earl of Buryan to Lady Helen Morris: this propitious event had taken place last Sunday at Grebe Castle which Princess Amadeo had rented from the bride's father for the months of June and July. The writers of Society paragraphs highly approved: an alliance between these ancient and ennobled lineages was most suitable. The girl was the most lovely of last season's débutantes, and very popular, and though she was of an impoverished family, the bridegroom had enough for both. Her face was already familiar to the readers of illustrated journals; indeed they were also familiar with her arms and her legs and a good deal of her back, for she was one of the earliest of the devotees of the sun and the sea, and many ravishing photographs of her on the sands of the Lido at Venice had decorated their pages last summer. Whatever she did, there was always a camera to record it and a paper to reproduce it. Sometimes she was coming out of the sea like Venus Anadyomene, sometimes she lay on the shore like an exquisite star-fish, sometimes she lounged in a deck-chair with a paper parasol and a cigarette in a long holder, sometimes she appeared with her hostess Princess Amadeo, at whose palazzo on the Grand Canal she spent these amphibious months. The latter was a handsome swarthy American who paid her husband a very substantial sum never to come near her. She was always in England for a few months before she went to Venice, and she spent the winter in Switzerland where she captained a bob-sleigh at St. Moritz, of which the crew consisted of women only. The summer suns of Italy and the winter suns of the radiant heights had permanently so coloured and dried her skin that she was like a very good-looking kipper, and she was known to her friends as Henry, an abbreviation of her christened name Henrietta. She was the most devoted friend of Helen's, and as Lord St. Erth's name was also Henry, it was only natural that, when the engagement was announced, he was dubbed Henry the Second.

There was a big week-end party at Hakluyt in honour of this event, consisting mainly of the friends of the young couple, and now for the first time the younger generation made an invasion in force. These were of all sorts and origins: there was one of Henry's friends and contemporaries at Cambridge, lately elected a Fellow of Magdalene: they called him "Tickets," and he

explained with some pride to Lady Buryan that this was
a nick-name given him because his father had been a
ticket-collector at Cambridge station. Henry protested: "Do shut up, Tickets," he said. "You are such
a frightful snob about your family." Then one of
Helen's friends kept a bric-a-brac shop in the Brompton
Road, and she had arrived driving herself in a car laden
with Victorian objects which were just beginning to
come into fashion again. These she had bought that
day in an auction at Woking which she had attended
on her way down, and an astonished footman went to
and fro from her car to her bedroom carrying in the
loot, wool-work footstools, wax-flowers, glass paper-
weights, and papier-maché boxes decorated with mother
of pearl. There was a young Duke, who did not talk
about his family at all: he was known as the Tin Duke
to distinguish him from the Iron Duke, and they all
called him Tinny. Altogether there were some twenty
of them.

Lady Buryan had never in her life heard so many
nick-names and Christian names; surnames apparently
hardly existed. They were all charming to her, deferential and attentive, but they seemed to belong to another
epoch: it was as if a picnic party of boys and girls had
invaded a Druidical temple. She had often had three
or four of such together here, and then, chameleon-like,
they had taken their colour from their surroundings.
Now, in mass like this, they had a collective colouring
of their own, and she was puzzled to know what that

was. Sometimes it seemed of the gayest hue; they all
jabbered and laughed together, while next moment
they were grave and serious, discussing the poems of
Ernest Dowson: they were like a flock of birds dark
against the light, and then they all wheeled together,
bright and silvery. Speech with each other was curiously telegraphic and in a code she was unacquainted
with. Their relations were intimate but wholly without
sentiment or sentimentality. A boy said "darling
Helen" to her future daughter-in-law, but that meant
nothing, or a girl said "Oh, village idiot," to her son,
and next moment he would be a darling too. But
when they talked to her, as they were perfectly ready
to do, they spoke altogether differently: it was as if they
talked in a language which they had learned in childhood, and still spoke very correctly, though the feat
implied care and an effort of memory. Most of them
did not touch wine at all, and in the after-dinner sitting
of the men, the boys sent it on undiminished or forgot
to pass it till reminded.

Then after dinner none of them wanted to play
Bridge, though there were four card-tables put out.
Might they play "Lights" instead, Helen asked Lady Buryan, and wouldn't she play ? Not very hard to understand: one of the circle began to talk in the character
of some man or woman known to all of them, and as
each of them guessed who was being impersonated, he
joined in too, talking in character. If he guessed wrong,
he lost a life. None of the elders felt equal to this feat,

and the younger lot all sat together in a circle on the floor. Some of them had lit cigarettes, and since smoking was not practised in the gallery, Henry took them all off to the smoking-room. At eleven Lady Buryan made the usual move for the women to go up to bed; "Lights" was broken up, and the girls quite cheerfully and politely went upstairs with her. The boys drifted away as their elders, with Lord Buryan in ruby velvet, came into the smoking-room. Soon Lady Buryan from her room opposite Helen's heard sundry taps at Helen's door. "Hel, may I come in ?" asked one. "You haven't gone to bed yet, have you ?" said another. From the sound of voices gradually increasing in volume she gathered that a contingent of them had resumed the game of "Lights." Somebody had forgotten to close the door, and his lordship convoying the rest of the men upstairs an hour later, found a fog of cigarette-smoke issuing therefrom and spreading down the corridor.

He went to his son's room, and was bidden to enter. Henry was half-undressed, cutting his toe-nails and one of his friends who had rowed for Cambridge in the last boat-race (a fact reluctantly admitted by him) was lying on his bed in pyjamas reading aloud:

> But when the feast is over and the lights expire,
> Then falls thy shadow, Cynara, the night is thine,
> And I am desolate —

"I want to speak to you a moment, old boy," said Lord Buryan.

"Rather," said Henry. "Don't go, Ralph: I want to hear the end of it."

He followed his father into the corridor.

"There are a lot of your friends in Helen's room," he said, "and the house is filling with smoke. Do you think you could tell them that it's really time — "

"By all means, father," said Henry, and in vest and trousers with bare feet he paddled down the passage and entered.

A lively chorus greeted him.

"Hullo, Henry Two," said one. "Had enough poetry ?"

"Hel's set a corker," said another. "Go on, darling."

"I say, let's go and bathe," said a third, who was seated by the open window. "I see a lake across there. Moonlight, midnight, et cetera."

"Sorry," said Henry, "but my father thinks it's about time to go to bed. And the corridor's reeking with smoke. Some bloody fool left the door open."

"Shut it then," said another. "Can't go to bed without guessing this."

"Really, if you don't mind," said Henry.

The cheerful assembly instantly dispersed.

ON Sunday morning Helen and Henry were the only two from the younger section of the party who joined their elders in the hall at ten minutes to eleven to go to church. There had been no real debate about it: it had been almost tacitly settled as they sat about on the ter-

race after the nine o'clock breakfast, that attending
morning service was too large a sacrifice of this June
morning, and the rest of them, not tied by blood or
prospective alliance to their hosts, had quietly vanished
till zero-hour was over.   It was too much: there were
limits.   In consequence the great loose-box with its
cushions and its prayer-books of the age of Adelaide was
but half-filled, and there was no need to requisition
fresh pews.   When the coast was clear, the rest went off
to bathe in the lake beyond the nine-hole golf course.
Lunch-time saw them all assembled again, charmingly
indulgent, but without much appetite, for the bathe had
been succeeded by a visit to the kitchen-garden, where,
after a square meal of fruit, they had crowned Tinny
with strawberry leaves as befitted his rank.   Lady Buryan could scarcely supply chicken-broth for them all.

Thereafter came further symptoms of disaffection: it
could hardly be called revolt, so passive was it and so
polite.   None of them wanted to play golf, for they
had walked across the course on their way to the
bathing-place that morning, and seen "the sort of
thing."   None of them cared to see cows milked by
machinery or to feel the fetlocks of King Pippin.
"What's the use, Tickets ?" said Helen.   "I should only
make some awful *gaffe* for I don't know the difference
between a horse and a cow, and I should mistake fetlocks
for forelocks.   Besides Henry and I have been burnt of-
ferings for you all morning: the heat in church was
something awful. My dear, the organ !   Handel's

Largo: devastating. We're not so strong as they are: we want to be let alone and slack it. I shall go to my room till all the pleasure-parties have started."

So some went to bathe again, and four of them, when the elders had gone to see the farm or to drive with Lady Buryan to the village on the Itchen — rather a long drive — where Isaak Walton used to fish in his later years, discovered the billiard-room, and played fives on the table there. The game was of short duration, for soon a violent scooping stroke by Ralph sent the ball crashing through the window. On the whole, it was better to say nothing about this accident, for it was quite a small pane, but it damped the fervour and so, having retrieved the ball from the herbaceous border outside, they pulled the blind down over the shattered glass, and put the cloth very neatly back on to the billiard-table. It was voted that in case the fracture was discovered, Tinny should own up, because he was a Duke. The four who had been playing wandered out into the garden again, and the two boys lay together in the shade on the lawn with a book from the library about Diane de Poictiers, which one of them read aloud, and then used for a pillow and went to sleep. But the flies were troublesome, and they strayed indoors again with the sense of being thwarted at every turn. They forgot about the book, which was found on the lawn by the party returning from the farm.

This gulf between the two generations had been partly bridged over by the tact of the admirable Josephine

Lister. She belonged to the younger set, but was several years older than any of them, being now close on thirty. She had been of the party in Helen's room last night, and she had not gone to church that morning, but by lunch-time her matchless tact perceived that there was discord in the air, and she exerted herself to harmonize it. So when plans were discussed, she dissociated herself from her inert friends, and was positively torn in two between the treat of seeing shire-horses and mechanically milked cows, and of visiting the haunts of Isaak Walton.

"I adore horses," she said, "and it's quite awful to be obliged to choose. But you don't know what Isaak Walton means to me. So English, so marvellously English. I couldn't bear to miss it: so may I come with you, Lady Buryan ?"

Off she went, thin and small and eager, in the motor with Lady Buryan, and the Curator of the Manuscript Room at the British Museum, and Helen's great aunt the Dowager Marchioness of Basingstoke, who had been kissed in her childhood by Lord Beaconsfield, and now recounted that experience. It thrilled Josephine.

"It's too wonderful !" she said. "How I envy you ! Was he terribly attractive ? I so often wish I was thirty years older and could remember the great days, for they were great, weren't they ? All that dignity and stateliness . . ."

Then there were her friends to speak up for, and without pause she went on:

"And sometimes how I wish I was younger," she said, "and was a real contemporary of Henry and Helen and the rest. They're all so nice to me, but then the quite young are the most adorable people. They're so frightfully intelligent and so appreciative. Helen said last night, Lady Buryan, that she had an absolute passion for you. And how handsome Henry is, and his quickness positively frightens me. They are all enjoying themselves so tremendously. Raymond Loshyer — he's the one with the glass eye; his father shot him in the eye, just one pellet, wasn't it terrible for them both ? — Raymond says he's going to pretend to be too ill to travel tomorrow, and so he'll stop another day . . . Oh, are we here, and is that the river where Isaak Walton fished ? It's too much ! And Mr. Arkenshaw has promised to shew me some day the first edition of the *Compleat Angler* which is in the British Museum in its original binding."

Josephine followed up the good work of bridging the generations by taking the most fanatical interest in King Pippin's pedigree: she would have liked to copy it out, but there was hardly time as she meant to go to evening service. At a bedroom meeting that night, care being taken to close the door, she was awarded a unanimous vote of thanks which, except for the noise, would have been carried by acclamation. They had all elected to go by the early train, with the exception of Helen, for Princess Amadeo was motoring up to London from a house in the neighbourhood and would pick her up. They dispersed very silently about two o'clock.

But Lady Buryan lay long awake though her husband slept peacefully by her side.   She was puzzled, she was disquieted: the young generation, when in force like this, was very hard to understand, and she felt she had set up no kind of relationship with any of them.   Least of all did she understand her future daughter-in-law.

II

AND all these imaginary scenes are a parable that sets forth by means of trivial incidents some of the under-lying differences between the two generations who were spending the Sunday at Hakluyt, namely those who were of ripe middle age in the years just preceding the war, and their sons and daughters who were then entering adult life, and were to form so large a part of what was to prove the lost generation.

Hakluyt itself, it is true, has been endowed with rather exceptional splendours, so that its tragedy (if it was a tragedy) might be the more marked, but all over England at that time were many houses of the type, now vastly diminished in numbers, where a hereditary line had lived for centuries.   The bigger owners had in-herited great wealth and a position now nearly vanished, and, on coming into their inheritance, had taken up the responsibilities which tradition attached to it, in a most conscientious manner.   They had these large houses in the country with rolling unremunerative parks and gar-

dens or they had places in Scotland with salmon rivers
and grouse-moors and deer-forests, and they entertained
with comfort and splendour both there and in London,
spending enormous annual sums on their sports and their
pleasures, the amenities of which were freely bestowed
on their friends. These large places gave employment
to a host of keepers, woodmen, gardeners and servants,
who were extremely well looked after: they had good
wages and healthy dwellings, and when they were getting past active work they were given lighter jobs
and pensioned in their old age. No conscientious landlord, as these mostly were, would have suffered a tenant
or a dependent who had served him well to come down
to the work-house, which in those days was the equiv-
alent of old-age pensions, and there was practically no
such thing as unemployment on such estates. All over
the rural districts of England reigned these small terri-
torial kings who identified themselves with their tenants'
interests, and who went to church on Sunday not only
because that was the proper thing to do and set a good
example, but because most of them believed in the God
whom they prayed to and praised there. They did not
trouble themselves over the mysteries of the faith nor
did they take the slightest interest in the doctrines and
disputes of theologians. Such things were the concern
of the clergy, and Lord Buryan would as soon have
thought of seeking enlightenment from his parson as to
the correct conception of the Real Presence before he
received the sacrament on the first Sunday of every

month, as he would have thought of questioning the engine-driver of the train on which he proposed to travel about his steam-gauge or the working of the slide-valve cylinders. He trusted the knowledge of those whose business it was to have these things in order. Besides, the constitution of England consisted of Church and State, and the hierarchy of the Church and the clergy under them were as valid an institution as the government of the day and the members of the Houses of Lords and Commons. It is not implied that all landlords were of this type, but there were enough of them to constitute a very solid power.

Possibly, had it not been for the war, the habit and outlook of the generation then passing through the decade of its twenties would not have grown more widely divergent from those of their fathers, than those of their fathers had been from the generation that preceded them. For every generation in turn has been impatient of current restraints and of shibboleths that seem to them meaningless, and each has made its successful revolts against such; or its revolts, as in the decade following on the accession of Queen Victoria, have been social reforms and a tightening up of lax moralities. These revolts or reforms are like the pulse that beats in the continuous flow of the blood, shewing the vigour of the life within: in another sense they are like additions made to some moulded or sculptured design, which, with their edges of juncture smoothed down and their roughnesses polished by use, have become part of the curve of progress or, if we deplore them, of decay. But there has always been a party of elders, silently in their lives, or volubly with their lips, protesting against such changes. Those who were of middle-age in the nineties beheld with horror the riotous abandonment of the generation then growing up, forgetting that they themselves had doubtless been regarded as Bacchanals by their elders twenty years before, while to the young of 1910 to 1920 those audacities of the nineties had become the humdrum and habit of normal behaviour.

But unfortunately there comes to the majority of those of middle-age an inelasticity not of physical muscle and sinew alone but of mental fibre. Experience has its dangers: it may bring wisdom but it may also bring stiffness and cause hardened deposits in the mind, and the resulting inelasticity is crippling. Those who suffer from it merely sit woodenly while the days stream past them: the days no longer nourish them or are digested. Nobody in the world (such seems to be the inexorable provision of Nature) is of any use unless he is still capable of assimilating new ideas, so that they work that change in him, which is needful for the due appreciation of changes. His Jeremiads about what the world is coming to may afford him a piquant though a bitter sauce to existence, he may hold forth about the good old days (unwittingly producing the impression that they were only queer old days), but he does not count, nor is there the slightest reason why he should. Only those of middle-age count who, though

they may not be able to initiate any longer, taste promise in the new wine of life, though they may personally
prefer the old.　The new wine may mature into a nobler
vintage than any that has yet been known, and to note
only its present rawness and acidity is to miss all its
potentialities.　In these years the young clusters were
to mature under fierce suns and such storms as had never
yet swept across the secure vineyard where they grew:
the berries would be shredded from their stems under
the pelting hail.　What would be the quality of the
diminished harvest that was not then battered and
burned, but duly went to the winepress, who could tell ?

But even before the dawning of the day of wrath, so
thought many of their elders, the young folk of this particular decade were different not in degree only but in
kind from those of the first decade of the century, and
from those of the nineties.　The latter had amused
themselves very thoroughly, and the girls had obtained
a far larger measure of freedom in their relations with
the other sex than had even been granted them before,
but they had been serious young people, too, full of
admiration and aspirations, and culture and high ideals.
That freedom the later generation had inherited and
assimilated, and now a new growth altogether was spring-
ing up.　A new female type, not a mere variation of the
old was evolving.　It was constructive, it was throwing
overboard the lumber for which it had no use, and which
cluttered up the spaces which it wanted free for its new
structure.　They accepted nothing in the validity of

which they did not believe, and they accepted everything
which gave the ring of solidity.   They no longer regarded home life as their destiny until they fulfilled
themselves in marriage, but revolted against its restraints,
going out to work as secretaries and saleswomen or setting up shops and supporting themselves independently,
though their parents were in good circumstances and
there was no need for them to do anything of the sort.
Others became newspaper correspondents, others took
up historical research or medical work.   Many of them
lived away from home in lodgings, two or three together, and there were many pairs of passionate friends
to whom men made no appeal.   They did not want
men: their work and their friendships among themselves
supplied them with means, with interests and with emotions.   The movement was not actually new, for the independence of women, their right to work and the immense gain to themselves in so doing rather than in
smouldering away by the domestic hearth had been
preached as long ago as 1850 by Charlotte Brontë.   But
it had been so sporadic that it had not presented the
appearance of a movement: here and there were odd girls
with odd notions in their heads, rather unfeminine,
rather queer.   But now the infection had developed
into an epidemic, and most of the girls were not unfeminine at all.   It seemed like a new type.

Simultaneously the suffragette movement grew rapidly in numbers and in violence.   There again the cause
of the movement was not new, for many exceedingly

able women, like the late Lady Frances Balfour, had long upheld the right of women who owned property or earned wages and paid taxes to have the vote. But the violent methods were new, and outrages of the most puerile kind were fanatically committed. Women of intelligence and good breeding, despairing of legal methods, became hooligans. They broke windows, they fired hay-stacks, they slashed pictures, they padlocked themselves to the railings of the houses of Cabinet Ministers, they made schemes for the kidnaping or shooting of Mr. Lloyd George when he played golf, and cheerfully went to prison, where they endured the pangs of hunger-strike and the ignominies of forcible feeding. They demanded to be treated like men, and then, not very logically, when they were so treated, they execrated the cowardly brutality of the stronger sex and cried out that chivalry was dead. Their more law-abiding sisters were deeply ashamed of them, and though probably a large majority of women were in sympathy with the object that the Suffragettes had in view, they deplored these silly demonstrations, which not only were highly unedifying in themselves, but injured rather than advanced the cause, for by way of proving their worthiness to exercise the responsibilities of citizenship these militant champions were only proving their worthiness to become the irresponsible inmates of a lunatic asylum. This view was perfectly correct, and it was not through these senseless outrages that the battle was won, but through the steadfast efficiency, self-sacrifice and service that women rendered the state in the day of trouble that was now imminent.

But as yet, except for the hysterical operations of the Suffragettes, the change that was undoubtedly going on in the position of women was not violent, and from outside there was no threat against the internal stability and security of national life, which was so characteristic of pre-war days. There were alarmists who insisted that Germany was not becoming a nation under arms for nothing, that she was accumulating material for war to an extent wholly unprecedented, that her fleet was yearly increasing in power and efficiency, but no-one paid any attention to them; it was more comfortable to remember that Germany was Lord Háldane's spiritual home. Then there were rumours that she was much engaged in financing Turkish enterprises, that her peaceful penetration there was proceeding apace, that she was even now in a position to dictate to the party of Union and Progress. The English Government, too, at one time had thought of doing a little counter-penetration and starting a bank in Constantinople as a rival to the Deutsche Bank, entrusting the establishment of it to Sir Ernest Cassel, but this had been given up. Turkey was a sick man, effete and bedridden, and if Germany chose to sit by his bedside and give him medicine it was no affair of ours, and she was throwing her money away. But as for Turkey being a sick man, it was quite otherwise. Germany's medicines had proved extremely tonic: the Committee of Union and Progress were most efficient administrators, and the invalid's army, drilled and organized by German officers, was becoming a very formidable body.   Already before the war it exceeded our own in numbers, was inferior in discipline to none and now its artillery was coming quietly and regularly in from Essen.   But all such talk was scoffed at as the gabble of idle alarmists.   They had attempted to get up just such a scare over the incident at Agadir in 1911. Besides, a European war was quite unthinkable.

CHAPTER III

WAR AND RUMOURS OF WAR

I

TO RETURN to the parable of the family at Hakluyt, the young couple were married in the winter of 1913 and set up house in Chesterfield Street. Lord Buryan also gave them a charming little Manor House just outside the Park at Hakluyt where they could entertain three or four friends on their own account: it would be very pleasant to have them close at hand for week-ends and holidays. But the arrangement did not work out quite as he and Lady Buryan had pictured it. They had imagined Henry and his wife and any guests they had with them constantly coming in to dine at the big house, not half a mile away, or dropping in to lunch after church on Sunday: there would be continual droppings in and goings to and fro. But it did not happen like that. At Easter, for instance, the two arrived on the preceding Wednesday, and Henry came in next day for a few minutes alone: he had to get back because they were expecting two or three friends and he was meeting them at the station. On Good Friday none of

them appeared at church or elsewhere, but there came a
telephone message in the evening, asking if Lady Buryan
would have tea at the Manor House next day. She
went, but found no-one in.   But she was actually a little
in front of her time, and sitting down to wait for them,
picked up a French book lying open on the table, called
La Bas.   A paragraph was enough: much perturbed she
laid it down again.   How could Henry allow such a
book in his house ?

Then he and Helen came in: with them was a big
brown woman, called Princess Amadeo. A strange
type, no specimen of which had ever appeared at Hakluyt in all the years of its Sunday parties.   Masculine in
dress and appearance, with cropped hair, she sat with one
knee crossed over the other, refused tea, and had a vermouth instead.   She had an extremely pleasant manner,
rather off-hand perhaps, but very cordial: she regretted
that she had not been able to attend Helen's wedding, for
she had been laid up at St. Moritz with a broken arm, the
result of a bob-sleigh accident.   Then a Cambridge undergraduate strolled in: his hair was longer than the
Princess' and his face was more feminine. He was
dressed in shorts with shirt open at the neck; he sat next
to Lady Buryan, and never had she seen so great a length
of bare leg.   *La Bas* perhaps belonged to him, for presently he took it up from the table and retired with it
into the window-seat, relieving her of her embarrassment.   A girl came in of about Helen's age: nobody
introduced her to Lady Buryan and she went to the

window-seat, and leaning against the boy read *La Bas*
over his shoulder. Presently she said to the Princess:
"Oh, Henry dear, your maid asked me to tell you that
there was a trunk call for you on the telephone an hour
ago from Babs. She wanted you to ring her up as soon
as you came in." "Thanks, darling," said the Princess,
and took her vermouth away with her adding a little gin
to sustain her while telephoning. Lady Buryan, when
she rose to go, hoped that they would all come in to lunch
after church next day, and she saw Helen's eyebrows
conveying an unspoken question to Henry the Second.
Might they come to dine instead, asked Helen, and of
course that was quite convenient. But the Cambridge
boy it appeared had no dress-clothes, so he and the girl
thought they would stop at home. Next day, Henry
came alone to church, and at dinner that night Princess
Amadeo inadvertently let slip the fact that they had had
the most enjoyable foursome that morning over the
Weyford links.

MEANTIME the building of Lord Buryan's village-club
was nearing completion: the roof was on, the floors were
laid, a pleasant garden with a bowling-green for summer evenings lay at the back. It was on rather a larger
scale than the original design, for there were quarters for
a caretaker and his wife: he had been head-keeper, but
was getting past his work, and this would be a good berth
for him. Over the porch and the open fire-place in the
recreation room was a limestone slab, like those above the

doors in the cottages, with a coronet, a large "B" and the date carved on it. Lord Buryan, during the next month or two often took his guests to see the place on Sunday afternoon, when they had visited the milking of the cows and the shire horses, and he hoped to have it open before the winter. It should have been ready before, but there had been trouble in the brick-laying trade, and the Trades Union had ordered its members not to lay more than a certain number of bricks a day. A scandalous piece of tyranny; the Trades Union seemed to think that they were dictators in all matters concerned with British industries. In that railway strike of 1911 it was entirely they who had made the men go out: the men had not wanted to. There was a fellow called Thomas in the House of Commons, and another called Mac-Donald who preached rank sedition: Lord Buryan thought that prison would be the best place for them. But the pheasants were doing well and there was promise of an excellent harvest.

As for plans, he and Lady Buryan were going to Aix for three weeks towards the end of July, for they both had twinges of rheumatism, and then to Scotland for a couple of months: a bracing climate and plenty of walking was recommended after the cure. Then Hakluyt again for the autumn and the shooting: the course of their lives was as uniform as the circling of a wheel on a smooth-running axle, and their movements as regular as the orbit of the moon. Henry would be with them for a while in Scotland, but Helen meant to spend the month

of August in Venice with Princess Amadeo.   It was odd
that she should wish to be a whole month away from
her husband, but Scotland, she frankly allowed, bored
her stiff.   For once, however, the invariable orbit was
dislocated by the pull of a greater force, and the Buryans
got back to England from Aix, cutting short their cure,
on the first of August.   War was declared on the fourth,
and Mr. Rudyard Kipling who, in the South African
war, had complained that there war "no satisfactory killing" for many months, was not likely to be disappointed
again.

MANY of the young men in the village joined up within
a few weeks of the beginning of the war, so too did most
of the gardeners and woodmen of the Park and the men-
servants in the house: their places would be kept open
for them on their return which, it was hoped, would be
before Christmas.   The elderly butler remained, also Lord
Buryan's elderly valet, and Lady Buryan advertised, as "a
lady of title," in the *Morning Chronicle,* for "two ruptured footmen": she would not thus be employing any
young man who could serve his country.   Henry had
got a commission in the Guards, and trained at Wellington Barracks.   Helen had secretarial work, and was with
him in London, and the two old people settled down at
Hakluyt to a new strange life.   The world-tragedy of
war was the background of it, menacing and frightful,
but the war in itself was not tangible or visible, only
manifesting itself in the actual routine of this quiet rural

life by a thousand annoyances and inconveniences,
which as the months went by were magnified and multiplied. There were no shooting-parties, there were no
week-end parties. Again there was the unfinished village club: it was impossible to get labour for its completion, and the damp and rains of the autumn got in
through the windows protected only by canvas stretched
across them, and crops of mildew grew thick on the un-
plastered walls. There was a big training-camp near by,
and when the raids began there were orders issued for the
darkening of lights in houses, and until the big skylight
in the hall was furnished with curtains that drew across
it, it was impossible to have any light there except
shaded lamps. Coke and coal were rationed and the
peach houses and vinery must be left unfurnaced. Soon
there was a call for big country houses to be turned into
hospitals for the wounded, and Lord Buryan's offer of
Hakluyt was accepted by the Red Cross. The long gallery was turned into the principal ward, the pictures
were removed, leaving square patches of unfaded colour
on the walls, and the Spanish silk was covered with white
enamelled canvas.

For a few weeks they lived in a corner of the house,
and Lady Buryan, in a nurse's uniform, became nominal
commandant. But the arrangement did not work very
well, and they moved into the Manor House. Petrol
was rationed, food was rationed, and though these de-
privations were nothing in themselves, the sense of being
limited and fenced about with restrictions was almost

incredible to folk who had never known what it was not to be able to have everything they wanted automatically ready for them.

Henry, after six months training, went out to the front, and now it was as if there was a jagged edge of the background of life penetrating into the foreground. They moved back to London in the spring, where they would be more in touch with news, and would also be near Helen.   But they did not see much of her, for she was at her work all day, and in the evening it was only natural that she wanted something more enlivening than a quiet dinner with them.   She would look in for half-an-hour on her way back from the office, but there was little to say.   She had heard from Henry, or she had not, and there was nothing to tell them about her work, which was of the driest and most monotonous sort. Soon she had to go, for some friend was back on leave, and there was a little theatre party, or his mother was giving a small dance.   If she was anxious about Henry, she let no token of that appear, and when one evening she told her mother-in-law that she had been to see her doctor and knew that she was with child, she announced this as a colourless fact that did not affect her emotionally. . . And all the time there was an air of silent reserve and resentment about her.   Somebody, not they particularly, but the collective body of the older folk, to whom they belonged, had so mismanaged affairs that Henry was out in that hell of fire and filth, and she occupied all day in a stuffy office, adding figures or making memoranda for her chief, when she should have been enjoying the banquet of her youth. Never in this year of her married life had she become in the least intimate with Lady Buryan, and now she seemed more withdrawn than ever.

Then Henry got a week's leave. He would be living with his wife in Chesterfield Street, but his father and mother had taken it for granted that he would be much with them. Lady Buryan had planned a quiet dinner for the four of them on the first night, and Henry no doubt would tell them all that was going on out there, and how near the end of the war was. For the next night she meant to get together a big dinner-party, for the third Henry would probably like a quiet evening again. But Helen said that this programme was impossible: Henry had already told her he had asked a lot of his friends who would also be on leave for the second night: would Helen ask as many girls of the right kind as she could get hold of, she knew the sort: on the night after they were going to a jamboree somewhere. Lady Buryan tried to be tactful and discerning over this: dear Helen perhaps had not considered that Henry would hardly care for a jamboree (was it ?). Would he not want to be quiet ? Helen looked at her as if she was next door to an idiot, but she was quite polite and explained that Henry would want to cram in just as much amusement as he possibly could.

The first quiet evening was very quiet indeed, and all expectations of hearing Henry talk about "what was go-

ing on out there" were disappointed. His father and
mother asked him questions which he answered as briefly
as might be: a dugout was a filthy hole in the ground
strutted up with timbers and populous with lice. He
drank a good deal, and he was rather on edge, for when
the ruptured footman (Lady Buryan had only been able
to get one) let a spoon clatter from the sauce-boat on to
the salver, he started violently. Then about the French:
no, he did not think they loved us at all; they loathed us
as they always had done and always would.

His eyes and Helen's met sometimes, as if something
was happening that they had both anticipated, and she
came to the rescue with a change of subject. How good
the spring salmon from Drumarden was: what a bore for
his father, said Henry, not to have been able to go there
either this year or the last. He talked of the horrid inconveniences they were suffering here in England. Not
possible for his mother to go for a drive ! Not possible
for them to have a sirloin of beef on Sunday ! And the
raids, and the darkened streets, and saccharine instead of
sugar, and margarine instead of butter, in spite of the
herd of Jersey cows. Awfully good of them to let the
hospital have it all. He could not imagine what the gallery would look like with its forty beds, and her sitting-
room as the operating theatre. There were silences.
There was a sense of strain, of grit in the wheels, of jerks
and stoppages, and as for talking about what he was
going through he simply refused. His manners perhaps
were not so good as they used to be, for when for the

second time she asked him when he thought the war would be over, he reminded her that he had already said that he had no more notion than an Esquimo.

Then he lit his cigarette before the port came round, indeed before she had finished her orange, and extinguished the dottel of it against the Sevres dessert-plate. She saw her husband wince at that; this dessert-service was very precious, for his grandfather had brought it back with him, when he returned from the Grand Tour. He asked her, before he and Helen went home, whether his father and she would not come to Chesterfield Street tomorrow evening, but his sketch of the manner of the entertainment was designed to give them easy excuses for not coming. There wouldn't be dinner, but a perpetual buffet from nine o'clock onwards: soup and sandwiches and dancing and sitting on the floor; and probably eggs and bacon towards morning: you could never quite tell what would happen. He was almost insistent that they should come as he observed the effect on his mother of his outline of the entertainment: she could not imagine herself in such an assembly, nor for that matter could he, and she found the most valid excuse when she remembered that it was the season of full moon. She had been at the theatre on the night of an air-raid last month, and had been obliged to take refuge in the bowels of the tube. A most unpleasant experience which she did not want to repeat. . .

Even as they said good-night the maroons banged, giving warning that an air-raid was imminent. Henry's face

went white. "Good God, these damned airplanes," he
said. "Good night, mother, we shall have to hurry home
if we're to get there before it begins. Come on,
Helen," and off they went into the night. It was
strange, thought Lord Buryan that, after all Henry had
been through, an air-raid should whip his nerves like that.
He himself took no notice of this "cursed impertinence"
of the Huns, but, disdaining the shelter of the basement,
read his evening paper with very fair attention, though
slightly sweating in the palms of his hands when the firing began. Tonight the noise of the engines overhead
was unusually distinct, a buzzing, rattling metallic noise
that sounded down the chimney as some machine passed
directly overhead. Then came an explosion that made
the windows rattle: that must be a bomb dropped not
far away, and soon after he heard the clanging of the
bell of a fire-engine.

He felt that he was "doing his bit" by not allowing
the laying of these murderous eggs to interfere with his
reading of the paper, and he recalled with pleasure a
story he had heard which showed that the English treated
them with the contempt they deserved. There had been
a Promenade Concert at the Queen's Hall, and it was
just drawing to its close when the warnings sounded.
No-one would be able to get home till the raid was over,
so Sir Henry Wood said a word to his orchestra, and they
played dance-tunes, and the area was presently full of
couples, waltzing or fox-trotting till the "All Clear"
sounded. Then the orchestra struck up "God Save the

King," and everyone sang it, and they streamed out into the street in rare good spirits.   So much for the panic that Germany imagined these air-raids wrought in London: an impromptu dance and then God Save the King !

But it was strange, he thought, how Henry's face had blanched just now: the younger generation, though gallantly doing their duty, had not perhaps quite the nerve of their fathers: he had been, as a young man, on Lord Wolseley's staff in the Egyptian campaign, and that had not unsteadied his nerves in the least.

II

It is the greatest pity that it occurred to nobody to write down at the time all the amazing stories concerning the war, sedulously circulated as reliable, which were entirely imaginary, and had no foundation of any sort in fact: a history of the war based solely on accredited rumours would have been an instructive psychological document, for the fact that these grotesque absurdities could be believed shows how powerful is the effect of jangled and excited nerves on our capacity for credulity.   These stories were usually prefaced by the suspicious words "I'm told that etc. . ."   You could then be tolerably certain that the narrator was also the inventor or had at least added some further picturesque decoration.   Those of German birth, however long they had been naturalized, and however firmly their interests were knit into those of their adopted country, were signally chosen to be the targets of these industrious romancers, chiefly women, who considered tha they were helping their country best (and most enjoyably) by disseminating fabulous tales about these: Sir Ernest Cassel and Sir Edgar Speyer, both Privy Counsellors were favourite cockshies. Concerning Sir Ernest Cassel, it was perfectly true that though he was up in London for several days in most weeks, he had never been there during the long series of German air-raids, and that was sufficient. It was therefore argued by people not otherwise insane, that the nights when he was at Brook House, his residence in Park Lane, were immune from attack. The method by which he communicated with the enemy was discovered also, and I was once gravely told that a wireless apparatus of secret design was installed on the roof of Brook House, and that when Sir Ernest was there, he informed the headquarters of the German air-force of his presence, adding that Thursday, Friday and Saturday would suit him. How else, pray, could I account for his immunity? Evidently he did not consider London a dangerous area, whatever the moon or the weather, but English folk, not having his advantage thought it was, and found that country-air, when the moon was large, was far better for their children. Sir Edgar Speyer had a house at Overstrand on the coast of Norfolk, and a somewhat similar wireless apparatus was devised for him. With it he was accustomed to chat with German submarines in the North Sea, and to give them valuable information. . . Then why, just before the war broke out, had a certain wealthy man, undoubtedly (or nearly so) of German origin, who lived near Colchester, been in such a hurry to finish his *en tout cas* tennis court ?　I was told why.　Below that *en tout cas* court was a solid concrete platform, and when the Germans landed, it would be most useful to them as an emplacement for a big piece of artillery which would be trained on London. But I repeat that my informants were not otherwise insane.　Probably owing to information thus supplied them, some of these submarines were certain to creep up the Thames, and at any moment they might lob a bomb into the Houses of Parliament, torpedo the railway bridges at Charing Cross and Blackfriars, or shatter the electric power-station at Lot's Road.　So convinced of this peril was a certain patriotic lady of my acquaintance, who lived on Chelsea Embankment, and had no other qualifications for the lunatic asylum that, in order to do her bit in defence of her country, she used to walk up and down the riverside for hours every day and peer for periscopes.　The August sun beat down on to the pavement, and the dazzle from the water scorched her face and terribly tried her eyes, and in the winter the bitter winds chilled her to the bone, but this admirable woman was determined that no submarine should wreck the power-station at Lot's Road while she patrolled the neighbouring water.　When there was a thick fog, London was in more imminent danger, for then indeed they might escape her vigilance, but she hoped that the atmospheric conditions which baffled her sharp eyes, might also baffle the steersmen of the submarines.

Then there were strange doings on the nights of air-raids in London. When the first Zeppelin came, an American lady living in Belgrave Square distinctly saw the murderous German faces of the crew leaning over the side of the gondola, and quite a quantity of people, on subsequent occasions, asserted that they had seen our anti-aircraft guns being galloped through the streets and firing at the narrow strip of sky between the houses. So interested were the officials who had charge of the defence of London in these manœuvres of which they knew nothing, that they examined a certain butler in a house in Chesham Street, who said he had stood quite close to one of these guns when it was fired. The flash, oddly enough, had not temporarily blinded him, though he was looking at the muzzle of the gun, nor had any windows been broken. It was puzzling, for the staff were under the impression that their guns were station-ary, set up in open spaces like Hyde Park. Again, I was informed by an Englishwoman lately returned from Paris in 1916 that the French reserves were entirely de-pleted and that every man was now in the fighting-line. When I expressed doubt, she said that Clemenceau had told her, so there was the end of that.

Most remarkable perhaps of all these fine flights of fancy was the cheering and wonderful news which was current very soon after the beginning of the war, that thousands upon thousands of Russian soldiers had landed at some northern port, and were passing through Eng-

land on their way to the Western front, for the entire
Russian front was fully manned, and these cohorts were
the surplus of the Eastern armies. They were seen
everywhere: trains full of them with the blinds drawn
down were constantly arriving at Euston at the dead
of night, and the highly educated porters recognised
that they were talking Russian. Other detachments
changed trains at Swindon, and though the month was
August, were observed stamping the snow off their boots.
Others marched from Ascot station towards the Sun-
ningdale links, for I was actually staying at a house on
the route when my host's butler told him that a friend of
his had picked up on the road a Russian *kèpi*, and he saw
that it was stamped inside with the name of a military
outfitter in Nijni-Novgorod. Incessant and widely believed as this extraordinary invention was, it was never
possible to get first-hand evidence: it was always a married sister of the housemaid or the nephew of the cook
who had seen them. Lord Kitchener's secretary asked
him if it would not be as well officially to contradict these
rumours, but he said certainly not, for they were productive of a cheerful and optimistic spirit: they bucked
people up.

Simultaneously from France came some beautiful
stories about the appearance of Angels who protected the
British troops (not very efficiently) in the retreat from
Mons. There were several versions of this encouraging
tale: some said that there had been only one or two of

these glittering beings who appeared to the harassed
troops, some that there had been a whole host of them.
But there again first-hand evidence was unobtainable,
and the story seemed to be news to those who actually
were in the retreat, just as the story of Russian troops
passing through England was news to the military au-
thorities at St. Petersburg and to our own War Office.
Both obtained considerable credence in England from the
same type of mind, and those who, in Lord Kitchener's
phrase were "bucked up" by the one, were equally
cheered by the other. Many kind women dropped a
tear of thankfulness on the comforters and bed-spreads
they were knitting when the parson who was taking tea
with them told them about the Angels at Mons. It
made them feel ever so much happier, and the thought of
the Russian troops pouring into France was full of glee.
Two nasty surprises for the Huns: what with angels and
Russians their west front must soon break. In 1917 the
Channel tunnel was finished, and thus our transports going backwards and forwards from France no longer ran
any risk from submarines. Yet the wildest of these in-
ventions was scarcely more ridiculous than the pronouncement by the Prime Minister after the close of the
war, that the allies would insist that the German Emperor should be arrested and tried. The main difference
between them was that many people believed that hosts
of Russians had been passing through England and nobody believed the other.

III

EVERY month that went by dug deeper yet and yet more wide, so that none should bridge it, the chasm across time that the war had made. Deeper yet, too, though not yet apparent because of the red fog of butchery, grew the psychical chasm between intelligent and thinking young men through whose ranks the shuttle of murder plied to and fro and the older generation owing to whose mad muddle and mismanagement this senseless slaughter raged. Admittedly the day had come when war was inevitable, and none but a handful of pacifists would have had it otherwise, but what of the years that went before? How had they used their power? To prevent and render impossible this colossal catastrophe? Not at all: they had done all they could, the statesmen of England, France and Germany alike, to further it. They had piled up armaments and launched fresh fleets; their chemists in a thousand industrious laboratories of the State had vied with each other in working out the formulas of new and more devastating explosives and of deadly gases: their steel-works had forged guns of larger range and more rapid fire; their mechanics had designed aircraft that would carry bombs to wreck a city and submarines that would pierce with their torpedoes the hulls of ships a mile away, and there were further devices against submarines, nets to entangle them, depth-charges adroitly dropped, and then presently the surface of the water was streaked with patches of oil from the ripped tanks below, and all was well. Millions upon millions of gold had been spent in perfecting these engines whose sole aim was slaughter, and now the youth of England was set up as targets to prove which nation had been the cleverest. It turned out that they had all been very clever indeed, for the results were highly creditable, but millions more targets were necessary before this important question could be finally solved. But none doubted that, things having come to this pass, there was anything for it but to see it through. The mischief was done when nations began to challenge each other on paper with the growing lists of their battalions and torpedo-tubes.

Then many of these young men had a bone to pick with God. Such a statement of their intention may sound gratuitously profane, but no other expression seems quite to convey what I mean. To say in milder phrase that "a wave of irreligion" swept over the young generation in the years 1914 to 1918 does not meet the case. For some years already a growing indifference to religious matters had been sweeping over them: it might be called a wave, or it might be called a tide. But there was no hostility about it, any more than there was when Darwin published his *Origin of Species*. Science then simply formulated certain incontrovertible conclusions which seemed to invalidate the first chapters of Genesis, but these conclusions were not designedly polemical. They were groupings of ascertained facts in natural history or geology, only incidentally controversial: their object was to search for the truth, and to get as near to it as possible.   Similarly, but in no polemical spirit, the exponents of the Higher Criticism of the New Testament, looked into the history of the founding of Christianity as revealed in the Gospels.   They examined these books as they would have examined any other documents that claimed to be authoritative, and pointed out historical discrepancies.

But now there was something different.   The fathers and mothers of most of these young men and women who were being targets to prove the efficiency of chemists, or were scrubbing floors in hospitals where the damaged targets were patched up again for future practice, had accepted Christianity as they accepted most other traditions and had brought up their children in a faith that to them was still a guide for life and a consolation in death.   But the children, particularly those who thought, and whose already existing emancipation demanded the right to use their intelligence, began to find very serious objections to taking for granted any longer the code in which they had been brought up, and made of this an indictment for prosecution.   They did not speak of it much, for that is not the English use, but many conducted, in camera within their own minds a pretty stiff cross-examination and they found the answers of the defendant highly unsatisfactory.   There was a crudity, of course, in stating things directly, or asking direct questions, but what (to be crude for a moment) about the efficacy of prayer, as they had been taught to believe in it ? They were convinced that the cause for which they fought was just, but petitions were not getting through: perhaps the line was blocked, for millions of Germans, young men and their parents, were in the same case, and the only conclusion was that God was not interesting Himself. Not long ago at Hakluyt the Bishop had asserted that religion was daily becoming a more vital force in the life of the nation, but it looked as if he was mistaken: it was the chemists and the gunners who had the last word.

I do not want to draw an unfair picture of this quarrel. There were thousands of young men, as padres at the front would testify, in whom belief in God was an unshakeable conviction, and who in danger, in bodily agony and in death found peace and consolation in their undimmed faith. There were thousands upon thousands again for whom religion had always been a matter of indifference, and to whom it remained so. But there were also those, not negligible in point of numbers, and far from negligible in point of intelligence, who quietly thought about it all, and found that the faith in which they had been brought up was not reconcilable with the horrors that were their daily bread. About the reality of them there was no doubt: to see your friend turned to tripe or a dish of brains before your eyes was actual, and they threw over the other not with indifference, but with the savage contempt of those who have been fooled. It was childish to talk of loving your enemies when you were going through hell yourself for the sake of maiming

or killing them as profusely as possible.   And what price
Divine Protection for non-combatants ?   There was
that padre (bloody fool) who ran out across a shell-
swept area to administer the sacrament to a man who lay
mortally wounded in front of a trench, and who was
like to die before they could bring him in.   A shell hit
him directly as he ran: he vanished like a property in a
conjuring-trick, and one couldn't help laughing and was
sick afterwards.

They lived in a world of destruction and fortuitous
death.   All was chance, and it was not even the Devil
who threw the dice, for he was part of the fairy-tale and
perished with it.   It had hardly been worth while to
pick a bone with it, for the only thing to quarrel with
was one's own credulity in having ever believed a tale
that broke down at so many points when put to the test.
Year by year boys fresh from school joined in the dance
of death, and sweltered in the reeking, stinking heat,
when they should have been playing cricket or swimming in cool waters, and they got trench-fever and were
gassed, and young limbs swift to run and ripe for love
were gashed by bullets and sawn off in hospitals.   The
fate of the world rested on their shoulders: they were the
bewildered scapegoats who were driven out into this
desert of death, to expiate the criminal pride and folly of
those who had been in charge of world-affairs while they
were yet unbreeched.   Save for rare moments of panic,
they maintained a cheerful carelessness, a studied uncon-
sciousness of the surrounding horror, for to think about

it, to realize it and to speak of it was to go mad. A few went mad, and with bandaged eyes awaited the volley they would never hear. The rest carried on, dumb and gallant, saying nothing, except in a few blurted words to a friend, of that smouldering focus of resentment and despair.

CHAPTER IV

JOYCE

THESE inarticulate reactions of spiritual revolt and the sense of the injustice of the whole damned mess which had brought these burdens upon the young were felt at home no less than on the various fronts of battle. The girls were scrubbing floors in hospitals, or working all day among innumerable files or mixing the treacles of death in munition factories. These were the years which nature had ordained to be full for them of the rapture of life, and here they were perhaps less mute but no less devoted than the boys and, like them, scapegoats for the sins and monstrous stupidities of those who had brought the world to such a pass. It was the most cruel hard luck that the catastrophe should have come now rather than sooner, when they would still have been children, or later when they would have had their beautiful time. But here it was, so why talk rubbish about it and pretend to accept it as the will of God ? It was hardly possible to go to church without being made sick with such futilities, or by reminders that He chastened those whom He loved. They could have done with fewer of these tokens of affection. Besides, after six

days of painting the wings of an aeroplane with dope
that smelt like pear-drops, who wanted to go to church ?
It didn't seem to do the slightest good, and it was more
sensible to be out of doors if it was fine, or lie in bed till
lunch-time if it was wet. Some of these girls had a
personal problem to solve, and a weighty decision to
make, though, indeed, nothing seemed weighty except
news from the front if he was there, and the scraps of
amusement which could be enjoyed in the intervals of
work: these certainly were not lightly to be foregone.

Of course there were thousands upon thousands of
other girls who throughout these years did their work
admirably and were not the prey of such disturbing reflections. But Joyce Anstey was not of them: she was
of a type that the war evolved, or at any rate made much
more common, and she had something she must make up
her mind about, as she lay in her bath towards lunch-
time that Sunday morning.

Bertie was coming home this afternoon, and they were
to meet in the evening at a party in a studio in Chelsea
given by Princess Amadeo. There would be nobody except her hostess above the age of twenty-two or so, and
she was to chaperone them all. Such an admirable
chaperon: she was always madly devoted to somebody,
and retired with him or her into a discreet corner and
writhed. The party began at eight: there would be a
cold buffet and endless champagne. You danced with
anyone you liked, whether you knew him or not: just a
glance of a particular sort was sufficient introduction

under the Princess's superlative chaperonage, and if it
was a success you exchanged names and presently danced
again, this time with Christian names, and possibly a kiss
or two. Your partner was not always a boy, for boys
danced with boys if they felt disposed and girls with
girls. Joyce herself thought that rather silly. Princess
Amadeo, more open-minded, danced with both. Paris,
with the French genius for nicknames had recently
dubbed her Madame Minotaur and a certain distinguished English General had likewise been called Monsieur Minotaur, but Paris did not imply that any scandal
linked them together; the Classical Dictionary would explain, and there was a pun, slightly indelicate, about
Crete where the Minotaur lived and the signification of
that word when accented.

It had been at one of these unprejudiced parties six
months ago that Joyce had met Bertie. He was dancing
with a boy, when she first saw him, and looking rather
bored, but they exchanged the glad eye, and he dropped
his willowy friend at once. After half-a-dozen meetings
they had got engaged, and this evening they meant
to settle finally what they were going to do about it. She
had no father, but both his parents and her mother were
strongly opposed to their marrying now, for the war, it
was believed (this was in the late spring of 1918), could
not last more than six months longer, as Germany was
beginning to crack and liquefy in all directions like ice
under a south-west wind, and their parents thought it
was more sensible to wait. There was something in this,

thought Joyce, for a friend of her's had been married last year, and her husband had been killed a week later: and there she was now, nineteen years old, with a baby born nine months after his death, and a widow's pension. A ridiculous position. On the other hand six months would be a long time to wait for a legal ceremony, and they were going to settle tonight whether they should be married quietly at a registry-office before he went back to France, or dispense with the ceremony. There was something to be said for dispensing with it, for if they got tired of each other before the war was over they could break their engagement without the sordid publicity of a divorce. It did not seem possible that they should get tired of each other, but you couldn't tell, and so why run the risk ?

Joyce rippled the steaming scented water, and pressed her hands upwards on her body from thigh to breast, and masséd her neck. She had had one adventure with a boy during the second year of the war: it had been a frolic just for the fun of it. Neither of them had taken it seriously and it came to an end quite amicably, as they soon got rather tired of each other, and it was all over long before she met Bertie. She had thought about it very little since, and never with the smallest sense of shame or regret, for it was entirely their own concern, and no harm had come of it, nor did she feel for a moment that she had violated the shrine of herself that ought to have been kept stainless for dedication. Such a notion was part of the old discarded shibboleths, pass-words that admitted you nowhere. Besides, to look at the matter fairly, how many men are virgin when they take their mates? A handful of cranks and milksops. She grinned as she thought of an antique story she had read the other day of how a young man about to wed came to his bride-to-be and told her with faltering lips and lowered eyes how once . . . And that sweet creature blushing violently said she would forgive him and never allude to his "fall" again, because he had been open with her! What would a girl do now-a-days if her future husband came to her with such a pack of rubbish? She would laugh and say "Oh, darling, how can you be such a liar and say it was only once?"

Were people ever like that, she wondered. Hardly possible. Girls and women, she would have allowed, were rather different from men. Promiscuity no doubt coarsened them somehow and they became — what was that word in the Bible? — yes they became lascivious and thought about nothing else. Bitches. But could that book by Thomas Hardy, *Tess of the D'Urbervilles*, ever have been psychologically true? Joyce's mother, Victorian to the marrow, had only two years ago said that she did not wish her to read it at present, so of course Joyce, though with some labour, read every word of it. There was a chapter in which on their marriage-night, just before going to bed, Tess and Angel Clare confessed to each other their previous sexual experiences: Angel Clare allowed that he had once been with a woman, and Tess, like herself, had once been with a man. This was such a frightful shock to him that he instantly left her, married but unwed, and she went back to her original seducer. Joyce thought she had never read anything so grotesque. Could any young man have been such an ass?

The bell for lunch rang, but she still lay in her bath, till her mother came and rattled at the door. She had mixed herself a cocktail before she came to her bath, and now, as she dried herself, she sipped it, and smoked a cigarette, continuing to think about Tess. Tess had been a fool to tell a man who, she ought to have known, was such a transcendent prig, but she herself had been quite wise to tell Bertie about her own experience. Naturally he had not minded an atom, indeed it had occurred to her that it was rather a relief to him to know that . . . As regards their possible marriage at the registry-office, she settled that she would do exactly as he liked.

For tonight they had made their plans. They would stop at the Princess' party for an hour or two and then go to his bachelor-flat in Beaufort Street close by, and sleep together for the first time: she would take with her the despatch-case which she used at the office, containing her new black pyjamas and a few things needful. . . That trick he had of wrinkling his nose when he was amused, that slight stammer when he was excited, that great yellow mop of hair . . . This would not be a frolic as her affair with Derek had been, for they had both been children, utterly shameless and full of laughter, ragging

and wrestling together, not needing each other an atom
but just enjoying each other.   This was different, for it
seemed to her that her physical passion for Bertie — how
she longed to be in the dark with him, still and tense ! —
was not a sundered pleasure, complete in itself, but that
he grew out of some intimate soil in her nature and had
his roots deep down in the centre of herself.   April:
spring-time; the singing of birds.

POWDER and lip-stick and rouge were beginning to come
into common use among her contemporaries, but Joyce
preferred not to try experiments with that olive paleness
of complexion which nature had bestowed on her.
Many other girls, she thought, would have looked far
more attractive if they had left their faces alone, but
they used these devices as signals.   They wanted to look
coquettish and cocottish and larky and ready for anything, and these bright flags would encourage the eye
of a desirable bashful and wave to him that *ici on parle
des amourettes*.   But Joyce did not want to give that
impression, for she was not in search of *amourettes*.
Besides, apart from that, make-up had to be exceedingly
well done to produce the right lure; otherwise it made
you look like a hag who plastered it on to conceal the
ravages of years.   Occasionally, if you were very tired
and felt like a worm, it gave you confidence to know
that your lips were vermilion, and that a streak of kohl,
daintily applied, made your eyes look bright.   But to-

day there was no need for that, and she hurried over her dressing and went down to lunch.

Her mother was a fortunate woman, for she had a friend who was a vegetarian with two vegetarian children, and who gave her all her ration-tickets for meat, in exchange for Mrs. Anstey's sugar-tickets. With these she could procure a solid undercut of beef for Sunday. How good it smelt! Joyce ate heartily, conscious of nourishment, and afterwards went out for a stroll in the Park in the clear spring sunshine. The southwest wind bowled shining white clouds across the sky, it raised big ripples on the Serpentine that set the tufted ducks bobbing up and down like tubby boats in a choppy sea, and made the clumps of daffodils nod gaily to each other as if they were talking of some joyful news that had just reached them. Joyce caught her mind behaving in a very Victorian manner: positively she found herself wondering whether the daffodils had heard that Bertie was coming back today. Fragments of old-fashioned verse, rather jolly, ran in her head as she looked at them: she could hardly help saying aloud:

> And then my heart with pleasure fills,
> And dances with the daffodils.

or:

> Oh! to be in England
> Now that April's there.

Perhaps in all women when they were in love, and knew that they would spend the night in their lover's arms, some streak of sentimentality asserted itself.

Her mother had gone to the afternoon service at St. Paul's, and when Joyce returned home, she found on the hall-table a letter for her which had just been left by hand. The writing, she knew, was that of Bertie's mother, and across the back of the envelope, when she turned it over to open it, were the words "Bad news." That could only mean one thing, and inside was a note from her and the War Office telegram to say that he had been killed in action yesterday.

She wondered whether someone had sent her this as a joke. She wondered whether God had got to know what she and Bertie had planned for that night and, in order to stop it, had diverted a bullet as it whistled by him to the required direction. She was not stunned, she did not cry, she sat and thought. Her mother would be in presently, and Joyce would have to tell her. Mrs. Anstey would fold her in her arms and weep, and say in a broken voice that trials and bereavements were sent us for some great and good purpose, though we might not be able to see at the time what that happened to be. She had done that when her husband was killed in the first year of the war, and without doubt she would do it again. Joyce wondered what would happen if she said to her mother that she quite agreed, and that she knew what the great and good purpose was, for she and Bertie had meant to sleep together at his flat tonight, and now they couldn't.   All this passed through her head, not as if she thought it herself, but as if it was presented to her on the screen at a cinema.

Joyce's mother returned from her service, and did all that might have been expected of her, even quoting the hymn "For ever with the Lord."   Soon Mrs. Anstey wore the girl's nerves to fiddlestrings: she spoke in a low voice; she said, "Darling, how brave you are being about it"; she laid occasional hands of sympathy on her head, she talked of the dead as having "crossed over," and what hosts of friends there would be to welcome him on the other bank !   It was all such rubbish: the same old fairy-tale; it was not even worth while to ask her how she knew there would be anybody there or if there was any other bank.   Mrs. Anstey had been engaged to dine with the vegetarian friend this evening, but when she took it for granted that she would stop at home, Joyce absolutely forbade it.   Presently she could stand her mother's sympathy no longer, and went to her room, saying that she would be better alone.   No: she didn't want any dinner, she would go to bed, and she hoped her mother would not look in on her when she came home for, if she was asleep, it would wake her.

She heard her mother go out, and soon solitude became as intolerable as her presence had been, and she could not face the darkness and the slow silent hours. Anything to divert that unending stream of thought that circled round in her mind that he was dead, that she would never see him again nor be with him tense and still in the dark, with her fingers in his hair, and her lips and her body pressed close to his. She wanted to be among people who did not know what had happened, and who would not look at her with solemn sympathising faces: she wanted to be back at her work again. But it was only just nine: there were thirteen hours to get through before that. Well; there was only one thing to do, and she got up and dressed herself in the frock she had intended to wear. A glance at her looking-glass told her that a touch of lip-stick on her mouth and of black below her eyes was advisable. Then with her latch-key, but without the despatch-case, she let herself out of the house, and went to Princess Amadeo's party.

The party was already in full swing, the big studio and a small room adjoining were crammed and, as everyone, dancing or not, was smoking, the air was thick with a bluish haze that made visibility dim, just as the gabble of talk rendered the blaring gramophone only faintly audible. Joyce was not hungry though she had not dined, but she went with a friend into the buffet, where she had a couple of glasses of champagne. That sluggish circling of one thought in her brain slowed up: it was as if a layer of ice formed over it, and the sun glistened on it, so that what lay beneath became invisible. There were heaps of friends about, and they all looked gay and jolly, and were ever so pleased to see her. Then suddenly she caught sight of Derek. Two years had passed since she had seen him, but they had not changed him an atom, he was still as cherub-faced and boyish as ever, full of sap, full of the grace of irresponsible animality. He had pointed ears like a satyr (how well she remembered that when she saw them again!) he was lissom, he was bubbling with that air of spontaneous enjoyment which she craved for as racked nerves cry out for morphia. Just now he was dancing with Helen St. Erth, and had not seen her yet, and as she looked at him, she felt some familiar thrill and prickling stir in her blood. Presently Derek — oddly enough Joyce could not remember his surname — saw her. He stared for a second, then recognised her, and at that moment Monsieur Minotaur came and took Helen away from him.

Derek came sidling across the studio towards her between the close couples. "Rather on," thought Joyce, "but not blotto. He never used to get blotto because he said it simply made you stupid, and that you didn't enjoy other things so much. But slightly tipsy, yes; and how killingly funny he was when he was like that. I've never laughed so much . . ." Half way across the room he was jointly and affectionately embraced by an epicene couple of disagreeable appearance: they might have been a girl and a boy, or, in the same order of identification, a boy and a girl. Or perhaps they were both of the same sex which may have been either: it was impossible from their faces and figures and gestures to be certain. Derek disengaged himself, and next moment he was kissing her.

"You darling," he said. "I've never been really happy since I saw you last. And I've been thrown over by the prettiest girl in the world, except you, whom I was en-

gaged to. Told me I was a bloody philanderer, just because
— well never mind that. Has Bertie jilted you too?
Madame Minotaur told me he was coming tonight, and I
don't see a vestige of his vulgar countenance."

"Nor you ever will again," said Joyce. "He was killed
yesterday."

"God! What bad luck!" said Derek. "Rotten
luck. Septic. Jolly sensible of you to come here and
put it out of your mind. No use in thinking: I should
go dotty if I thought. There'll be time to think when
it's all over. Let's go and have a drink. Drink, not
think."

"Darling, haven't you had enough?" said Joyce.

"No: 'another little drink wouldn't do me any
harm,'" quoted Derek "then I shall be utterly o k.
Come on."

She had another glass of champagne, she danced with
him, and the remembering blood purred in her veins.
She noticed a red ribbon on his tunic and asked what it
was. He acknowledged, as if rather ashamed of it, that
it was so. She questioned him further and he told her
that there had been a pal of his whom he simply adored,
who had been shot in the groin and lay out in No Man's
Land howling and writhing. So he nipped over the
parapet — it wasn't more than a dozen yards or so —
and brought him in, in the hell of a funk all the time that
he would be plugged in the bottom.

"Frightful piece of luck for me," he said, "but it
turned out really to be an awful sell, for Kenneth died

an hour afterwards.   Let's go and sit out somewhere.
Ever been into Madame Minotaur's bedroom ?   A great
voluptuous bed big enough for three, and a huge silver
crucifix immediately above it.   Made me roar with
laughter: damned funny. Or what about another
drink ?   And when am I going to see you again ?
Properly, I mean, or improperly if you prefer that way
of putting it.   Do !   We've both had disappointments,
and it will cheer us up.   We did have fun, didn't we ?
How about tomorrow night ?   My father's away:
sumptuous mansion in Lowndes Square all to ourselves.
You remember it: several times."

Joyce had nothing to do to-morrow night, and she
promised to go.   So the despatch-box with the black
pyjamas and the few things needful would be used after
all, though not quite according to plan.   He was a
darling: he was so gay, and he wanted her and she him,
and she hungered for the frolic of the flesh and its almost
innocent shamelessness.   She herself, it struck her, was
really like Tess, going back, when her own man had cast
her off in favour of harps and hymns on "the other side,"
to her seducer.   As to what her mother would say when
she knew she was going out, she cared not at all: probably Joyce would tell her that she was dining with
Bertie's people, and if she found out afterwards that she
had not been there, what did it matter since nothing
mattered ?   But she thought she would go home now,
and Derek whistled up a taxi, and got in after her.   She
lay in his arms, with eyes shut, saying over and over to

herself that he was Bertie.   Suddenly with a violent re-
vulsion as swift as a spasm of sickness she pushed him
away.   "You beast!" she said.   "Leave me alone.   I
hate you, and I don't want ever to see you again."

The taxi stopped at her mother's door.

"Good Lord, w'off I done?" said the astonished Derek.

"Nothing.   Not your fault.   But I can't."

"Right-o," said Derek.   "Kiss me, and say you forgive
me for nothing at all.   And let me know when you feel
you can.   Any time during the next week, darling: I'll
chuck anything for it.   Oh, tell the jarvey to drive back
to the Minotaur's."

She let herself quietly in.   The house was dark, so evidently her mother had no notion that she was not in bed.
She did not turn on the lights, but felt her way upstairs
by the banisters.   She listened for a moment by her
mother's door, but all was quiet, and then let herself into
her own room.   Was she drunk, she asked herself.   No
doubt she was, but that was all to the good for she would
sleep.   She undressed quickly and got into bed.   Derek's
face hovered in the darkness, and she remembered his
surname for the first time.   And the house in Lowndes
Square, she remembered that too, and his room, and the
fun of it.   She had been a fool, and she would certainly
ring him up tomorrow morning.

THERE were many of these Joyces and Dereks.   The
girls were working hard, and the boys were fighting like
devils, and in the flower of their youth they were being

mown down like the hayfields of June to save the nation from perishing. They all knew that, and though not a single one of them would have said so, it was like a free-masonry between them. They were not the least proud of what they were doing, they detested the necessity that had been put upon them, and they refrained even from thinking about it. All those horrors must be put out of mind. They must be buried, as if beneath a shower of rose-leaves, under any pleasure of the moment that could cover them up for half an hour. And for themselves they demanded, in payment for services rendered, a complete independence in the conduct of their private lives; they were going to have no interference there on the part of those whom they were saving from the consequences of their own mismanagements. Their elders could not dispute their right: they had earned whatever liberties they chose to demand.

CHAPTER V

EARLY REACTIONS

I

ON ARMISTICE DAY the streets of Boston, U.S.A., were filled with processions of riotous rejoicing, and some of them carried fine large banners, with the satisfactory legend, "We won the War." That same day there was an English gunboat in the harbour which gaily beflagged herself, and to one of these flags some humorous person, who had been ashore and seen the banners, attached a small label on which he had printed the modest words, "And we helped." Then the gunboat, with a broad grin, put to sea. . .

It was over, and totally apart from the huge and heartfelt reactions were minor ones: restrictions would be relaxed and life would be comfortable again. Lord Rosebery (than whom there was never a more level-headed and incisive thinker) had said, now three years ago: "The worst of the war is that it's such a bore." Many people considered that a very dreadful and cynical thing to have said, but their real reason for murmuring "Hush !" was that it summed up, without any nonsense,

exactly what they themselves felt, and they did not like
such a petty sentiment openly expressed: they had an
uneasy qualm that he was reading their secret thoughts.
But his remark was perfectly true and not in the least
cynical. He was not talking about the heroic and tragic
side of the war: he took for granted that everybody ex-
perienced the strain and the anxieties and the danger of
its hideous realities, and merely pointed out another objection to it which everybody except an idiot must feel,
and nobody but a hypocrite need feel ashamed of expressing. The liberty of daily life had been curtailed by
numberless and most inconvenient prohibitions and regulations. Lights in the street must be darkened and lights
in houses obscured after nightfall, so that the glow of
London should not guide the raiders to their destination,
though in spite of these precautions they always seemed
to find their way without much difficulty. If you
dined out or went to the theatre when nights were
moonlit there was always the risk of an attack from the
air before you got home; then you had to wait till it was
over, or scurry along through deserted streets with the
rattle of engines overhead, the harsh barking of anti-
aircraft guns, and the occasional thud of some abominable explosion. If you were at the club, you had to
order drinks the moment dinner was over, in case you
might feel thirsty two hours later: motors could not be
used for purposes of pleasure, and if you went by train,
as likely as not you had to travel in the guard's van, and
it was impossible to obtain a passport to go abroad, unless

you were on an official errand of some kind.   Rations of
butter, sugar and meat were cut down to derisory proportions, and, if leaving home, you had to remember to
furnish yourself with ration tickets.   All the amenities
of life which one takes for granted were withdrawn, and
the whole thing was a dreadful bore, but nobody said so
except Lord Rosebery.   As soon as the war was over
this minor reaction of relief speedily made itself felt,
and nobody wanted to hear anything more about the
boring subject.   In consequence the flood of books concerning the war which presently poured out from every
publishing house in London roused only the most tepid
attention.   Many of them were extremely well written,
they recounted experiences and adventures of the most
interesting kind, but nobody wanted to read them because they dealt with that topic of which everyone had
had more than enough.   It was years before the public
cared to hear any more about it, and then, oddly enough,
it was the translations of German war books that first
took hold.

THERE had been other profiteers besides the great whales
who had made fortunes and peerages out of the nation's
need for ships and coal and food; there were minnows
as well, and a peculiarly loathsome type of such, small
in actual number but wholly execrable, was the so-
called "mediums" who made brisk business with widows
and childless mothers.   It may be said that credulous
folk have only themselves to blame when they let go of

common sense to clutch at anything, however fraudulent, that may bring them comfort. But they sorely needed comfort. They had prayed that their beloved should be kept safe from the terror by night and the arrow by day, but prayer had not availed, and the great silence had fallen. They now longed to get some sign that a husband or a son was still individually alive, and a friend, in similar case, would tell them of the unspeakable consolation that she had found in *séances;* she was convinced that she had got in touch with her dead, and he had told her that all was well with him. In consequence hundreds and thousands of the bereaved, chiefly women, flocked to these practitioners. Demand, as always, created supply, for there was an unusual number of folk who longed and hungered to know what had become of the unimprisoned souls they had loved on earth, and in consequence an unusual number of otherwise ordinary persons, again chiefly women, who were found to be ready, at a small fee, to tell them.

Now the subject itself is of universal and transcendent interest. It is impossible to conceive any discovery that could be made in the realms of human knowledge comparable with a proof or indeed with very strong evidence that the individual is not extinguished by death, but that individuality survives and that communication can be established between the two worlds: no such solvent for the bulk of human sorrows could be imagined. Evidence does exist, strong enough to convince trained and scientific minds, accustomed to sift phenomena and re-ject all that could possibly be accounted for by manifestations of natural laws, such as telepathy or thought transference, and a residue remains which is accepted by men of the highest reputation in science, like Sir Oliver Lodge and the late Sir William Barrett, and by eminent lawyers like the late Sir Edward Marshall-Hall. All these had psychical experiences which they considered inexplicable except on the theory that individuality survived corporal death, and that individual discarnate spirits could through certain channels communicate with the living. Such communications are for the most part exceedingly trivial, they often contain errors of fact, and, as far as I am aware, not one has yet given any informative picture of the conditions under which individuality persists after the death of the body. Perhaps it is impossible that we could understand an existence in which time and space have no part: perhaps no idea of it can be conveyed in human speech which only deals with human concepts. But among these trivialities there have been given pieces of information which could not have been known to the medium, and were unknown to the sitter (whose mind therefore cannot have been "tapped" by the medium) and these have subsequently turned out to be true. The Society for Psychical Research, also, has been for many years investigating such messages, which purport to come, chiefly through automatic script, from the dead. Those who have studied them (they are exceedingly dry and difficult) are satisfied that they contain evidential matter. These conclusions arrived at by highly intelligent people should be regarded with the greatest respect by those who have not made their study in them.

But those mediums who sprang up like mushrooms during the war, and whose *séances* were grotesquely and transparently fraudulent can only be regarded as swindlers battening on the credulity of those who were starving for comfort. I attended several of these callous performances, and the following account, though it may possibly combine details drawn from more than one, is substantially correct.

Five women, all in deep mourning, had come to find consolation in their bereavements. There was also an elderly man who, so he told me, sat with this medium once a month in order to talk with his sister, who had died many years ago, as a child. My friend and I, who had come to observe, completed the circle of enquirers. The medium, a middle-aged woman, sat next her brother, and when the circle had been formed the lights were turned out, and the only illumination was a ruby-shaded candle that stood on the mantelpiece. The medium had thus every facility for cheating: neither she nor her brother nor the room had been searched, the light was so low that no quiet movement of her or her brother could be detected, and as they sat next each other it was perfectly easy for them to detach a hand from the circle. Her left hand and his right hand could be busy without any of the sitters being aware of it. A good deal can be done with two free hands in the way of manipulating properties and distributing spirit-touches. In the middle of the table round the edge of which our hands were joined, thumb to thumb and finger to finger, stood a cardboard megaphone known as a trumpet, similar to that through which the coach of a rowing eight talks from the towpath to his crew. Through this we hoped to hear the direct voice of departed spirits: it was within easy reach of the free hands of the medium and her brother.

The medium "offered prayer," and we said "Amen." Silence. Then she began to breathe heavily with a snoring sound. This subsided, and her brother told us that she was in trance: we might therefore expect that her control, who was the spirit of a Red Indian squaw, called Bluebell, would soon take possession of her. Pending Bluebell's arrival, he suggested that we should sing "Lead Kindly Light," because Cardinal Newman often came to these *séances*, and the singing of this hymn would gratify and encourage the departed prelate. Sure enough, we had hardly begun the second verse, when a stentorian voice, thick in volume and like a fog-horn, joined our scrannel choir, singing the air of the tune (Dykes in A flat) an octave below the trebles, and so that was the Cardinal. Soon after a luminous cross appeared hovering and bobbing about somewhere above the centre of the table, and then the Cardinal blessed us, and went away, I suppose to attend another *séance*. A slight rattle on the table indicated that he had replaced the megaphone.

There was a pause, then a sound of girlish laughter, and a woman's voice said, "Good evening, dear friends," and those who had been here before, evidently a majority of the circle, knew at once who this was, and replied, "Good evening, dear Bluebell." Then Bluebell said that there was a young man with her who had passed over in the war, and he longed to talk to his mother, if she was present. His name was Henry. But no one claimed Henry, and he went away. An older man, said Bluebell, took his place (apparently at the far end of a telephone between the quick and the dead). He had brown eyes and brown hair with a little grey in it, and his nose and his chin were what Bluebell would call medium. His name was Walter, and he had another name too, which she could not quite make out, and she thought he was called by the other name. . . Then out of the darkness there came from the woman sitting on my left a little sob, and she asked if his other name, by which he was called, was Bob. It was, and Bluebell said it was her husband, who had passed over in the first year of the war, or it might have been the second, and she could speak to him. Her voice was trembling, and she whispered, "Oh, Bob, how lovely that you've been able to get through! Tell me what you're doing." There was silence, and Bluebell said he was collecting power to speak to her. After a while he got enough power, and he said in a rather low hoarse voice that he was in a lovely place, much lovelier than anything on earth, but difficult to describe. He was very happy and very busy, helping those who had passed over after him, because they felt a little strange at first. They could not understand that they were what is called dead, and they weren't. And she, his wife (name not disclosed), mustn't mourn for him any more, because he was so happy. Then his voice faded to a whisper, and he could not say any more now because the power was fading out, but he would try to lay his hand on her shoulder as he used to do. From somewhere close at hand, not localisable in the darkness, came a whisper, "Do you feel my hand, darling?" and she said, "Yes, dearest."

Bob faded out to the sound of a musical box. Soon there came a childish piping treble saying, "Is 'oo there, Dickie?" and the elderly man who came to talk with his sister, who had died in early girlhood, said, "Yes, Effie, dear." Effie, it appeared, had not grown up since she had "passed over" at the age of ten; she remained a child. This was puzzling. I could not see how it would work out. For if, on the same analogy, a man's mother had died at the age of twenty, and he lived to be ninety, he would find, when he passed over, that he would be seventy years older than his mother. But there was no time to follow up that complication, for Effie said that the power was coming through "booful," and she thought she could materialize some little piece of her. So we sang a verse of some other hymn to help, and presently there appeared in the centre of the table a small white hand, faintly luminous, as of a child. It terminated at the wrist in folds of muslin. The fingers were rigid and motionless, but the whole hand moved with little jerks from the direction of the medium towards Effie's brother. He was sure it was Effie's hand, and while he talked to Effie he was allowed gently to stroke it. . .

There is no use in continuing the account of such drab charlatanry. Bluebell came again, dropped a flower on the table, and then said goodbye, for the power was going, and we were told to sit with our hands still touching till the medium came out of trance, for otherwise she would receive a fearful shock, which might even be fatal. My friend and I agreed in a whisper to risk this, and quietly withdrew our touching hands, thus breaking the circle. A minute or so afterwards she came out of trance quite uninjured and without any shock, but the pause no doubt had been useful for the storing away of the properties, child's hand and so forth. The lights were turned up, and the woman who had talked to Bob was tearfully radiant.

Now these mourners were just as sane as those who looked for periscopes in the Thames, and believed that Russian battalions were passing through the country, and hardly more credulous. No one could grudge comfort to those who were bewildered by their bitter losses, but it is sickening to think from what trumpery cheating they often derived it. There have been dupes and swindlers in all ages, but this particular form of swindling increased enormously during the war. A peculiarly repulsive feature in it was that the swindlers blended religion and trickery together: hymns were sung and benedictions pronounced while the apparatus of fraud was being got ready, and the loftiest emotions of the mind were being played upon to render the sitters more gullible to the shoddiest illusions.   This profiteering over bereavement was very lucrative: there were eight sitters at the *séance* I have been describing, each of whom paid a guinea.   That was not a bad wage for sitting in the dark for an hour.

ENGLAND was inclined to agree with the grinning gunboat putting out from Boston harbour, but she formed the less justifiable impression that the millennium was about to dawn.   Those who were fortunate enough to see good in everything were not slow to discover that, bitter and bloody as these years had been, they had made it impossible that there should ever be another war. How those responsible for the conduct of national affairs, not only here but in other countries, set about securing that, belongs to a later chapter, for they are busy at it still.   For the present there was the task of industrial reintegration to be attended to, and that must be the first concern.   On paper it looked simple.   The factories which had been converted into manufacturing places of war-material, such as steelworks, shipyards or chemical works, would resume the industries of peace, and those which for lack of man-power had been closed would re-open again.   The girls and women who had been employed in factories would go back to their proper sphere in domestic life, the men of the demobilised armies would take their places, and with the enormous losses the nation had suffered, there would naturally be work for all. Not a man — England would see to that — who had given up his employment at the call of his country would find himself out of a place.

With war no longer possible, the competition in rival armaments which had been so ruinous even before the war would cease, and an age of unexampled prosperity would begin. Income tax, it is true, had risen to unheard of heights, and highly taxed incomes, it was admitted, crippled the hands of capitalists. But that was due to the appalling expense of the war, and now, automatically, since that expense was over, it would subside again. There had been a time when Mr. Gladstone, as Chancellor of the Exchequer, had pronounced that a shilling in the pound was far too high a rate, and nobody really expected it to go below that figure for the present. Wages were high, but the cost of living would now go down again, and wages would follow. Like the general subsidence of a rough sea when the gale has ceased to blow, we should soon have a halcyon calm. Again, America, France, Italy and England were now bound together in bonds of brotherhood that could never be loosened. There were some war debts, it is true, to be adjusted and paid, but a thing like that could never cause difficulties or unpleasantnesses between those who had saved the world from being ground under the iron heel of Germany. They would look into each other's eyes, grasp

hands and say, "How can you speak of such trifles ?"
Besides, all these debts would have to be paid by Germany, said Mr. Lloyd George merrily. A heavy bill:
£600,000,000,000 was a rough estimate. How would
she raise it ? That was her business.

This is no caricatured picture of the Fool's Paradise
which, for a couple of years after the war was over, no
one pointed out was the most unstable of fantasies.
There was a tremendous boom on the Stock Exchange
and shares soared: Shell Transport, for instance (£1
shares), stood at over £14. This boom was significant
merely because it was a symbol or a symptom of the insane illusion that, the war being over, an era of security
and prosperity was coming, and it is as difficult to account for it now, on the basis of intrinsic values, as the
South Sea Bubble, or as the affair of Mme. Humbert's
famous safe, in which, so she assured astute bankers, were
certificates worth millions and millions of francs. They
were satisfied that it did without any examination of its
contents, and advanced more money. When, eventually, the safe was opened it proved to contain a few buttons, but was otherwise empty. In the same way, it
was generally believed, without any scrutiny of assets,
that, the enemies of peace being now in the dust, the
coffers of the rest of the world, which served them decently before, must presently be bursting with wealth.
It occurred to nobody that during the last four years the
man-power (which in the last simplification is the earning power) of all nations concerned in the war, except

America, who had won the war, had been decimated, and that the milliards of money spent in causing this decimation had been productive of nothing whatever except destruction of capital and of death. The shell that cost a hundred pounds (say) to make had given work and wage to a certain number of men, but the shell when finished and sent out on its job destroyed far more than the capital that had been spent in its manufacture. If luck attended it, it caused death and mutilation, and the ruin of buildings: if it had no luck it and its cunning mechanism, the hellish energy expensively stored in its smooth steel sides, were all wasted. Indeed, the more it fulfilled its purpose the greater was the resultant annihilation of capital: a bomb adroitly let loose from an aeroplane might possibly destroy a thousand or a million times what it had cost to make, and the world was correspondingly poorer for its success. Naturally, when nations are at war, destruction of the enemy's wealth in men or material is the main object of their activities. But the total result on Armistice Day was that every penny that had been spent, whether on a bullet that found no billet, or on a shell that demolished a corner of Rheims Cathedral or shattered its irreplaceable glass, had been destructive of wealth. There is productive expenditure and there is destructive expenditure: the man who buys manure and hires a gardener to dig it into his vegetable beds is spending his money productively in the reasonable hope that the earth will repay him his capital with a dividend added.   So also is he who digs in the bowels of the earth to find gold.   But every penny spent on the war was lost.   In twenty years' time or perhaps fifty the carefullest economy might conceivably make good the Bedlamite extravagance of the war, and England be as rich again as she was in 1914.   But the notion that an immediate era of wealth and prosperity was coming was just as Bedlamite.   Not she alone but the whole world was for the time bankrupt, and it thought that it had only got to draw cheques to itself to restore its depleted exchequers.

England of all the Allies (Russia for the present having ceased nationally to exist) was the last to recognize the truth, because she was accustomed to consider it quite impossible that she should ever be poor, and her collective mind could not grasp such a conception. Moreover, unlike the French, to whom economy is a natural instinct, she was as yet constitutionally incapable of thrift, and when she did get some fleeting and unpleasant glimpses of the real state of things, her remedy was not to be thrifty but to be spendthrift, and the successive governments of the day, whether Conservative or Labour, though widely differing as to their methods in unbridled expenditure, were at one over the principle. But that was still in the future, and the tragic history of it, perhaps not yet complete, was to become a problem, vastly complicated, not for England alone but for the world.

APART from this approaching financial débâcle, not as yet even dimly apprehended, it was soon clear that the values of all that concerned the social life of the nation had changed. Chief among these changes was the whole status and position of women. Up till the time of the outbreak of war the spirit of respectability in women, even more than in men, had been deeply outraged by the violent deeds and martyrdoms of the suffragettes. But now when the war was over, and the burning questions then left to smoulder out were rekindled again, there was no need for them to renew their campaign. Women had shewn that they were not only steadfast and reliable workers, but were capable, individually and collectively, of sound organization and of shouldering responsibilities. The nation could not have pulled through had not women taken the place of men in the management and administration of all kinds of business hitherto believed to require masculine brains, and they had proved their entire efficiency. No one, not even those who had been most bitterly opposed to it, any longer wished to deny them some form of suffrage, but they had won it not through their antic exhibitions of lawlessness before the war, but through their wisdom and their demonstrated worth during it. It was granted them not in any spirit of patronage or of giving a prize to a good little girl, nor by the grace of superiors but by the willing justice of equals. With this, as an undisputed corollary to their right to have a voice in the elections to

Parliament, came the right to be themselves elected.

But the suffrage was not the greatest of the emancipations that women had won during the war. They had been chauffeurs, constables, electricians, chemists, doctors and nurses, and perhaps the only branch of industry in which they had not, subject to certain limitations in physical strength, shewn themselves at least the equals of men was, ironically, that of dressmakers. In secretarial work they were both cheaper than male labour and, on the whole, more efficient. Many directors of companies and managers of businesses preferred, when the war was over, to retain their girls instead of reverting to demobilised young men. The latter, in any case, would have to be trained afresh, even if they had had any experience of the kind before, and begin, at a rather mature age, at the bottom. The girls on their side preferred to retain the freedom and wage-earning of employment to a reversion to the sheltered life. They had shewn themselves amply capable of being efficient workers when the national need required it of them, and now, when there was no longer any call for that, work had become an instinct. Independently of their wage, it gave scope for the employment and development of their qualities. Dr. Johnson, in one of his more questionable pronouncements, said that no man likes to work, and that he does so only because he needs money. That was certainly true of himself, because he had a genius for conversation, and was most congenially employed not when he was writing "Rasselas" but browbeating Boswell. But his generalization does not hold: the majority of mankind prefers work to idleness, for they are using their powers, as, in point of fact, Dr. Johnson himself was when he was talking. Certainly thousands of women and girls who, till the outbreak of the war, had droned their lives away in a vague comfortable discontent, found that, after having tasted the sting and sweetness of occupation, however monotonous in itself, they were most unwilling to go back to the deadlier monotony of having nothing to do. They demanded also, as the worker has every right to do, livelier relaxations and a greater measure of liberty when the day's work was over: latchkeys were multiplied and the domestic hours by the fireside curtailed. They left their homes in increasing numbers, set up in flats with a friend or friends to share expenses, or lived in hostels for women where they had practically complete liberty.

It is undeniable that the war, with the calls it made on the employment and the energies of women, hugely accelerated this movement towards independence. It had begun, as we have seen, before the war, and what the war had done was to demonstrate on a vast scale that women were capable of doing the work which had hitherto been considered the province of the male. It was no use, as some old-fashioned malcontents did, to call them unsexed, for they were nothing of the sort; they were only bent on using the gifts which the war had shewn they possessed. That was all to the good, for surely the greater number of efficient workers that a nation breeds the greater is the efficiency of the nation. That there was an enormous number of men out of employment at the time was merely incidental: it did not touch the principle of the matter, nor was the principle affected by the fact that there was not enough work for everybody. Women had become competitors with men in a way they had never done before, and were showing that in every branch (save in dressmaking) they were formidable. "Self-expression" became a common word in the vocabulary of the day for there was much of it about. . . The student of language in the future will observe that the adjectives "septic," "crashing" and "devastating" belong to the same epoch: they were synonymous.

This competition manifested itself in the arts as well as the industries: an unprecedented number of women, for instance, took to writing novels and proved their competence. There had been women, Emily and Charlotte Brontë and George Eliot, in the first ranks of English novelists before, there had been "best-sellers" and hugely popular writers such as Marie Corelli, and serious thinkers like Mrs. Humphrey Ward: it was this spate of female authors of fiction in competition with men that was new. And how the conditions of that competition had changed ! Robert Southey had once told Charlotte Brontë that "Literature cannot be the business for a woman's life, and ought not to be": and so convinced were she and her sisters that no woman writer would be fairly judged on her merits, if it was known that she was a woman, that they had adopted *noms de plume* which did not betray the secret of their sex, and under cover of Currer, Ellis and Acton Bell, hoped to get not necessarily a favourable but at least an impartial judgment from critics and readers, which would not otherwise have been theirs. Even after Charlotte Brontë had published the best seller of the year in *Jane Eyre* (though Thackeray's *Vanity Fair* was then coming out in parts) she was still acutely anxious that her sex should not be known when *Shirley* was published. But her secret leaked out, and though her fame was already established by the prodigious success of these first two books, she wanted to publish her masterpiece *Villette* anonymously sooner than incur the prejudice against a novel known to be written by a woman. Next to her in the succession came Marian Evans who, for the same reason, preferred to make her appeal to the public as George Eliot. But time by now had brought its revenge to the misjudged sex, and if today a young man wanted to secure a prejudice in favour of his first venture as a novelist, he might seriously consider whether he would not do well to adopt a feminine *nom de plume* and, if his name was Desmond, call himself Desdemona. He would probably have a far better chance of instantly becoming "a force to be reckoned with" or "the possessor of genius, that lightning of the mind." Charlotte Brontë today would certainly not dream of concealing her sex or, when it was known, of following up her success by anonymity, for she was fortunate enough to be a woman. Her sex

which had once been a handicap was now a definite asset.
The chivalrous Victorians, to whom women were
charmers and sylphs and fairies, were perfectly certain
that they had no brains and ought not to adopt literature as a profession, because the pretty things were quite
incapable of writing.   Now the wheel has turned, and
though chivalry is accounted dead, women's brains are
more respected than men's.   Not for a moment do I
say that women have not fairly beaten men out of the
field in fiction, or that the discoveries of fresh feminine
genius made every week in the columns of the most
authoritative reviewers are not justified: I only note the
complete reversal of sentiment towards them as authors.

PROBABLY every generation in turn has been amazed at
the reticence which its fathers and mothers preserved in
the elementary facts of natural history that concern the
human race: animals were different, it was not shocking
that a bitch should have puppies or a cat kittens.   But
in the year 1910 a spinster of forty once told me that her
mother had just informed her that a married friend of
hers had found a little baby boy under the gooseberry
bushes in her garden: was not that a pleasant discovery?
Such an instance of parental discretion was certainly exceptional, but the mother, not, I believe, an idiot, still
thought that this was the proper way to tell even so mature a virgin about the place where babies come from.
Previous to marriage such a mother had a heart-to-heart
talk with her daughter in the gloaming and told her very

delicately what the girl knew quite well already. Boys
for the most part were left to discover such elementary
facts for themselves, and it was assumed that when they
were about sixteen they knew them: this was crediting
them with strange backwardness. But a rather advanced parent of my acquaintance told me that when
his boys went to a public school he wrote each of them,
the day before, a long and careful letter speaking of the
internal treasure which their Creator had thought fit to
put into his body, and warning him of the disastrous
consequences of its misuse. He was surprised that I
considered this unnecessary and rather shocked at my
suggestion that he should try the converse of this pa-
ternal plan, and get his boys on the eve of their going to
school to write him a letter stating all they knew on such
subjects. Then if there were any *lacunæ* in their equipment he could supply them, and not be obliged to write
so long a letter. All such system of prudent precautions
and timely revelations was, of course, nearly obsolete before the war, but with it there came a freedom of discussion between the sexes of the young about such matters
as had not been known before. The change was sudden:
freedom broadened quickly down. There was no subject that was taboo any longer between the girls who had
worked in munition factories and the wards of hospitals
and the boys who had gone from school to the trenches.

But it is the greatest mistake to imagine that these
boys and girls who talked so freely had minds a whit less
clean or a smudge more dirty than those of their more

reticent parents: their minds were precisely the same, and it was only that the tongue was given a greater freedom in intersexual talk. Rather nonsensical barriers had been carried away by the raging flood of naked realities that had swept all before it. Just as they had no longer any use for fairy tales, so they had no use for the avoidance of topics which were common knowledge. Nor could they bother to practise the gradually growing intimacies of more leisurely days. If a girl and a boy liked each other on a first meeting, there was no time to get acquainted in the old methods, to remain Miss Jones and Mr. Smith, to lunch with his aunt and play lawn tennis at the house of hers. He would be out at the front again in a few days, and they accelerated. When the war was over there would be time enough to look into the finer shades of each other's natures: for the moment eyes were bright and youth with the first down on its lips was gracious, and the scythes of death were sharp.

This sense of there being no time to spare (for who could foretell about next week?) and of the utter unimportance of trifles produced a corresponding change in manners. The politeness, the deferential courtesy, especially to elders, which had been supposed to be a sign of good breeding, was largely the result of leisure, and now that leisure was so cruelly curtailed, manners became more brusque. Besides, it was the generation of the elders which had brought about this grim business, and since the juniors were pulling them out of their mess, they must be content with that and dispense with deference. There was not time for insignificant observances, to ask if you might smoke, to request an introduction, to "place a chair," to continue to smile and listen to a septic or a crashing bore, and why stand up if you were tired ? In these relaxations the elder generation, to do them justice, cordially concurred. Who could refuse any infinitesimal indulgence to those who were so gallantly looking on the face of death ? When the war was over the old formalities could be brought out again, like a box of pretty toys. . . Everything — so thought those who did not think — would be as it was before, when the war was over: fairy tales, pheasant shooting, church on Sunday morning, manners and the leisurely circuit of the port after dinner before cigarettes were handed. Mourners would be comforted, the old security would return, and the ruthless days would melt into the background of life and all trace of them disappear.

But what these seniors had not reckoned with was that the ruthless days had begotten a certain stubborn ruthlessness, hard to define but impossible to mistake, and it was included under the term self-expression. It did not affect or infect older men and women, whose formative years were past. They were only thankful that the dark days were over, and that they could return, as they hoped, to their businesses and diversions. It was confined to a certain extremely intelligent section of those who were still young and who had been lopped of the legitimate birthrights of youth. They knew that it could not have been otherwise: they had willingly given

what they could not, first by self-respect, and then by
compulsion, withhold, but life had cheated them, and
the years which should have been the heirlooms in memory of their middle and old age, the years when they
should have been dreaming dreams and seeing visions and
making magic were a swarm of festering recollections to
be forgotten if possible.   They wanted never to hear the
war mentioned again, they had been swindled out of
what was legitimately theirs, and they intended, ruth-
lessly, to make the most of what remained to them of
youth.   Hence the phrase not so much on their lips as
in their hearts, self-expression.   They had had enough of
discipline, of stepping forth from a hell of discomfort
to be targets, of boredom punctuated by moments of
terror, and they intended to keep the liberties they had
earned.   The girls quite agreed; they had had enough of
being scullery maids, and neither proposed to be bored
any more, nor to submit again to the traditional discipline of peace, such as their elders imagined would now
be re-established.   Self-expression was like an unspoken
oath of allegiance: doing as you pleased, and, having got
rid of shams (or treating them like Aunt Sally), behaving as your whim or instinct prompted, and eating just
such apples of good or evil as your appetite desired.
There was no self-assertive gabble about it; it sprang
from a sense of justice, it was a bill that must be paid,
and those who presented it were inexorable.   The
liberties granted them during the war must be permanent: there must be an end of antique cackle-codes and

fantastic restrictions, and there must be no further tax
on the freedom that had been so murderously taxed already.

Back came the boys and men in their demobilised
thousands, wanting work and eager to work. But in
spite of the reiterated slogan that none should want it
and not obtain it, it was speedily evident that there was
not work to be had. The disorganization was far
greater than anyone had anticipated: men did not step
back into well-paid places, but into no places at all, for
industrial centres had dwindled, land had gone out of
cultivation, offices were being worked with diminished
staffs, and girls and women were being employed in
them.   Places were exceedingly difficult to obtain, even
for those who had previous knowledge of the work they
wanted to resume, for boys who were too young to serve
in the war, and who had continued their education, were
now trained and occupying junior positions which their
seniors by four or five years would otherwise have occupied: elderly men occupied others.   Those too young for
active service, those too old and women were in possession, and they, too, were being discharged from munition
works and the innumerable departments which the war
had brought into being, while the industries of peace had
yet to be reorganized.   The whole machinery of industry had to be reconstructed from top to bottom, and
instead of there being work for all, the spectre of unemployment began to materialize.   The demobilized were
the first to suffer from its hauntings.

II

IT so happened that I was in fairly intimate touch with a large number of young men who had joined up, from school or the University, on the declaration of war. Various causes, both work and games, had brought this about: I had spent a series of winters in Switzerland where such came out for the Christmas holidays, and assisted many aspirants to the acquisition of the outside edge and its ensuing developments, others, terribly keen on literary pursuits, had confided manuscripts to me; one way and another interests and sympathies were open doorways through which I had been permitted to enter and find myself at home once more in the dream country of youth. The doors were still open, and often it was sunny within, but at other times there were twilights and silences, broken as the dusk gathered with hints, brusquely and telegraphically delivered, of the trouble.

One of these young men, for instance, who had married a year or so after the war was over, had set up house, but he was still out of a job, and now the house must be let, and they must take a couple of furnished rooms. The marriage had been a mistake, but one of those mistakes which are the only way of setting things right, for a child sickly from birth had been born not so many months afterwards. Another had had shell-shock and though he seemed to have got over it his eyes were now beginning to give bad trouble, and he must throw up his job (he was one of the fortunate) and go to live in the country for rest and quiet. His father was a widower, the country parson of a remote parish, ritualistic and narrow-minded with a tendency to drink too much. But there was nowhere else for Lionel to go. Six months complete rest might arrest the damage, but the chances were that he would become completely blind. Another had lost his left hand, so there was no more golf: was it worth while, he wondered, to learn to play with one hand ? Perhaps it was better to chuck it altogether. None of them groused, though sometimes there were these twilights and silences.

But then one night when these three had been dining with me a sort of memory-storm, sudden as a tornado, descended on them: a window, so to speak, always kept discreetly latched, blew open, and until it was secured again, a very bitter blast drove in.

Dinner had been hilarious, and afterwards we went upstairs to play bridge. There was lying about a book containing Laurence Binyon's noble poem "For the Fallen" and, while I was bringing out the card table, John of the amputated hand found it, opened it at this poem, and began to read it to himself.

Then he gave a sudden cackle of laughter.

"I say: damned good stuff," he cried. "All about our little lot. Listen !"

He read it aloud and, as he read, the other two sat down at the card table as still as if they were being photographed. When he had finished they were silent, and the three looked at each other. I remember that I

did not like that silence, and tried to break it by telling
them to come and cut, but they took no notice.   I knew
also that I had ceased to exist for them: the three were
alone.

Then Lionel, he of the troubled eyes, said quite
quietly:

"Well, I do call that 'andsome.   For the fallen!
And we're those that are left, who are going to grow old.
Lucky dogs, aren't we?   And what does the fellow
know about us?"

"Can't say, I'm sure," said John.

Timothy, the married man, plucked the book out of
John's hand and opened the piano.   He put it on the
music rest and striking up a valse tune from some old
revue, sang to it.   Here are the tune and the words:

They shall not grow old   as we that are left grow old.

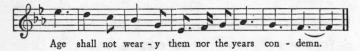

Age shall not wear - y them nor the years con - demn.

"Sing up, you cripples," he shouted, as the storm drove
in.   "Spit it out!   Think of the fallen!   Aren't we
lucky?"

The other three joined in.

"Goes damned well," said John.   "Come and dance,
Lionel.   Play it again and again, Tim."

He took hold of the boy who had to go and rest in
the country, and they pranced round the room together,

bawling out the words at the top of their voices. Half a dozen times they went through it, and then Timothy stopped playing. He banged the lid of the piano down, and shut the window through which this blast had been blowing.

"Bloody rot!" he said. "Sorry for making such a row. Aren't we going to play Bridge?"

"Do you remember the bridge over the Marne?" asked Lionel.

"Oh, dry up!"

And that was all.

Then arrangements had to be made. Somebody dealt for John, and he built a palisade of sheltering books, so that he could lay his hand face upwards on the table, and play from behind it: a light must be placed close to Lionel's elbow, so that he could see his cards when he held them close to it. It was chatty Bridge, it was hectic Bridge, with loud recriminations between partners, and it was very cheerful Bridge and there was a prodigious quantity of whisky drunk. Some hours later it was discovered that the last District train to Richmond, where John's family lived, had gone, and so he telephoned to his mother to say that, as it was a bit late, he was sleeping with me in London, and would she please send up a bag with his day-clothes in it early next morning. Very early: he had to be at the office by ten: ripping evening: good night.

So that was that, and gaiety reigned again. Presently people grew hungry, and we explored the kitchen and larder and found sufficient ham and a loaf of bread.

When the others had gone, we made up a bed for John in the dressing room next door to my room, and he called to me to see how nimble he had become at undressing with only one hand.

"Sit down and talk for a bit," he said as he got into bed, and slewed himself aside so that I could sit there, and put his left arm below the clothes. So we talked for a bit on all sorts of subjects: the difficulty of making people converse naturally in a book; the possibility of going out to Switzerland once more next winter; the chance of his puppy pulling through distemper, but of course there was not a word about what had happened just before we played Bridge. Eventually I went to bed, and through the door I heard John whistling the tune out of the revue, and then suddenly in the middle of it he dried up and clicked off his light.

I lay awake with the tune and the words they had sung to it running in my head. Till then I had not known how bitter was the blast that blew outside the window, usually so carefully closed, though I had suspected something of it. In spite of the hilarious evening and the hectic Bridge some part of those boys was out in the storm still, and it wailed for lost years and lost friends, and anguished with the wounds of the spirit for which there was no cure. They say that some men who have been flogged with the cat are never the same again: physically they recover, but the memory of the savage deliberate brutality of what they have been through festers within: perhaps here there was some similar injury. But probably I had exaggerated the whole affair, giving it a meaning that it did not bear. Of course they had entirely misinterpreted Binyon's words, but they had been a spark that set something afire.

Yet I was right, and even now that sense of the searing horrors they went through, even though they suffered no physical damage, of the incomprehension, even in those who loved them best, of what ailed them, of the apathy of the nation, in general, in spite of Cenotaph services and silences, to the consequences of the war on them, still festers and perhaps will never heal. Certainly it was with a startlingly vivid memory of the evening I have been describing, that I read an article in the *Evening Standard* on Armistice Day 1931. The writer had spent his twenty-first birthday in the trenches, and I quote from what he said fifteen years afterwards: "Sometimes I feel like an old man, for I seem to have known intimately more dead men than living ones. . . When after the war [my generation] came back blinking, bewildered, it had to get a livelihood, and do it when everybody seemed to be greedy and grabbing. Can you wonder that we seem at times a trifle hysterical, rather bitter ? Perhaps we don't: perhaps we seem jolly healthy-minded fellows, but then you are not there when two or three of us are gathered together. . . Sometimes I wonder whether any of us are quite sane."

Reading that, I thought he spoke not for himself alone, but for the three young men who sang "They shall not grow old": they meant just what he said, though they did not express it so publicly and so explicitly.

CHAPTER VI

THE SHADOW FALLS ON THE PARABLE HOUSE

SO MUCH for the ferments, secret for the present, that were working in those who came back and would grow old, some of them disabled, and many out of the jobs that they had left when they were needed elsewhere. They had laid down their pens or their spades or their books, whatever it was that had been earning them their livings, and when they returned others had taken them up and were sitting on their stools. . .

WHAT happened at the parable house of Lord Buryan was typical of another dislocating experience, not tragic, and not dangerous to life and limb and sanity, but to those who suffered such things bewildering and disconcerting to the highest degree. The great house emptied by degrees of its patients: some got well, some were moved to hospitals for the incurable, some died; and six months after the end of the war it was ready for its owners to take possession of it again, and transform it back to its accustomed uses. The beds were cleared out of

the long gallery and the smaller wards, the white
enamelled canvas was removed, and once more the Spanish silk glimmered richly on the walls. The pictures
were brought up from the cellars and rehung on their
proper patches of unfaded colour. The Bellini and the
Botticelli and the Titian glowed there again, Landseer's
hinds surrounding a magnificent stag were recalled, and
the Greek youths and maidens of Lord Leighton, the
Rossetti and the Edwin Long, and the signed engraving
of Queen Victoria in deepest weeds gazing at a bust of
the Prince Consort. Back came the Aubusson carpet,
and though the smell of benzine soon evaporated, no
amount of airing would get rid of the faint odour of
disinfectants that hung about the rooms and passages.
Some of the peach-trees in the glass-houses had died,
for one of the winters had been fiercely cold, and no
heating, in the rationing of fuel, had been possible, but
fresh trees were planted, and the great Hamburg vine
that sprawled through two houses was none the worse.
Part of the lawn in front of the house had through some
mistake been dug up and planted with vegetables: the
Red Cross was most apologetic, and had them uprooted
and the desecrated area returfed. But for that and the
persistent odour of disinfectants, the house and garden
were soon themselves again.

But the neglect into which the park had fallen would
take longer to repair. Undergrowth was thick and
rank, thickets of bramble had grown up, and the nine-
hole golf course long unmown and untended was merged

in coarse grass. For five years no pheasants had been reared, and the hencoops had rotted, and a tree had fallen across the nursery where the chicks were raised. All this could be restored, though it would take time, but there were some changes which would need centuries to repair. Timber had been wanted for the shoring up of trenches and dug-outs, and Lord Buryan had instantly had a big section of the woodland felled. Though in what had been shadowed and unsunned spaces there had sprung up with the ingress of light an innumerable company of flowers, anemones and willow herb, bluebells and primroses, the antique and loftier glory was gone, and of it only the sawed off stumps of the trees shewed where the secular towers of foliage had stood. But the need had been met, and though he lamented the nakedness, he did not regret what he had done.

Then there was the village and it had suffered irremediable losses. Half a dozen of the houses were occupied by widowed women, in another dozen the sons would come back no more, and now along the village street could be seen young men with a limb missing, and one was blind. Something must be done for these: a boy with one arm was given such work as he could manage in the garden or at the farm, but what of the blind one ? He was totally apathetic: he had refused to stay in an institution where he would be taught to make a livelihood, and had come back home, quartering himself on his mother and making no effort to grapple with his darkened life. He shuffled about, feeling his

way by the palings of the cottage-gardens, till he came
to the public-house, where he waited to be treated to
drinks.   A number of young women had gone: town
life with its allurements and employments had seemed
more attractive.   Some had been married, some ought
to have been, and there was what is known as "a sad case"
on one of the farms.   A girl had come back in the winter
and given birth to a baby.   She ran away again as soon
as she was recovered, leaving her baby there, and now
her father and mother would have nothing more to do
with her.   A very sad case indeed, thought Lady Buryan,
but her parents could do no more for her if she was like
that.   The parents were much to be pitied.

For men who were able-bodied there was plenty of
work, but wages had risen, and so, enormously, since the
time when Hakluyt was in full flower, had income tax.
There would soon, it was supposed, be a far higher rate
in death duties and succession duties, and Lord Buryan
was no longer young.   He saw, large though his income
was, that he must cut down expenses if he was to render
a creditable account of his stewardship of his inherited
wealth.   He might have to let, or even sell, his place in
Scotland.   That would be a very distasteful thing to do,
for he loved to have it full of friends during the two
months that he was there and give them admirable stalk-
ing and shooting and fishing.   Also the crofters were of
the host of dependents to whom he had duties: they and
their fathers and grandfathers had served his family for
generations.

But there was no use in anticipating such gloomy contingencies, and for the present there was much to be done at Hakluyt. First of all came the village club-rooms and these must be taken in hand and finished. The damp had got in badly; floors had to be renewed and wooden fittings, but a couple of months saw it complete. The furnishings were ready, tables and chairs and druggets, and it was opened during the summer. A war memorial was but a small item; a larger one was that of the park palings which had occupied his attention just before the war. It was not possible now to think about replacing them with a brick wall, but it was bad economy to let them get worse. The work must go on quietly, until good times came again, as they undoubtedly would, now that the colossal expenditure of the war was over. It had cost the nation, he was told, a million a day. Probably exaggerated.

Then came the boom on the Stock Exchange already alluded to, and prices soared. Lord Buryan often said that the men on the Stock Exchange were very knowing fellows, and now they felt sure that an era of prosperity was coming. No doubt that he had been unduly pessimistic in ever dreaming of selling, or even letting, his Scotch fishings and deer-forest, and he refused an advantageous let to a young Englishman who, if he had not done very well in the war, had done remarkably well during it and, in answer to an enquiry from an American millionaire who wanted to buy the whole estate, and thus own a little strip of Scotland from sea to sea, replied that he had no thought of selling. He went up to Drumarden this summer, for the first time since the beginning of the war, and he and his friends had marvellously good sport. There was a fish of forty-five pounds killed in the river, four royals were shot, and the grouse-driving had been remarkable. Nature seemed to endorse the signs of returning stability.

Then Hakluyt again. He had, in that period of pessimistic economy, decided to rear no pheasants, but partridges were abundant, rabbits had increased beyond all bounds, and one of the battues, rather bloody and unsporting affairs, but necessary for their decimation, had yielded a record in mortality. They were sent to hospitals in their hundreds, and were most thankfully received. He also laid down twenty dozen of 1918 port: the bin was labelled "Peace Port," and was not to be touched for twenty-five years.

But — the feeling was indefinable at first, though hauntingly persistent — the prosperous and respectful village had somehow changed. Making all allowance for the sad case, and the blind young man who would not work, and for the houses that had lost their bread-winners, there was something queer and sultry, as if with approaching storm, about the general atmosphere. The village-club, for instance, built and furnished by Lord Buryan at such expense, was not a success. The sub-scription to it, with all its amenities, central heating in cold weather and fire of logs, its temperance bar run

at a loss, its chess, draughts, bagatelle and supply of
papers and magazines, was nominal — five shillings a
year — and this he would not have imposed at all except
for the feeling that he, the landlord, and they, his tenants,
were a corporate and co-operative body, and must work
together: the sound old principle.   But very few men
joined: they seemed to prefer the public house, or to go
over to Weyford and see the cinema there of an evening.
Sometimes there was no one in the club at all, and the
coffee at the refreshment bar, at the price of a penny
for a large cup, diffused its fragrance in vain.   Sometimes three or four men assembled, and since playing-
cards were not provided, as being likely to lead to gambling, they brought packs of their own.   Lord Buryan
looked in now and then after dinner, driving down from
the Park in his evening clothes on surprise visits, to see
that everything was comfortable, but not stopping long
lest his presence should embarrass the members: occasionally he played a game of draughts or drank a cup of
coffee, for which he paid his penny.   He said it was
quite as good as what my lady gave him at home.

One night there was no one there, and he found among
the illustrated papers a copy of a Socialist organ, which
he had certainly not ordered to be supplied: it contained
a very fierce attack on landowners.   He read a paragraph or two of it, and chucked it back on the table,
resisting the impulse to throw it into the fire.   That
would not be right: clearly this unclean rag was the

property of some member of the club and, though proprietor, he was only a member himself, drinking his coffee and looking at the papers.

Presently a man came in whom a week before Lord Buryan had dismissed from his employment as a wood-man in the park for flagrant poaching: he had not prosecuted him. The man took no notice whatever of him, but picked up the Socialist paper, and established himself in front of the fire and read, chuckling to himself.

Then attendance at church on a Sunday morning had fallen off, and whereas before the war the church was full to the west door, there were now lines of empty pews, and the congregation, whatever it was, no longer rose to its feet as the party from the Park entered. Lady Buryan's choir practice on Saturday afternoon was even more sparsely attended: the small boys and girls who sang treble and alto were there in sufficient numbers, but there was a sad lack of men to take the tenor and bass parts.

Again it had always been the use to sing carols from house to house on Christmas Eve, at the lawyer's, at the agent's, at the Parsonage, at the detached villas beyond the village street, and the waits finished up at the Park where, after the "First Noël" (and the last) they were sumptuously entertained at supper in the house-keeper's room. Nothing could have been more democratic: Lady Buryan accompanied the songsters, singing alto herself, and beating time for the others, and she walked

with them from house to house in her sable coat, and, if
the evening was inclement, brought down with her half-
a-dozen old umbrellas, so that the choir should not get
wet as they stood to sing.   When they got back to the
Park she sat down to supper among the rest, not even
taking the head of the table, and the breeched and white-
stockinged footman did not pay her any particular attention; those were the orders.   She was not helped
first, but in her turn, and the butler handed mince-pies
to his own son, who was a shrill and notable songster,
for they were all of one family tonight, in the equal
fellowship of Christmas.   But this year, when first the
Park was open again, no adequate choir could be
mustered, and the carols were given up.   Then on
Christmas night there had always been a Christmas Tree
in the hall.   Lady Buryan took the greatest trouble over
its furnishings: she had the complete list of the children
and their ages, and there was a suitable present for each
of them, ranging from dolls for the youngest girls and
clockwork trains for the youngest boys, to work-boxes
for the elder girls and pipes and tobacco-pouches for
the young men.   For the parents there were silk scarves,
pull-overs or rainproof coats.   These were ranged on
tables, and Lord Buryan gave the women their presents
and Lady Buryan the men.   But this year there was
some odd stiffness and lack of cordiality: the supper that
followed was a silent affair, and the guests went home
unusually early.

On New Year's night there was always a servants'

ball. It began with Sir Roger de Coverley, the butler
leading off with my Lady and my Lord with the housekeeper. But this year, the butler, very deferential and
diffident, put it to Lady Buryan that he and his lordship's valet and the ruptured footman were the only
men in the house and that the women (the difficulty
about getting servants at all in the country had begun
to be acute) were not quite of the sort to which her
ladyship was accustomed. He had talked it over with
the housekeeper and, if her ladyship would excuse him,
they both thought that it would not quite be such an
evening as they had always enjoyed so much in previous
years. So perhaps . . . And she thought so too, and
there was no servants' ball.

There was something wrong: it was hard to define
what it was, for such symptoms as these were so slight,
but there were others also rather more legible and more
puzzling. The wife, for instance, of one of the lodge-
keepers who had also been a gardener had lost her husband
during the war, but Lord Buryan had allowed her (she
was a capable woman) to stay on there, and supple-
mented her widow's pension up to the full wage her
husband had earned. Now she took into the house, as
a lodger, the young man who had been dismissed for
poaching: there was scandal in the village about them,
and it was supposed that they would be married before
long. She was quick to open the gate, she dropped her
curtsey as usual; the man's face could often be seen at
the window looking blankly out, or he would be sitting

smoking in the porch and not stand up as the motor passed. Lord Buryan consulted his agent about this: it was most unsuitable that a man caught poaching should be lodged within the Park gates. The agent talked to the woman, trying to make her see that it ought to be a matter of good feeling on her part not to let a room to a poacher who had been very leniently treated.

She turned nasty. She had always been allowed to let a room: she had done it with his lordship's full knowledge for years, and she meant to go on doing so. His lordship, of course, might turn her out if he liked, but her husband had given up his life for his country after serving him faithfully for fifteen years, as his father had done before him. The agent told her that Lord Buryan had not the slightest intention of turning her out, nor did he wish to prevent her having a lodger, but it must not be this one. Thereupon she gave notice and the two took a couple of rooms in the village. The feeling there was that she had been shabbily treated.

The mere fact that there could be any argument about Lord Buryan's wishes in a matter of this sort, especially where his view was so eminently reasonable, was an indication of the nature of the change that was going on. It kept revealing itself in one way or another, like glimpses of distant lightning that shewed a storm was brewing somewhere among the clouds which, after the brief serene moment when the war was over, were collecting in every quarter. He had always been the most kind and generous of landlords, identifying himself with his tenants' interests, and the change was not in him. They on their side had been wont to obey his wishes, even as they obeyed his orders, knowing that he was master, but equally well knowing his goodwill: they had been content with their relations to him, accepting them, as he did himself, as part of the established order of the British Constitution. Things no longer worked quite smoothly: it was as if a piece of grit had got into the bearings of the machine, or as if some essential part of it, axle or piston rod, was ever so slightly misplaced. The sense that there was something awry hung in the air just as the smell of disinfectants lingered in the gallery.

The financial side of his affairs began to worry him, for he had lived nearly up to his income, though without ever needing to think about economies. But supertax which he, like many others, had hoped would diminish now that the colossal expense of the war was over remained unmitigated. There were huge debts to America which must be repaid, whereas the debts of other allies to England were not being discharged: unemployment was rapidly increasing and with it the crippling burden of the dole. Death duties and succession duties had risen, and it began to seem probable that at his death Henry would be unable to live at Hakluyt unless by the sale of his Scotch place he could raise a sufficient sum to pay those duties. He consulted Henry on this, for his consent was necessary to break the entail, and Henry very willingly consented to the sale of

Drumarden. Neither he nor his wife cared in the least about the Highland life and for the last two years he had only been there for a week or two and Helen had spent August and September in Venice. So Drumarden was put up for sale, but the American millionaire who had wanted to purchase it before was no longer a buyer, and the young Englishman who had done so well during the war had attempted to do better during the boom that followed it, and had lost a very large sum during the ensuing slump: he no longer wanted to obtain a lease of it and Lord Buryan had to look about for other ways of retrenchment.

The succession duties on Hakluyt he found could be evaded if he made it over to Henry by deed of gift, and himself lived for three years more afterwards: the place would then not be liable to succession duty when Henry came into it. This was done, and though he lived there exactly as before, the house and the park were no longer his, but he was his son's tenant. This went against the grain: the sense of proprietorship, even though his own son was the owner, was gone, and though the sense of proprietorship may be deemed an emotion of little worth, he missed the consciousness of it. He was not quite so intimately identified with the place as he had been before; it was not his with the old solidity.

Then there were his daughters' portions to think about: he made both of them an allowance of two thousand pounds a year and, by his will as it stood at present, they would each receive on his death the sum of fifty thousand pounds. What with rising taxes and his failure to sell the Scotch estate he would like to pay that over to them now, and thus to free it also of succession duty. He would not be the poorer for it in the way of income, for the allowance he made them represented four per cent on this capital.

Rents from the farms on his property had been falling off. Farmers were having a bad time, and he had in many cases been obliged to reduce their rents in order to enable them to make a decent livelihood. Others had not renewed their leases, and had gone to live in towns in manufacturing districts where they hoped to earn a better wage for themselves and their children than farming had lately been bringing them in: moreover in towns there were more diversions, cinemas and what not, instead of long winter evenings in sundered homesteads. A good many farm labourers had thus been thrown out of employment: they also had migrated to towns, and now in the village there were a couple of dozen cottages vacant. There those well-built comfortable little dwellings stood, smokeless and cold, and the gardens in front, once neat and fragrant, degenerated into weedy tangles. To walk down the street now and observe all these signs of neglect was like entering some familiar room in his own house to find the paper peeling off the walls, and the paint discoloured and the carpet in holes.

All these shrinkings of income, with the prospect of more in the future, not only made economies necessary, but some realisation of property, if at his death he was

to leave his daughters provided for as they had been led
to expect, his wife in a befitting dignity, and Henry well
enough off to live magnificently at Hakluyt according
to the Buryan use.   He himself had been brought up in
that tradition: he had come early into his inheritance
and for over thirty years had kept that tradition up
with all its institutional extravagance, its large hospitalities, its responsibilities towards tenants and dependents; and the due discharge of all these was bound up together and formed the code of the duties of that state
of life to which he had been born.   The idea of selling a
single yard of the park was abhorrent, land like that to
his sense was a peculiarly personal, indeed almost a sacred
possession.   We may call it a "hereditary taint," but
there the taint was, and it was incarnate in his bones and
marrow.   But there were the pictures, notably the Bellini, the Botticelli and the Titian.   They were all quite
first-rate examples: before now he had been offered exceedingly large sums for them, but these offers had come
from America, and he regarded his pictures as part of
the wealth of England, things belonging directly to him,
but essentially to her, and not to be sent overseas and lost
to her.   Now he got an expert down, and on his advice
offered them to the nation at the price of £100,000,
which was a considerable reduction on the offer made
him before the war from America.   But this would
provide the sum he needed for his daughters' portions,
and he would thus make these masterpieces a national
possession for ever.

Socialist organs made fine play with this. A cartoon appeared entitled "The New Poor." It represented him standing on a step-ladder taking one of these pictures down, and the caption ran:

The Earl of Buryan (*to his wife*), "Really, my dear, times are so bad that I positively cannot afford to have a hundred thousand pounds hanging on the wall like that."

The Countess of Buryan, "Oh dearie me, to think it should come to this !"

This cartoon, snipped out of the paper, was sent him, and the postmark on the envelope was Hakluyt.

His offer remained open for three months, but at the end of that time not one-third of the required sum was raised. So for a while yet the pictures remained on the walls. Then a dealer offered him the price the nation had been unable to raise, and he sold them. To say that he actually missed them in the sense that he mourned their absence would be a gross overstatement. But they had been a pride, a part of the splendour that was passing not from Hakluyt alone, and the two unfaded oblongs and the circle of unfaded Spanish silk where they had hung was a perpetual Ichabod. Not a tragedy in any sense of the word, but the glory was departing.

Perhaps what brought the change most woundingly home to him was the complete indifference of Henry and his wife to it. Indeed, it was more than indifference, for both of them, in attitude and outlook, were types of the change itself, and were in sympathy with it. They were floating along with it, as on some broad-moving stream with whose motion they moved, and it seemed to them as if the old landmarks were slipping out of sight, lost in the mists that formed over them or as if they were falling behind by some retrograde movement of their own. It was but seldom that they came to Hakluyt at all; life in London was the only unboring form of existence, for London now was in blossom, like the gorse, all the year round, and their names became a *cliché* in smaller paragraphs of the press, as having been seen lunching or dining at restaurants, or as guests at some much advertised party of nimble, climbing hosts. Helen's clothes, the style of her hats, the length of her skirts and so forth were the weekly comment of society journals. She figured much in their illustrated pages: she was Cleopatra at some charitable entertainment of tableaux, she was Diane de Poictiers at a fancy dress ball, and the new decorations of her bathroom, the thin onyx slabs in the window, the pink tiles of the floor, the black enamelled bath with three steps leading down into it, were the pictured subject of an appreciative article, and even the diet of her Pekinese dogs, though not illustrated (nor would it have made a pretty picture, as it consisted of raw ox-liver) was easily worthy of record. All this was apostasy from the decorous tradition of reserve in which the Buryans, old fashioned and Victorian even before the war, had always lived. It troubled the old couple: once Lady Buryan had tried to speak to Henry about it, but he received her fumbling attempts to indicate that she was driving at with such blank uncon-

sciousness of what she could mean, that she could not
state what was in her mind.   He merely said that Helen
had looked quite divine as Cleopatra, and that the children's hospital had benefited enormously by the show.
As for the question of expense, her new bathroom with
all its fittings was a present from Princess Amadeo.

The Manor House, just outside the park, which Lord
Buryan had designed to be a country house for Henry
and his wife, was thus very seldom occupied.   Henry
was in the City now, director of one or two companies,
and partner in a stockbroking firm of good repute, but
his father had thought that Helen would occupy it during the autumn and winter months with her two children, and that he would come down there for week-ends
and holidays.   The children, two boys (that was satisfactory), of whom the elder was now seven, were there
always, for country air and exercise were so much better
for them than living in London, but weeks passed without their parents ever seeing them.   When this had gone
on for some months, Lady Buryan suggested that the
boys should make their home at the big house: their
grandparents would be delighted to have them there.
Helen was cordial in her thanks — she was always
charming to her mother-in-law — and she thought it a
most ideal arrangement: she would love to think that
the children, such ducks, would be there.   It solved a
difficulty which had bothered her, for she was sure that
the country was better for them (how well it suited
them their health and sturdiness testified) but she could

not leave Henry alone in London all the week, and as for
the week-ends it had happened again and again that they
had been prevented from coming down, as they had
meant to do, by something unexpected turning up
which kept them.   Of course the children's nursery-
governess was an admirable woman, but it would make
all the difference if they were at the Park.   The transference was duly made, and the Manor House stood
empty.

Henry and she came down to Hakluyt one Saturday
morning early in December.   A white mist dismally
blanketed the countryside, the winter dusk soon fell,
shutters were put up and curtains drawn, and an interminable evening was in prospect.   They were only
proposing to stay for one night, and to drive back to
London on Sunday afternoon, for though they had
come down from a sense of duty (it was many weeks
since they had been) duty did not call so shrilly as to
cause them to stay over the Sunday, for Pamela Rockingham, at whose house one was sure of an amusing evening, was giving a party on Sunday night.   Officially
their reason for going back on Sunday was that Henry
must be in the City at a decent time on Monday morning, and that meant a horribly early start.   There was
no one else in the house; there were just six of them, a
couple representing each of the three generations.

After dinner Helen and her mother-in-law had left
Lord Buryan and Henry in the dining-room, where the
port would go to and fro twice, and the bell be then

rung for coffee and cigarettes; the children had gone to
bed, and there would be at least half an hour of this
tête-à-tête. Helen still continued to address her
mother-in-law as "Lady Buryan," for that ice had never
been broken, and in answer to a question she was saying
that she was afraid they would not be able to get down
to Hakluyt at all at Christmas: Henry had managed to
get a fortnight's holiday, and he and she were going to
rush off to St. Moritz for a spell of winter sports.
Henry had not been very well (nothing to worry about)
and his doctor had said that the tonic air with effulgence
of frost and sun was just the thing to set him up again.
Of course it would have been lovely to take the children
too, but they were a little young for that at present.
As for expense, they had had a great piece of luck, for
she and Henry were both dreadfully hard up, and they
never could have afforded it just now, when business in
the City was so bad. But a friend of Henry's, Mr.
Blumenthal, one of the fortunate new rich, had built
a big hotel at St. Moritz, and he had begged them to
come out there entirely at his charges, board, lodging
and journey all included, and be bell-wethers, so to
speak. He was advertising the hotel extensively: there
were little paragraphs in the papers — had not Lady
Buryan seen them ? — to say that she and Henry had
taken rooms there, for he thought that their names
would attract the sort of people, the rich and the climbing, whom he wanted to get. Many of them used
Switzerland, now that it was so popular in the winter,

as a header board from which to plunge into social success.

"Of course it's all hideously snobbish," said Helen lucidly, "but Mr. Blumenthal was dreadfully keen for us to go, and as a matter of fact, so he told me, the hotel is filling up marvellously. And it's wonderful for us, as we should never have been able to afford it, and a couple of weeks there will do Henry no end of good."

Dead silence: to say that Lady Buryan was aghast at the scheme which seemed to Helen so natural and such a piece of good fortune, would not be an overstatement. It deeply and genuinely shocked her to think that her son and daughter-in-law (herself "one of them") should be using the privileges of their birth and position as a bait, dangled by a Mr. Blumenthal, for climbers and snobs. Helen wished she had not told her, but now it was too late.

"But, my dear, just think!" said Lady Buryan at length. "You and Henry are being paid — for that's what it comes to — to be touts for his friend's hotel. I've no doubt that Mr. — Mr. Blumenthal is an excellent fellow in his own way, no doubt at all, but surely — I know you'll pardon me — when you say it is all hideously snobbish, aren't you countenancing that and taking part in it ? Do you know I hate the thought of it ! . . . My dear, please let me pay for your visit. So good for Henry, as you say, and after all he's my son: so let your holiday be my Christmas present to both of you."

Helen was touched by the old lady's earnestness and

generosity, but how absurd it was, how utterly out of date !

"Dear Lady Buryan," she said, "it's too sweet of you to suggest that, but I'm afraid Henry has consented and the thing's done. Besides I know you and Lord Buryan are hard up, too, or you would never have sold those pictures, and have wanted to get rid of Drumarden, and I couldn't dream of putting you to such an expense, a very big one, I assure you. Mr. Blumenthal has engaged berths for us and Henry's servant and my maid on the Engadine express, so that we shall have them on the journey, and he's given us a suite of rooms on the first floor, two bedrooms and a sitting-room and bathroom for us, and rooms for the servants adjoining. I don't know what it wouldn't run you into. And as I say, it's all finished: Henry received the tickets and vouchers for the rooms this morning. And Mr. Blumenthal is awfully pleased at the way the hotel is filling up. He says we're the best bargain he ever made."

Lady Buryan, though really troubled, had in a converse sense, an eye on the gallery: she hoped, that is to say, that the gallery would not observe. "Well, if it's done, there's no help for it," she said. "But I do trust it won't be known. Mr. Blumenthal, I hope, will hold his tongue, and I'm sure you and Henry will. I certainly shan't tell Buryan. It would distress him very much."

Helen laughed. That sort of reticence (no talk, no scandal, hush it up !) was equally old fashioned.

"I'm afraid a good many of our friends do know," she said. "Pamela Rockingham asked Mr. Blumenthal to dine with her, though she had never in her life set eyes on him, and told him point blank that she longed to go to St. Moritz, but could not afford it. A pretty firm hint, wasn't it, but he wasn't taking any. Devastating for poor Pamela: how we laughed ! She was furious with me for being a better draw than her."

Helen rose, and putting her coffee cup down on the chimneypiece (how she wanted a cigarette !) glanced at her image in the looking-glass above it. She had been rather hurried over dressing for Henry had been occupying the only bathroom anywhere near their room with the double bed in it, and now, quite automatically, she took out her lipstick to repair the neglect of her haste. The glass was brightly lit by the great chandelier on the ceiling and, looking into it, she could hardly help laughing, for she saw that Lady Buryan had perceived what she was doing, and that her face wore a pursed expression. Not till then, honestly, did she remember that her mother-in-law had very decided views about the way young women made up their faces in public. She was sorry: she would have let her face alone if she had thought of it. Then Henry and his father came in from the dining-room, and she made the excuse of seeing whether the children were asleep, in order to have a cigarette. They talked till half past ten, when Lady Buryan was sure she must be sleepy after her long drive,

and the little family gathering dispersed. Breakfast
at nine as usual in the morning, so that the servants
might be able to get to church.

But all the evening these two generations, typical of
those in a thousand other homes, had been ill at ease and
ill-fitting. The jars, except for the treated jaunt to St.
Moritz, which was terrible from Lady Buryan's point
of view, were infinitesimal: none of them mattered in
the smallest degree, but collectively they made a total
that resulted in a continuous discomfort. There was
no freedom in their talk; some topics were taboo or
gibberish to the elders; others, to the younger, merely
hopelessly dull. Lady Buryan, for instance, had never
heard of Ciro's, nor did she know and how could one
explain what the 'Chelsea crowd' was ? It was just the
Chelsea crowd. Helen on the other hand could not
feign the least interest in the admirable qualities of the
new village nurse, nor Henry in the Bible classes of the
new parson. There was scarcely a subject of common
interest between them, except the two boys, and even
there was no close bond. Manners had changed, reticences had been relaxed, reserves had been loosened, and
perhaps one may liken the old conventionality with its
proprieties and wellbred quietness, and withal its pom-
pousness, its decorousness-at-any-price, and its con-
sequent hypocrisies and loss of naturalness, to a bundle
of miscellaneous documents, some valuable, on vellum
and in a beautiful handwriting, eminently worth pre-
serving, some rubbish, and already ripe for the waste-

paper basket. Once, an elastic band, with firm soft pressure, had easily bound together this collection of codes and ordinances, and it had been compact and solid. But the binding band loses its elasticity; it becomes brittle, and if an attempt is made to stretch it, it snaps, and all the hoarded documents are scattered on the floor.

So THE two young folk, leaving the children at Hakluyt, went out to St. Moritz. Mr. Blumenthal travelled with them, and he lunched and dined with them on the train. The champagne and the liqueurs were of his ordering, and his the discharge of the bill, for they were his guests from the departure platform at Victoria till they reached the arrival platform on their return, and thus the train was his house and he their host, just as when they got to St. Moritz the hotel was his house too: no wonder Pamela Rockingham was green with jealousy. Of course they had their reciprocating duties, and they both understood that. It was their part to be very friendly and cordial with him, and call him, by request, by his Christian name. Helen waltzed with him on the ice, and he came to play Bridge in their sitting-room. But that was not disagreeable, for he was a very good card-player, and an expert on skates. In person he was a good-looking fellow of Henry's age, with sleek black hair and naturally vermilion lips, quite pleasant, laughing a little loud, and a trifle too fond of exclaiming to Helen when she came down to dinner, "My dear, you

look *too* divine tonight " and of using Henry's Christian name on the curling rink more frequently than was
absolutely necessary, calling him Harry: this was a mistake, for never in his life had Henry ever been addressed
like that.   But he had paid handsomely for such privileges, and it never entered the head of either of them to
disallow his right.   Perhaps there were rather more
duties attached to the post of bell-wether than Helen
had anticipated: new arrivals were always introduced
to her, if they had taken sufficiently expensive rooms:
she was *ex officio* hostess at fancy-dress balls, welcoming
arrivals from other hotels, admiring their costumes; she
gave away prizes at ice-gymkhanas, and when the *föhn*
blew, making skating and ski-ing impossible, she took
an active part in indoor games.   She posed for the
photographers of illustrated papers, her lissom figure in
trousers and pull-over was reproduced in Benjy Blumenthal's advertisements, and she felt it only reasonable that
she should discharge these decorative functions in return for such lavish hospitalities.   Henry, it is true,
absolutely refused to lecture on "My Experiences on the
West Front," but otherwise he was as docile as his wife.
On the last evening of their stay they gave a large dinner
party at Blumenthal's expense, and Henry made a speech
saying that he hoped to come out again next year; his
health and Helen's was drunk with musical honours, and
they signed menu cards for their guests, and everybody
sang "Auld Lang Syne."   Their railway carriage next

day was a bower of floral tributes and boxes of chocolates which Helen sent to the 'chicks' at Hakluyt, and they both thought themselves exceedingly fortunate in securing so luxurious a holiday entirely free of expense.

CHAPTER VII

THE SHADOW LENGTHENS

I

THE CONVICTION that the old days of affluence would speedily return was now weakening a little. An uneasy feeling got abroad that the mere fact that England had lost millions of her workers, and spent milliards of money on the engines of destruction was not in itself productive of wealth. There were pessimists, not many of them as yet, but level-headed folk, who said that a period of exceedingly lean years was at hand, instead of a period of fat years, and that the nation ought to realize that for the moment it was poor. Unemployment was mounting, capital was ruinously taxed, and the conversion of the workshops of war into the manufactories of the implements and provisions of peace was not proceeding as it should. But the idea of England being poor was too ludicrous to be entertained for a moment, and the government with a magnificent gesture pledged itself to pay the interest on its enormous debt to America, though England had cancelled much of the debts owing to her from the allies; 54% was remitted in the case of France, and 75% to Italy.

The wholly unwarranted boom on the Stock Exchange had collapsed, for the public was shy of putting their money into shares which steadily depreciated, and the stockbroking firm in which Henry was a partner was doing no business at all.   Both he and his wife were extremely extravagant people, accustomed, if either of them wanted something for which ready cash was not needed, to get it, and a domestic conference that was presently held revealed the fact that in spite of treats to St. Moritz, they were living hopelessly beyond their means and had a formidable overdraft at the bank.   A generation ago, two young people in their position would have let their house in Chesterfield Street with its onyx bathroom, or have shut it up with a caretaker in charge, and retired for a year or two to the Manor House at Hakluyt where they would have lived rent-free, and economies would have been easy: Henry would have taken a bedroom at his club, and rejoined Helen and his boys on Friday evening until Monday morning.   But such an expedient was not worth discussion: it never entered the heads of either of them that it was possible. The autumn evenings were closing in, what would Helen do with herself night after night when dusk fell and curtains were drawn, and she was shut up in her neighbourless box ?   She could dine, of course, at the Park, spending a domestic evening with the old people, but who could stand much of that ?   Certainly not she: she could more easily imagine herself reading a book at her solitary dinner, and playing patience afterwards.

During the day she would have her children with her, she could teach them, she could go out with them, but two young boys of eight and six could not be companions, and even though they were her own sons she felt little or no maternal interest in them.   Again she detested the country occupations of driving and walking, and though she enjoyed skating in the exhilarating air of St. Moritz, and swimming in the languorous seas of the Lido, it was the milieu, the cameras and the costumes that lent them a charm: as for exercise in itself, she had the serene health that often goes with apparent fragility, and in London she never set foot out of doors except to cross the pavement to a friend's house.   And the week-ends when Henry would rejoin her would be hardly more tolerable than the rest.   They were quite good friends, and got on together very decently when there were plenty of people about them, but they had no desire for undiluted companionship.

In London they went about together to a reasonable extent; they might perhaps dine together at the same house, and then, as likely as not, they parted, going to different entertainments, and saw each other no more that night.   Once they met on their own doorstep at half-past two in the morning, coming from opposite directions.   Henry had evidently drunk rather too much, and Helen with friendly tact went up to bed at once, saying that she was horribly sleepy, and never alluded to the incident again.   They drifted about in the ceaseless tide that ebbed and flowed through dance

clubs and studios and cocktail parties and flats converted
from mews.   Many of these wanderers drank a good
deal, some were married: there were inverts among them
and the normal only gave faint grins of indifferent derision at what was no business of theirs.   It was idle to
apply stereotyped standards and accepted moralities to
those who had spent four of the most impressionable
years of their lives among shells and bullets, among the
racks and irons of a mental torture chamber.   All were
consciously or subconsciously eager to make good the
years they had lost, by dyeing the present with deeper
colour, and by giving life now the quality of their days
of leave during the war, by distilling from desire and
whim as much self-expression as it would yield.   The
French for "self-expression" definitely became "*Fay ce
que voudras.*"

To Helen the call of the flesh meant very little: marriage had not ripened her, nor yet maternity.   She had
done her duty in bearing two healthy sons, and that,
she considered, was all that could reasonably be required
of her in the fulfilment of her marriage-vows.   Men
with their gross contracts and insistent, intrusive needs
rather disquieted her, and her intimacies were with those
of her own sex.   She wanted Henry to leave her alone;
as long as he did that she did not really care whether he
took his ardours elsewhere, provided that he behaved
with discretion and did not make such scandal as would
cause her to appear in the truly ridiculous rôle of the
slighted wife.   She had long suspected that he was hav-

ing an affair with Pamela Rockingham, with whom she
was quite good friends, but they were managing it very
well: they did not appear together overmuch, or exchange those foolish bovine glances that give everything
away.   They did not cause the kind of talk that would
be annoying, and not for a moment did she think of
Pamela as a "rival."   She was not competing, indeed,
she was quite content that Pamela should take him off
her hands.   But they must use the liberties she granted
them with discretion, and at present she had no fault to
find with them there; in return for these liberties she
must have her own.

Intellectually she was of finer fibre than he, with
subtler curiosities and perceptions, fond of peering into
the subaqueous caves that underlay the placid and shining surface of human nature, of parting the aromatic
seaweeds that lined its edges, and finding there strange
oblique animals, and this moving tide of her contemporaries gave her plenty of scope for her investigations.
She had by reason of her beauty and her charm a power
of enchanting and of winning confidences and, wife and
mother though she was, she most made friends with, she
attracted and was attracted by, the queer and the exceptional, by men who treated her like a comrade, and
women who adored her.   Unemotional herself she was
more interested in women than in men and felt herself
intellectually and ethically at home with them: this was
nothing new, for even in her girlhood her greatest friend
had been Princess Amadeo, and her indifference to the

encroachments of Pamela, and in particular to her own children, was merely a confirmation of it. So, in return for the liberty she granted Henry, she assumed her own freedom to cultivate the friendship of those with whom she felt a kinship.

All this was common ground between the two when they had their conference over their financial affairs; so, too, was the impossibility of giving up their life in London and economizing at the Manor House at Hakluyt: other methods of retrenchment must be found. The immediate cause of the conference was that Henry had received a perfectly polite note from his bank, calling his attention to the amount of his overdraft, and an equally polite note from a firm of fashionable dressmakers, asking him to pay the enclosed account, long overdue, for goods supplied to her ladyship. He gave Helen a very decent allowance for dress and purely personal expenses, and this bill for fifteen hundred pounds was outrageous. It was no use, he said (opening the debate) his trying to economize, if she was so ruinously extravagant. But Helen had a retort for that. She had seen in the shop window of a famous jeweller's in Bond Street a perfectly fascinating bracelet in the form of a snake. The rippling back was a patterned diaper of small rubies and emeralds, the head a mis-shapen pearl with diamond eyes. Barbarous, but with a *chic;* she had wanted it very badly. Then one day she had seen Henry come out of the shop; she had waved to him, but he did not see her and, crossing the street, she ob-

served that this glittering bauble had gone from the
window. She enquired, and found it had just been
sold: it had been taken from the window that very moment. Two days afterwards she saw it adorning Pamela's well-shaped wrist. So now, when Henry called
attention to this unpaid dress-maker's bill, she laughed.

"But I expect you have unpaid bills, too," she said,
"though they don't send them in to me. What about
that delicious snake-bracelet which used to be in the
window at Galopin's ? Unnecessary to go into it further, of course, because these are subjects which we are
quite right to avoid. As to my bill I agree it is monstrous. Let me see it, please: I don't think I looked at
it when they sent it in last. I'll try to be less expensive,
Henry" — she laughed again — "but you must try, too.
Curb your generous impulses. Now let us go into everything very carefully."

Then they talked over, quite neutrally, their own
poverty and that of their friends in general, and
Helen wondered whether it was the cross-word habit
that was responsible. All sorts of clever people spent
hours every day doing cross-words when they might have
been employing their brains in making money. They
laughed over that and, still chatting, they went upstairs,
and she sat in his dressing-room a few minutes till suddenly it struck her that he might think she was making
hints, flying signals to him, and she made an abrupt
departure, not noticing, of course, that a half-bottle of
champagne was standing on his dressing-table. The

door of communication between their two rooms was locked on her side, so she went round by the passage, and presently heard the pop of a drawn cork. So that was all right. . .

HENRY was now, it may be remembered, the actual owner of the house and park at Hakluyt and of the estate and farms belonging. For all practical purposes the transference had brought no change: his father still lived there, receiving the rents and paying the upkeep, but legally the estate was his son's. A few days after this friendly and futile conference, the representative of a building agency came to see Henry, with a proposal that might perhaps prove to render the need for rigid economies unnecessary. Weyford, the small country town three miles from the village of Hakluyt, was expanding as a place of residence for those whose business took them up to London every day. The train service had been lately accelerated, the admirable golf links were an attraction, and the company which was developing the district desired to know whether negotiations could be entered into for the purchase of a substantial strip of the Park, which bordered the road towards Weyford, for building sites. This strip was, it is true, within sight of the house, but quite half a mile away, and there was no design of erecting a row of eye-sore, gimcrack villas, but commodious and well constructed houses on the plan of a well known architect, each standing in an acre or two acres of ground.

The company also would plant, if desired, a row of trees between them and the big house, so that in the course of twenty years or so the new buildings would be entirely concealed.

Now Henry had a perfect right to make this sale without consulting his father. Lord Buryan had by deed made over to him the possession of the Hakluyt estate on the understanding that he should be tenant for life of the Park, and that the amenities should not be interfered with. Personally, Henry considered that it was the greatest stroke of good luck that anyone should want to buy this outlying strip of land, the sale of which, at the figure suggested, would relieve himself and Helen of all their financial difficulties. But it did not even enter his head to close with the offer: he said that the agency would have to wait a few days for his answer, and he went down to Hakluyt to consult his father.

The interview was a painful one to the older man and tiresome to the younger; the two quietly and politely enlarged the gulf that already had grown wide between the two generations. His father did not dispute Henry's right to sell, nor did he contend that the sale would encroach on the amenities of his life there. But if he had ever foreseen such a contingency he would never have dreamed of making over the ownership to his son. That had been done simply and solely in order that Henry should, at his death, enter on his inheritance without such cumbering succession duties as would make

it impossible for him to live at the Park.   His objection
to the sale was, if Henry wished to put it that way,
purely a matter of sentiment.   That was all.   He was
aware that Henry could do exactly as he chose. . .

The two children made a joyful irruption into the
room.   They were a little shy of their father, whom
they had not seen for so long, but perched themselves
on the two arms of their grandfather's chair, and shrilly
told him, as they were wont to do, about their ride.   As
they prattled to him, he encouraging them, Henry saw,
and believed that his father meant him to see, the ease
and affection with which the boys treated him, and to
draw the contrast which was obvious enough.   The
gulf that separated him from his father seemed to rip
open further, and sunder him from the youngest generation as from the older.   Physical fatherhood and no
more connected him with those handsome brats.   They
were the children of a woman who meant nothing to
him, and to whom he meant nothing.   They had spent
a few hours of passion together, but those had made no
growth of friendship between them nor any sense of
identity with the fruits of it. . . The old man, sitting
there, with his ludicrous notions of the sanctity, no less,
of ancient and landed property and of the continuance of
the Hakluyt line, was far more closely linked with them
than he, and they were being brought up in the tradition of an age long past.   They went to church with
him on Sunday morning, they were taught to lift their
hats when a decrepit old farmer touched his, they were

taught to say "Thank you" when the butler gave them their roast beef. Drop by pompous drop it was being instilled into them what a grand thing it was to be the Lord of Hakluyt, and how courteous you ought to be to your inferiors, giving yourself no airs, but deeply conscious of your own position and its responsibilities, and remembering, especially in church, that all were equal in the sight of God.

But how obsolete, how radically snobbish was such a creed: how strange that anyone could still subscribe to it. But his father was still teaching the tenets of that creed to the children! It was as if he was bringing them up to believe in totemism or some ancient heathen mythology. The old régime was being exploded all over the country, like munition dumps on the Rhine, and yet the reports of it seemed not to reach these remote sanctuaries. Should he take the boys away, thought Henry, to live with Papa and Mamma in London?

The children went to get themselves ready for tea, shutting the door very judiciously behind them. Excellent manners evidently.

"About what we were saying, father," said Henry. "If you feel like that I must give it up."

Lord Buryan stood up: he was still taller than Henry but bent, and certainly he looked much older lately.

"But can't you understand?" he said. "It amazes me. The place has been in the possession of your fathers for three hundred years. Doesn't that mean anything to you? You were brought up here: you shot your first snipe on the ground you want to sell."

Henry laughed.

"That's really rather far fetched," he said. "I remember you told me that when you were a boy you saw a Lord Westminster who had shot snipe on the site of Eaton Square. But that didn't prevent him from building houses on it. However, there it is. You've got your point of view and I mine. I think you ought to be satisfied with the fact that I've given in to yours."

"I must ask you to remember that you're speaking to your father," said Lord Buryan, "and not to tell me what I ought to be satisfied with."

"I'm sorry. But please remember, yourself, that I'm doing what a good many sons wouldn't have done."

"Obeyed their father?"

"It isn't quite a question of obedience. I'm doing what you wish."

"A father's wishes in a matter like this, when I was a young man, would have been accepted without question by a son," said Lord Buryan.

It was no use talking like this, thought Henry. He did not want to be disrespectful to his father, and he felt that he himself had behaved extremely well.

"Well, goodbye," he said. "I think I shall start back to town."

"But you are going to stop the night, aren't you?"

"I meant to, because I thought we might have a good

deal to talk about.   But there's no more to be said.   I'll just see my mother and have a cup of tea with her, and then I'll be off."

The old man was silent for a moment.

"Henry," he said at length, "I want you to tell me if you had any special or urgent reason for wanting this sale.   Things going badly in the City?"

"No business at all," said Henry.

"Debts?   You or Helen?   You're neither of you very good at economy, I expect."

"They can wait," said he.

"Let me know what they are.   All of them, mind, not a part.   I'll see if I can help you."

"Thanks very much, father," he said.   "I'll make them out when I get home.   Rather a big overdraft."

II

To continue the decline of the parable house, the parliamentary election of 1924 was approaching.   The division in which Hakluyt stood mainly consisted of large landed estates, and it had long been regarded as an absolutely safe Conservative seat; even in the violent epidemic of Liberalism in 1906 when the very pillars of the Conservative Party, like Mr. Arthur Balfour, came crashing down, it maintained almost unimpaired its huge Tory majority, and at the last election there had been no contest.   But now the present member was retiring, and Henry had been asked to stand.   It was largely in deference to his father's wishes that he did so: Lord Buryan had represented the constituency before he succeeded to the earldom, and once more there was tradition at stake. Again no contest had been expected, but not only Labour but also the Liberals put up a candidate. A dirty trick, though Lord Buryan, of that ancient and fast dwindling party, for their man could not conceivably get in, but he would no doubt poll at the expense of the Tory vote, and thus assist Labour just at a time when it was most important to form square against it. But it was soon evident that the Labour candidate would be very dangerous indeed. He was a very able young man, a born orator with a charming manner and a voice of stentorian gold, and by birth and marriage he belonged to the landed classes. He had been a friend of Henry's at Cambridge; he had even stayed at Hakluyt, and his attacks on capitalists and landowners were based on the knowledge that his upbringing had given him. He had served in the war, enlisting in August 1914 in the ranks, and had risen to be a colonel with the D.S.O.

The war was his platform, and it had been a capitalist war. Huge fortunes had been made by shipbuilders, colliery owners and the like, and as a reward for their noble patriotism they had been created knights and baronets and peers. But it was the workers who had won the war, and the reward for their patriotism was to find themselves, those who were fortunate enough to return at all, out of work, with no one caring a brass farthing what happened to them. It was no light thing

(he told them) for a man who had been born and
brought up in surroundings of wealth and luxury to
attack the class to which he belonged, but it had been
a matter of conscience. His wife — she was sitting by
him, and was an exceedingly goodlooking woman —
was heart and soul with him, and they had thrown in
their lot with the workers. He considered it a privilege
to have been selected to besiege this stronghold of Toryism. A hopeless task, was it ? That remained to be
seen. As they knew very well there were many large
landed estates in the constituency: a dozen men by the
mere fact of their having been born the sons of lords
or of Abraham, Isaac and Jacob owned the land from
which workers brought them in their revenues, and a
day of reckoning was coming for them. They had
their great country palaces and their town mansions and
their deer forests in Scotland, and there some of them
had lived for centuries without stirring a finger to increase the wealth of the world, but merely spending and
squandering on their luxuries the incomes that the
workers earned for them. They spent fortunes yearly
on raising pheasants in order to give entertainment for
a few idle autumn days to a dozen idle friends. Half
the year their palaces stood empty while they lived in
town so that their wives might exhibit to each other, at
ball and opera, their tiaras and ropes of pearls. Some of
them, no doubt, were kindly men, and he wished them
no ill, but this hereditary domination must be broken.
He was no friend to anarchy and revolution, such as had

ruined Russia, but what he was out for, and what he
counted on the electors to back him in, was the return
of a Labour Government to the House of Commons.
As for the sons of Abraham, Isaac and Jacob, why did
they not go back to their native land instead of singing
the songs of Zion by the waters of Babylon ?   The reason was plain: there was more oof in Babylon.

This renegade was, unhappily, making notable head-
way in the constituency.   He was a far better orator
than Henry, his personality was far more vivid, he was
quick at repartee when he was heckled, he had wit and
fire, and he sowed his seed with a far defter hand in a soil
that was rapidly becoming congenial.   Henry, by contrast, was rather pompous, he spoke of the century-long
connection of his family with the district, of the way
in which they had always identified themselves with the
interests of their tenants, of the dangerous unrest that
was going on in the country, a disease for which the old
prescription of mutual trust between employer and employed, landlord and tenant, was the only specific.   He
spoke through a mask, he spoke without fire, for nothing was further from his heart than himself to continue
the tradition.   And Helen was no use at all: she drove
about, looking lovely.   She made house to house visits,
but there was an air of patronage and condescension
about her, which did not conceal her own boredom with
the uncongenial task.   At Hakluyt village Henry held
his meeting in the clubroom: the hour was half past
eight in the evening, a stormy night, and the family at-

tended in splendour, Lord Buryan in dress clothes, wearing the Garter, and Lady Buryan and Helen sat glittering by him. Dennis, Henry's eldest son, was there too, the prettiest little boy, caressed by his mother, and with difficulty keeping awake; the presence of the three generations, it was thought, would be an appeal to the sense of stability and continuity. That was the traditional mode, but just now it was strangely outmoded: there were too many diamonds and too much little Lord Fauntleroy, and it gave handles for sarcasm to the opposition.

Then an unfortunate incident occurred: the Labour agent asked leave for his candidate to hold his ensuing meeting in the club, and Lord Buryan refused: it was too much to be requested to supply accommodation for the preaching of doctrines which he held to be little short of blasphemous. The club was his property: it was built on his land and he had paid for every penny of the cost of its construction and furnishing. That was a hideous mistake, as the Labour agent gleefully discovered, for all matters connected with the management and use of the club were, by its constitution, to be determined by the votes of its members, Lord Buryan himself having only the casting vote. As President, he had subscribed to these regulations in the days when any opposition to his wishes if he had expressed them was a thing undreamed of, and now at a meeting of the club, summoned for the purpose, it was decided to grant the use of the recreation room, which he had refused. The meeting accordingly was held there, and fine capital made out of this history. Among the speakers was the ex-poacher in a red tie. He had just married the widowed lodge-keeper, and anybody who saw her could see why. He recounted the story of how his wife had been turned out of the lodge, where her first husband, who had given his life for his country, had served his lordship faithfully for fifteen years.

This incident, small as it was in itself, bewildered and enlightened Lord Buryan. It seemed to clip together and bind into a homogeneous bundle so many other disconnected happenings. It gave them coherence and significance: there was the enlightenment, and the meaning of it was bewildering. He was being pushed out: it was as if part of his own house was thrown open to the public. It was even more intimate than that: it was as if some power which had always been in his control and at his command was ceasing to function; as if almost, in the gradual loss of the authority and prestige that had always been locally his, he was losing part of his identity by physical paralysis. Once again he took the chair for Henry at Weyford. He was heckled and interrupted; he was asked what he had done with the hundred thousand pounds he had got for his pictures. Monstrous intrusion as this was on his private affairs, he was ill-advised enough to answer. He was not, he said, a penny the richer for that, for he had devised it to his daughters. . . Loud laughter. Shouts of "Charity begins at home !" . . . "Keep it in the family !"

Polling day arrived.   Once more that afternoon the express had been stopped at Hakluyt Station, for a large party including an elderly Royal Princess was assembling for three days' shooting, and dinner, not less stately than before, was almost over when Henry came in with the news of the result of the election: the Labour candidate had got in with a substantial majority.   He sat down in his vacant place for his belated dinner, and almost immediately the quiet conversations were resumed again.   It was certainly frosty tonight and there were good hopes that some woodcock might have come in: that tankard had belonged to Queen Anne, there was the Royal monogram on it: how sad and unexpected was the death of the Italian ambassador.   Then Lady Buryan caught the Royal eye, and the glittering procession of women passed out into the gallery; the men closed up and the admirable port went round on its journeys.   There was nothing to be said about the election, but it was as if a man's hand might almost be seen tracing "Mene mene" on the wall.   There were coffee, liqueurs and cigarettes; then Henry took the men to join the ladies, and Lord Buryan stopped behind to have a word with the head-keeper about the partridge-drives tomorrow.   He followed them soon; there was defeat visible in his slow movements.   The popping of fireworks in the village and the upward rush of rockets could be heard in the library when Bridge was going on, and the Princess inadvertently asked what was happening: was it a birthday ? . . .

CHAPTER VIII

SENSIBLE ARRANGEMENTS

I

MEANTIME there was growing up the generation of those who had been just too young to serve in the war, but old enough to observe and assume the unlimited license so rightly granted to their elder brothers and sisters when on leave from the various fronts or from their work in hospitals and factories. They were now entering on that period of years which their immediate seniors had spent in service. The latter had been deprived of all the natural expansions and enjoyments which were the proper birthright of those years. Many of them were sore and bitter with the elder generation whose bungling in world affairs had been redeemed by their own self-sacrifice, and now they saw their immediate juniors securely enjoying all that they had missed, and adopting, without having raised a finger to earn them, the chronic privileges of their own short periods of remission. They pursued their uninterrupted course from school to the University or went into business as clerks or apprentices in positions which their

elders who were now finding employment hard to get
would naturally have occupied during the years of the
war.   This could hardly be helped, for a boy of seventeen
or eighteen fresh from school is more readily chosen for a
junior post than one of over twenty who has had a
four years hiatus in books or figures or languages.   The
younger ones had stept, or were stepping, into the shoes
of the elder, and they were having the good times their
elders had missed, and enjoying the liberties their elders
had earned.

There widened between the war-generation and their
immediate juniors a chasm like that which already separated them from their elders: jealousy, unexpressed in
the main, but deeply felt, went to the digging of it.
The younger were reaping where others had sown; they
had not come in even at the eleventh hour to work in
the vineyard, and behold, all the arrears of wages due to
those who had borne the burden of the day were passing into their pockets.   In addition to this jealousy, the
war-generation hated and despised them for other reasons.   Had they been (so their elders dumbly felt)
worthy inheritors of the security and of the liberties that
had been won for them, had they carried on a virile
tradition, and set themselves, now that fate had placed
in their hands the fruits of victory, to labour with any
sort of manliness in the vineyards that blood and self-
sacrifice had cleared for them, their elders, though envy-
ing them, would not have despised them.   But they
were slack and effeminate, they were bloodless and dilet-

tante; they had no gusto nor appetite even for their pleasures. Boys and girls alike made themselves sticky with cocktails and apathetically cuddled up against each other. They waggled and were willowy, they sat in rows on sofas and read illustrated papers, they called each other "egg" and "old thing." They had no guts, no ideals, no vitality, and not even any active viciousness.

All this — the verdict of the war-generation on those who succeeded them in the enjoyment of the years they themselves had missed — had a certain amount of truth in it: there was a section of them who justified it. The note was to be languid and indifferent; an epicene fatigue was the fashion. It is quite possible, as has been suggested, that the rationed food of four years, which for them were the years of growth and of the storage of nervous force, had been insufficient, and this may have been partly responsible for that unrobustness for which the war generation despised them. They had inherited liberties for which they had not worked, but they made only the feeblest use of them. In rare hours of energy they roused themselves to a monkey-like activity, they squealed and chattered, they thought it admirably humorous to go to dances to which they had not been asked, they organised nocturnal treasure-hunts and made the small hours hideous with their mirth, and they thought that their antics were the lovely frolics of the young and April-eyed bringing gaiety to a sad old world. They were in fact the Bright Young People,

a definitely post-war product and an unmitigated
though happily an ephemeral nuisance.

Such was the opinion of the war-generation, who were
tired and bitter, and who felt that they had made their
sacrifice, and now the world passed them by. The
bitterness, of course, was not universal, nor anything
like it, nor were the antics of the others, but both were
widely prevalent in the years that succeeded the war.
Every Armistice Day, in memory of the fallen, a silence
of two minutes fell on the roar of London, but that was
soon over, and then London went to work and play
again in happy forgetfulness of those who had not fallen.
There were the Bright Young People busy with their
self-expression in fatigue during the interludes of their
antics, but had not the others expressed themselves, too,
when they were their age, out in France ? The younger
lot did not reciprocate the contempt of their immediate
elders who, they believed, had done very well in the war:
they were simply indifferent to it. Besides, the war was
over, and the war was a bore, and nobody had any interest in it. Devastating ! Never had anything become ancient history so quickly: 1914 and 1066 were
about equally remote.

II

Dusk deepened into night over the concerns of the
parable house, and the night was starless. Helen and
Henry drew further apart, for he had become infatu-

ated with Pamela Rockingham, and London, usually
content to smile indulgently on such affairs, and go on
its way without ill-natured comment, began to laugh
not very kindly. It was a pity to behave like that: they
were being silly, they were calling attention to themselves. How unnecessary, for instance, to go and stay
at the same hotel at Brighton for a week-end — not
ostensibly together, of course, and going down by different trains, but simultaneously by accident — unless
they were actually asking for the kind offices of the
Divorce Court, in which case it would have been simpler
to have gone down together, signed in the visitors' book
as Mr. and Mrs. Jones, and have done with it. What
made London laugh more was that Helen went off to
spend July and August at Venice with Princess Amadeo.
While she was there, she got a letter from Henry saying
that Pamela's husband was bringing a divorce suit
against her, with himself named as co-respondent.
Would Helen think it over, and let him know what she
felt about it, what she was inclined to do ? He would
like to marry Pamela.

Helen and her friend had long confabulations over
this question, as they lay on the sands at the Lido.
There were a great many things to be taken into consideration before she could make up her mind whether
to divorce Henry. She was angry with him, for she
had given him liberty to do as he liked, and he ought
to have shewn greater discretion. He had made a fool
of her, for the wife of a man cited as co-respondent in

an undefended suit was an object not of pity so much as of derision. She had not been clever enough to keep her property, she had failed in charm and alluring quality, and let another woman annex it. Henry deserved to be punished for that and, as he was head over ears in love with Pamela, it would serve him right if she refused to divorce him and thus prevented his marrying her: that would be disagreeable for Pamela, too. . . Then again there were her own prospects to review. Lord Buryan was old, and of late he had been failing: that election of a Labour candidate had been a real shock to him, and it seemed to have weakened, odd though it appeared, his hold on life, and his grip was relaxing. In a few years now, in all probability, she would be Countess of Buryan, and she must figure up what that was worth in itself, and try to realize how much she would dislike seeing Pamela in the place that would have been hers. Pamela deserved to be punished for her indiscretion, and Pamela would certainly not like being deprived of the privilege of becoming an honest Countess, and remaining a decoronetted peeress. Then there were her two sons: if she divorced Henry, the custody of them would certainly be assigned to her, and that would be a nuisance. She could not imagine herself saddled with the care of two growing boys. For the present they could remain at Hakluyt, but afterwards? . . .

These very sensible considerations, the desire to punish Pamela and Henry for their stupidity, and her entire lack of maternal affection counselled her not to divorce him but to forgive him. "And that's so weird and subtle," said Helen dreamily, "for the real proof of my forgiveness would be that I *should* divorce him."

On the other hand, now that his affairs were to be made public, she had no taste for standing permanently as the odd (though wedded) member of that stale triangle which was so banal whether at the theatre or in actual life. She had had enough of Henry (and he apparently of her) and the only reason for keeping him would be the advantage to herself of becoming Lady Buryan. Money need not bother her: Henry her husband would be bound to give her a substantial alimony, and Henry her friend coupled the agreeable qualities of wealth and devotion to her. Princess Amadeo had been against the marriage from the first, she had told Helen that she was not a woman to whom wifehood and motherhood are instinctive cravings, and the event had proved her wisdom. Now as they lay basking she strongly advised Helen to let her husband go, and her arguments were weighty. Helen would be cutting off her nose — that lovely nose — to spite her face if she refused to divorce him, she would be punishing herself much more than she punished him. Did she really want to be Lady Buryan except for the barren satisfaction of standing in Pamela's way? It might have been fun once, when there was plenty of money attached to it, and when Countesses counted, but what was the use when they counted no longer, and the estate was so impoverished? Besides, Henry might get tired of Pamela

and insist on Helen's living with him again, and then, if
she refused, as she certainly would, he might divorce
her. Why risk being Pamelized herself? Surely it
was far better to give him plenary forgiveness and
divorce him at once. And something could surely be
arranged about the boys. How would it do to make a
private agreement with Henry that he should take the
custody of them, if she let him go? . . . That was not
much to ask, for after all they were his sons.

But it was time to have a final swim before lunch; let
the whole thing simmer in her mind. It would not be
a bad plan to telegraph to Henry, suggesting that he
should come out here for a day or two. With him here
in the flesh, she would be able to picture much more
vividly what it would be like to be still tied to him instead of regaining her liberty. The Princess would take
a nice room for him at the hotel, and he could have
his meals with them at the palazzo. That would be
better than his staying there.

This eminently sensible and modern arrangement was
carried out, and Henry arrived two days afterwards.
They all went out together in the Princess's steam-
launch to the Lido, and spent the most promising morning on the sands and in the sea. Both Henry and his
wife were eager that the Princess should take part in the
discussion, for both thought very highly of her judgment. She was a sort of umpire, a chairman to call
them politely to order when there appeared a note of
personal grievance in the debate, and under the tact of

her presidency and the sympathetic warmth of her reasonableness, they took to calling each other "darling" again. The impending divorce suit, Henry II explained, would not be defended ("Very wise, I think," said Henry I in the most appreciative tones) and Helen could thus get her divorce on those grounds, without Henry being obliged to resort to those crude and farcical expedients which would otherwise have been necessary. He willingly accepted the suggestion that he should have the custody of the children, and he felt sure that Pamela would feel as he did. At present, till — well, till things were settled, they had better go on living with their grandparents who were devoted to them. A couple of hours' pleasant discussion, punctuated by refreshing visits to the sea, was enough to convince Helen that the loss of the pleasure of preventing Pamela from becoming Lady Buryan would be more than compensated for by not becoming Lady Buryan herself.

His father, Henry was sorry to say, was very far from well. He had had two or three attacks of dizziness which made Lady Buryan anxious. They were slight, and not very alarming in themselves, but in an old man it might point to some mischief going on. Henry had written to him just before he came out to say that Lord Rockingham was instituting divorce proceedings, for it seemed wise to tell him that by letter, and wait till he had got used to it a little, before going to see him. He was afraid he would be very much distressed and shocked, and now he would have to tell him that this second divorce, his own, was to follow: perhaps that had better wait for a little, for probably he would begin to wonder quietly in his own mind what Helen was going to do about it, and when he was told, he would find that he was already sub-consciously familiar with this contingency. Certainly, thought the Princess, this would be the kindest way: Henry showed great consideration for his father.

Then it was time for lunch; and in pyjamas and dressing gowns they went to the Princess's tent, and had an admirable little repast, with an interesting conversation arising out of this topic. Lord Buryan and his wife, they all agreed, were the most high-minded people in the world; they never swerved from their principles, nor failed in their duty. But they were also the most static, and they had remained completely unaffected by the vast change that had taken place in all the revaluations and revisions of thought and conduct. They were as firmly rooted in the past as those two Cromwellian oaks on the golf course at Hakluyt Park. They had both inherited their convictions like inalienable heirlooms of the mind, and that was why the situation now developing would be such a blow and bewilderment. It was the tradition to be beyond reproach in their married lives: literally there was no family scandal of the sort to form a precedent. Henry felt morally certain that since his father's marriage he had always been faithful to his wife, and she to him, and he could guess what this double divorce would mean to him. It was tradition to have double beds and untarnished silver or golden weddings, but God knew, remarked the Princess, what emptiness of heart and yearnings and achings had been smothered, like Desdemona, under those connubial pillows. Had the blameless Buryans not paid too high a price for their faithfulness, a price out of all proportion to its value? Of course they must have, time and again. Then there was the publicity as well with its huge headlines: luckily there could be no long reports of the trials, for the suits in both cases would be undefended. Lord Buryan belonged by conviction to the system of Court etiquette: divorce and remarriage were still barriers there to State balls and garden parties and Lord Buryan too felt that such people had disgraced themselves, and it was right to treat them like pariahs. Helen argued that it was only being found out ("like you, darling") that stamped the stigma of Royal displeasure, for the Lord Chamberlain, as Prime Minister of morals, must know very well that quantities of the most distinguished guests at these functions had not invariably been Sinaitic in the observance of their marriage vows. Henry agreed: that was what he meant by Lord Buryan's conviction on these subjects, and the fact of his intimacy with Pamela, now to be revealed and acknowledged for the delectation of the world, would distress his father far more than the actual exposure of it. . . Then Helen's bill of divorcement would follow, and Henry could not guess how his father would take that, so it was wiser, as they had agreed, not to risk an immediate disclosure. For there were two lines of thought among the Victorians and he did not know to which his father belonged. One held that a wife ought not to live with a notoriously unfaithful husband and was right to be legally freed from him: the other that marriage was indissoluble; she had married him for good or ill, and she must bear her lot in silence, hold her head high and wear her diamonds as usual. Naturally they all smiled a little as they discussed these antique superstitions and shibboleths, but then Lord Buryan genuinely believed in them, and they were trying to look at it all from his point of view. He had been a very kind father, too, and generous; not long ago he had paid up Henry's and Helen's debts in full. True, the sale of a strip of land was all that was needed, but Henry was glad that he had settled to respect his father's wishes about that before he knew he was going to have his debts paid, and that he had not insisted on his right to sell if he chose. . . There was a unanimous feeling of regret that the old people were bound to be very much distressed.

By a natural digression the talk drifted to the more cheerful subject of Helen's parents. They were both of a more modern mould, in fact they could be called completely post-war. She had taken to authorship and he to dancing, and on most nights now he dined at the new Sybaris Club, where the proprietor was delighted to give him his dinner free, for the sake of the *cachet* his presence conferred, and he danced half the night and was as fresh as a daisy in the morning. Her mother meantime had become a most efficient breadwinner, and after writing a series of signed accounts of race meetings for the press, for which she was paid fifty pounds each, had been easily persuaded by the editor of the *Sunday Spice-Box* to write her autobiography. It had appeared as a serial there and in America, and had just been issued in book form under the title of "Memories of a Marchioness." Helen had received a copy of it the week before, and since then there had been three reprintings of it. "Darling Mummie," she said. "Isn't it nice for her? She has made £8000 out of it already, and nobody ever dreamed she could earn a penny. Henry I. and I have been reading it aloud, and when one of us got too hot and ashamed to go on, the other read, while the first cooled down. For sheer shymakingness it beats everything: I will lend it to you, darling. You see Mummie's nearly seventy, if not quite, and there's chapter after chapter about all the smart young men, names given of course, who were madly in love with her when she was a girl, and how they stood on chairs in the Park to see her, and rode horses up marble staircases to bring her flowers to wear at a ball: like the worst Ouida. Then she describes how marvellously she used to play golf, and how she certainly would have won the Grand National if women had been allowed to ride, and how she encouraged poor Daddy to propose to her by going to his bedroom one night at a house they were staying at in mistake for her own. Then she prints all the letters that the German Emperor and Dr. Nansen wrote to her:

I expect she made those up. Then there are masses of photographs of her when she was young. I don't think they're really all photographs of her. One, I'm pretty sure, is of Mrs. Langtry, some years earlier than Mummie's time, but what does that matter ? Of course she was never a lady, and that has come in useful at last, for that's what makes the book such a howling success. Really, darling, I don't think I can lend it you, for it would make you ashamed of having married me !"

"And is any of it true ?" asked Henry.

"Oh, yes; I should think about half. Daddy's delighted with it: he takes it to the Sybaris Club and reads it during dinner."

Henry laughed. "Anyhow your parents have moved with the times," he said, "whereas mine have not only remained as they were thirty years ago, but as their parents were seventy years ago. If only my father would understand that !"

"Yes, but you can't belong to two generations," said Helen, "you've got to choose. In fact, Mummie almost belongs to the next generation, for she does things that none of us would dare to do. For instance, there's a lot about that nigger of hers, who gives lectures. She's always going about with him, and she says that the reason of all the trouble the world is going through, is that we don't understand the black races. That's the most shymaking part of all. Daddy wrote to me to say that he didn't much like that chapter. He thinks she will really get talked about, if she isn't careful."

The afternoon was gorgeous: they sat about in the sun and bathed again, and there were many bright-hued friends on the sands who were most interested to see the three together.   Henry had intended to go back to England next day, but their conference had been so harmonious and he was so friendly and pleasant that the Princess and Helen persuaded him to stop for another twenty-four hours.   It was a long journey to make for the sojourn of one day, there could be no such hurry as that in going to see his father: besides there would certainly crop up some minor questions about the house in Chesterfield Street, which Henry had devised in his will to Helen, about the Buryan pearls which her mother-in-law had let her use as her own, or about the children, which had better be gone into at once.   So they all went out to the Lido again next morning, and in the evening there was a most agreeable little dinner at the Princess's palazzo, with a dozen cosmopolitan guests of charming manners and advanced views.   Venice was in *festa* that night and they went out afterwards in gondolas to see the *gallegiante* and the fireworks.   Henry left next day, but found, on enquiring for his bill, that there was no bill, for he had been the Princess's guest.

HE sent a telegram to his father to say that he would arrive at Hakluyt that evening, for there was no good in putting this interview off: he was anxious to know how his father had taken the news in his letter.   His car met him at Folkestone, in order to save the journey up to London, and it was towards sunset when he passed up the village street. There were a few men standing about who touched their caps as he drove by, and he casually wondered why they looked so solemn and un-smiling. Then he turned in at the lodge, and there passed him a car coming out: he rather thought that the man driving it was the local doctor. There was the glade where the pheasants were reared, and there the church and the long walls of the kitchen-garden with the glass roofs of the greenhouses showing above it, and he came into sight of the great house glowing in the flames of the sunset. The flag on the turret above the front door was flying at half-mast.

He went through the hall into the gallery where he found his sister, and learned that his father had died that afternoon. Lady Buryan was upstairs, and she wished to see him as soon as he arrived. She told him what had happened. Lord Buryan had received his let-ter two days ago — or was it three ? — three days ago it must have been. He had brought it to her, and began to read it her, but he had stopped and handed it her to read for herself. He had said something about the dis-grace, just a word or two, and then all day had not spoken of it again. He had taken Henry's boys out for a ride that afternoon, he had strolled in the garden and then he had written to Lord Rockingham. He had brought her that letter for her approval. "It was just such a letter as your father would have written," she said. "I need not tell you more about it. . ." She sat very still and dry-eyed as she spoke, with long pauses between her sentences, never looking at him.

"But he said not another word to me about what you had written to him," she went on. "He could not. That evening the new parson and his wife came to dinner, and your father was just as usual. Rather silent, as he had been lately. He sat up very late that night, all by himself. When he came to bed I tried to make him speak to me about it all, but not a word. He got up very early, before I was awake. After breakfast he came to my room. I was frightened: he looked very strange, and his face was flushed. He asked me if I would come to church with him, for we must pray together. And then he staggered and fell. A stroke: he never recovered consciousness. I telephoned to you and your sisters, but you were in Venice by then, and I telegraphed, but it must have missed you. Your father died this afternoon."

She rose.

"You must leave me now," she said. "I shall not come down tonight; one of your sisters will have dinner with me up here, and I shall see you tomorrow. I will not add a single word to make more bitter the remorse I know you must be feeling, nor can I give you a single word of comfort."

"But, Mother — " he began.

"I can't bear any more just now," she said. "Goodnight, Henry."

CHAPTER IX

ICHABOD

I

THE TWO undefended divorce suits went through in due course, and within a year Pamela and Henry were married. It would have been easily possible for them to have kept Hakluyt open, and lived there much in the old manner, for Henry had succeeded in selling the Scotch estates at a noble price. But neither of them had the slightest intention of so doing. They were not of the breed that could ever tolerate the traditional stateliness, nor be hampered by the endless trouble and expense that it entailed. Large parties and the provision for their entertainment in the country were an unmitigated bore to all concerned: moreover there was to their more modern minds a sort of snobbery about that, an ostentation in the possession of great parks and gardens and galleries and greenhouses. Dinners at restaurants with a dance club to follow, in a crowd of friends, were a far cheaper and vastly more enjoyable mode of entertainment, and there was no responsibility about it: the food was quite good and there was the band and the floor for dancing provided without a hostess's supervision, and London was far cheerier in autumn than days of shooting in the misty woodland.

So there was no need to discuss the question of living at Hakluyt at all. They would both have hated it, they would have been bored stiff not only by its isolation but by its entertainments, for who wanted to have the same set of friends on his hands all day? And what were they to do when they had not people with them? Go to see the cows milked, as in the old days, or take long drives to lunch with equally stranded neighbours, returning to dine solemnly together and play patience or read a book? That style of life was outmoded: incessant movement and diversity of ready-made amusements were what the new style demanded. Above all, one must never be bored: if the shadow of that spectre threatened to fall across one in London it was easy to dodge it. There were theatres and music and restaurants and dancing and Bridge, and there were always plenty of friends in London now every month of the year. But what was to happen to one in the country when, at the early close of the winter's day, the servants came round and put up the shutters and drew the curtains and shut one up, as in a box, till morning? Not Hakluyt at that price.

So they kept the Manor House at Hakluyt as a country cottage where they could go with two or three intimates for Sunday golf. They lived at their house in Chesterfield Street, and Henry bought a delightful villa near Cannes to escape the gloom of the English winter. Hakluyt Park was for sale, and though they neither of them dared hope that such a monstrous white elephant would find a purchaser, they had a tremendous stroke of luck. The admirable Mr. Blumenthal, whose hotel at St. Moritz was milling gold, and who regarded gold as a stud-farm to breed more gold, had heard from Henry that he wanted to sell that strip of land along the road by the Park for villa residences, but that his father had been opposed to it, and now he put forward a much bigger proposition. The expansion of the neighbouring town of Weyford was proceeding a-pace, the value of building land there was mounting, and Blumenthal enquired whether "Harry" would consider selling not the strip of outlying land only, but the entire park and the house. He had big ideas: his plan was to re-sell large plots of building ground and to make a superb golf links in the park, with the house for a residential club-house. There would be croquet lawns as well, and many tennis courts. He would have to form his syndicate, he would have to get some of those golf-experts down to see if they could guarantee a really first-class links, and he would be deeply grateful if Harry would give him a month's option before he entered into any other negotiations. A week before those days were accomplished the purchase was made, and a six-figured cheque followed.

Then there was all the furniture of the great barrack to be sold, for the club-house must be furnished in a different style altogether, with quantities of small tables and leather chairs instead of the huge mahoganies and Venetian thrones, with lockers for golf clubs instead of painted *cassoni*, with the Blackheath print and photogravures of famous golfers on the wall, and with new bedroom suites instead of the old cumbrous gear. It was settled to hold so miscellaneous and important a sale in the house itself, for Hakluyt had a *cachet* of its own, and dealers came in their shoals, for who could tell what unsuspected treasures might lurk in the pantries and passages and bedrooms of a house that had remained secure and wealthy and unravished for three centuries ? This proved to be the case, and prices took eagles' wings over an Elizabethan silver ewer and rose-water dish and a pair of flagons of the time of James I. There was a wonderful Chippendale cupboard in the housekeeper's room, there were first state mezzotints by J. R. Smith mixed with worthless steel-engravings in the bedrooms: never was there such a medley of things good and bad as the old house gave up from its unweeded spaces, all part of its growth and its stability. The three renowned Italian pictures had gone, but there was a panel from an early Dutch triptych that had hung modestly in the shadow of an immense Victorian cabinet in Lady Buryan's sitting-room, and over this two eminent picture-dealers had a notable duel. These spring tides in prices were balanced by corresponding ebbs: the Landseer of a stag with his hinds round him, commissioned from the artist by Henry's grandfather, fetched only fifty pounds, and the huge Edwin Long, the proud purchase of his father and the glory of the long gallery since the sale of the Italian pictures, was sold for about the price of its frame.   Against this decline again must be set the sale of the Spanish silk that covered its walls, and of a fifth century Greek bronze which Henry could not remember ever having seen before.   The books in the library, well bound volumes of standard works, were sold by the foot: among these there were tragedies. *Pickwick* in its original parts, with the paper covers removed and bound up into two neat morocco volumes was on these unscrutinized shelves and a similarly desecrated first edition of *Wuthering Heights*.   And the heavy Victorian furniture, sideboards and massive tables and mahogany bedsteads were sold almost by the hundred-weight.

When the disposals of each day were over, a host of vans and carts bore away the purchases, and at the end of the fifth day the rooms were empty and echoing. And now the house lay dying, breathing its last, for all the tokens of its past, which were its life-blood, had been drained out of it, and its deathbed was lonely, for it was deserted by the race of which it had been the cradle and the home; it no longer lived in the hearts of those whom it had nursed and sheltered so long, and their fellowship with it was over.   The hour of its dissolution had come and it looked out mournfully from its uncurtained windows as from dying eyes.   It had seen days of waste and splendour and magnificent hospitalities, but perhaps the noblest of its ministries was when its stately chambers were wards for the wounded. Generation after generation had been born and had grown up under its roofs, passing out in the fullness of years to their resting places in the churchyard near by, and now it was needed no more. But Henry was delighted with the sum that the auction had realized; he had not expected nearly so much, and again he made a purchase at Galopin's shop in Bond Street, as a fairing for Pamela.

But presently all was bustle and movement again in the empty shell, under the driving power of Mr. Blumenthal. Carpenters and builders invaded it, and they put up partitions in the great bed-chambers on the first floor, cutting them into new shapes and sizes, and they installed many new bathrooms and convenient places. The long gallery was divided into a sitting-room and a card-room; there was a new table put into the billiard-room, and the marble-floored hall was covered with a thick-piled red carpet, which made it much cosier, and it became a most comfortable lounge, whereas before it had had no function except as a repository for hats and coats. Then, since there was to be a ladies' links in the Park as well as the men's, one wing of the house was made into their residential quarters, and the divided library furnished them with a spacious dining-room and sitting-room: there were also rooms for refreshment and intercourse common to both sexes. The staircase at that end of the house led to their bedrooms, and above were the bedrooms of the waitresses, very neat in their white caps and aprons.   Mr. Blumenthal also arranged that specialists in hair, nails and complexions should be in attendance every Sunday, and Lady Buryan's sitting-room, divided into discreet compartments was furnished with the equipment of their craft.   This establishment was open to men also.

Simultaneously with all these great improvements indoors, the two golf courses were being hewn out of the park, and the architect gloated over so noble a site for his new cathedral.   The glen where the pheasant-coops had been made a beautiful short hole: it narrowed as it approached the green, and a sliced ball found bunkers, and a pulled ball trouble in the rough.   The marshy land where Henry had shot his first snipe was drained, for boggy places are tiresome hazards, but it was left tussocky and reedy for righteous punishment.   Once carried, a second long shot, avoiding the dip where guns used to be placed at pheasant-shoots for the high targets that rocketted over the beech trees, would reach the green.   Then came the Warren Hole: for weeks ferreting and trapping of rabbits went on: the whole village lived on gratuitous rabbit.   After that regiments of trees, the finest in the park, must be felled, and the tall obelisk to the first Earl of Buryan removed, for an obelisk, like a tree, was an undesirable hazard in the fairway.   The grass lawn in front of the house furnished room for four *en tout cas* tennis courts and a nine-hole putting course for diversion on summer evenings.   The

row of peach- and grape-houses in the kitchen-garden
was removed, and a room for the caddies, a shop for
clubs and balls and repairs and a house for the professional took their place, but the furnace and the pipes of
the central heating were retained to warm the lot of
them. The accomplished architect of the links regretted that the church could not be scrapped, for this
would have given him scope for a very fine eighteenth
hole ending close to the house. He hoped that hymns
and organ-noises would not disturb players on the ninth
tee.

The success of the club was assured before it was
opened, for, irrespective of the excellence of the links
and the luxury of the residential club-house, the President of the club was a Royal Highness and the Vice-
Presidents included the Tin Duke, Henry, and the amateur champion of the year *ex-officio*. None of these, of
course, paid entrance fee or subscription, but they attracted just those who would be willing to pay any
amount of both, and who would be likely to bring down
their friends at a ruinous green-fee, and have champagne
for lunch. A future like that of Le Touquet was confidently prophesied for it. There was no crossing of an
unquiet sea to arrive at it, but only a motor drive from
London or an hour's journey by train. The commodious villas, with charming gardens attached, rose rapidly
on the outskirts of the Park, and the farms that had been
scarcely able to pay their way, even with the help of a
generous landlord, found a ready market for their meat

and poultry and vegetables, without the cost of transport and the profit of shopkeepers and middlemen, for
all these new residents required good feeding, and every
week-end the club dining-room was full of hungry
mouths.   The unemployment in the village disappeared,
for a numerous company of caddies was needed, and the
upkeep of the greens gave work for many hands.   The
village club built by Henry's father for the young men
of the village, for chess and draughts and bagatelle, the
reading of illustrated papers and the enjoyment of non-
alcoholic refreshment, was leased to a cinema company,
and licensed to sell beer and spirits.   It had long been
quite unused for the purposes for which it was built, but
now it brought him in a very pleasant rent.   He was
Captain of the golf-club for the first year, and on the
opening day drove the first ball up the glade where the
pheasants used to be reared, and topped it heavily.   He
dined in the old dining-room, attended an amusing
cinema show in the old village club, and (such are the
marvels of modern science) saw a picture of himself
topping the ball from the first tee.   The house was be-
wilderingly altered, but he could locate the bright cheerful room in which he slept as having once been part of
his mother's and father's bedroom.

So the parable-house, typical of hundreds of others on
smaller scale, passed away. The tradition that had
maintained it and in days gone by had deeply founded it
in the soil of England was weakening, and the floods

came and the gales of war blew upon it, and it crumbled. There were forces acting from below upwards that contributed to its disintegration, for the war had brought unrest and unemployment, and Socialism had made use of these against once wealthy landowners: Labour at Hakluyt had stormed a Conservative stronghold, and all these were potent influences. But apart from them, the tradition was in this as in other cases abandoned by those in whom it was vested. Many of the new generation of inheritors were indifferent to it, and dissociated themselves from it: its foes, for they were no less, were of its own household. In all ranks of ownership, from the great landlords, who turned their estates into limited companies, down to the small country squire, who sold his outlying fields, they felt no personal dynastic responsibility as their fathers and grandfathers had felt for the welfare of their tenants; land and dependents became a nuisance if they entailed the duty of living on straitened means in the country when increased taxation had curtailed the diversions and hospitalities to which they were accustomed. It was more cheerful and cheaper to live in London in a small house for the dreary autumn and winter months, and shut up the country-place. In many cases to live on the larger scale was no longer possible, sheer necessity was the cause of that curtailment, but personal preference also had a loud voice in the matter. Long weeks in the country were dull.

This restlessness of mind and need of constant change

particularly possessed those who had served in the war
and were still in their twenties or their early thirties
when peace came. Many wanted to work, but there
was no work for them, and this craving for diversion
was like some sort of mental St. Vitus. Various causes
contributed. There was the half-sub-conscious instinct
that whispered to them that five years of their youth
had been filched from them and they were owed a compensation for that. Then there was the revolt from the
past and from all its staid old ways which was already in
active ferment before the war, and resumed its efferves-
cence now. Less obvious on the surface, but none the
less existent, was a scare of loneliness, seldom spoken of;
so many of their contemporaries, friends and lovers, had
been mown down by the scythes of death, and the bereaved remnant must cling together and make the most
of what remained of youth. They resented the imbe-
cility of their elders, whose mismanagement had brought
these things upon them, they detested those who,
slightly junior to themselves, had escaped their own fate
and assumed their privileges, and they were a generation
apart. They had stood the brunt of it all, they had
done enough duty to last them a lifetime, and they intended to enjoy the diversions of their own devising, and
to express themselves in any manner they pleased. Anything consecrated by use must go: there must be new
modes to fit the new world, jazz music with its synco-
pated rhythms to typify the unrest and the jigging
fidgetiness, novels whose text was casual adulteries, to

signify that a moment's whim was more potent than exploded moralities, a troupe of niggers to take the place of old-fashioned revues: there was a thrill to be got from niggers. . . Or was it that Nature was trying to find some unheard-of glue that should join together the broken edges of the fragments into which the war had split the nation, something to make a coherent whole again ? Everywhere was revolt against the old order, and the fate of Hakluyt was typical of the rest.

II

TYPICAL also of the new mode was the sequel of the harmonious triangular conference on the sands of the Lido. Henry's new ménage went as merrily as marriage bells, though none had been rung in the registry-office where Pamela had been made an honest countess. There was money enough now (that was the great thing) to enable them to live exactly as they pleased, and they were both of one mind about not having any children. Besides, Henry's youngest boy was now thirteen, and it would be like having two generations to bring up simultaneously. Their house in London was small, but they would both have hated having a large house, for who wanted to entertain largely ? A few only of the great London houses were still in possession of their owners, and there the old stately ways went on, with powdered footmen and dinner parties of thirty or forty, and couples going down arm in arm, as in the Methuselah

days of Buryan.   The "old crusteds" was their name for
such, in allusion to the port that went solemnly round
after dinner.   But neither of them moved any longer
in such circles, apart from which most of the big entertaining was done by Americans and other aliens who,
in the old-fashioned way of the New World, still delighted in Duchesses and took the vast empty houses in
the country from owners who had not been able to dispose of them to such advantage as Henry had done.   In
London these hospitable folk gave innumerable dinners,
and had cotillions and cabarets, and were an immense
godsend to those who thought that every hour not spent
in a crowd was sixty minutes wasted.   They were not
always quite up-to-date, and in their anxiety to make all
their guests known to each other, sometimes introduced
quite old friends.   This had happened to Henry and
Pamela, for on the eve of their marriage they had been
dining with a new trans-Atlantic hostess, Mrs. Horatio
Bedders.   Henry had had a card given him by the butler, indicating that he was to take Lady Rockingham in
to dinner, for Pamela still kept her old title till the new
one was ready.   Mrs. Bedders asked if he knew her, and
he said no, and was duly presented.

Mrs. Bedders sent Pamela a most expensive wedding
present to atone for her stupidity, and made a dead set
at them both.   They were the sort of people she most
wanted, for nobody's photograph appeared so frequently in the pages of illustrated papers.   She was a

phalanx in herself, and bore down all opposition. Pamela
had received four invitations from her by successive
posts, and so had christened her "Four-Post Bedders."
She had taken a lease of Mornington Castle in Kent, because it "tickled her to death to live in a castle," and one
Sunday afternoon the entire Russian ballet gave a performance in the banqueting hall. Pamela went to that
sumptuous entertainment without Henry, who could
not bear any more Bedders for the present, and just as
the special train chartered for the guests was moving out
of Charing Cross Station, Helen, Countess of Buryan
(for so she had continued to call herself), ran to the
open door of the carriage, and sprang almost into
Pamela's arms: this dramatic moment was snapshotted
by a photographer on the platform. Being true citi-
zens of the modern world, they were delighted to see
each other, and naturally had a great deal to say: instantly they were "darling Pamela" and "darling Helen,"
and talked incessantly all the way down to Mornington.

Helen had only just come back from Italy: she had
a flat with a *scala particolare* in Princess Amadeo's
palazzo in Venice, and had been there all the spring.
The Princess was coming to England next week: Helen,
for the moment, as she quaintly said, was *en garçon*.
Not a grain of awkwardness impeded the cordial progress of their talk; as for jealousy, or anything of that
sort, how could there be any since they both were so
thoroughly contented with the new adjustment of their

lives ?   Pamela explained why Henry was not here, and
Helen asked after her sons.   They were perfect dears,
said Pamela enthusiastically, she was devoted to them,
and they could not have been nicer to her if they had
been her own, probably they would not have been so
nice.   They were both at Eton now, and Dennis, the
elder, was in the eight or the eleven (she always mixed
numbers up) but, whatever it was that Dennis was in,
it rowed: at least eight boys rowed and Dennis steered.
He was such a handsome boy, as of course he had every
right to be, darling, and was immensely popular: her
own boy who had just left was devoted to him.   So nice.
Pamela was going down to Eton on the fourth of June
to see Dennis cox — that was the word for steer — his
eight.   Helen ought really to come down too to see him
and Francis, for they had both grown enormously since
she had last seen them.   It would be delightful if they
could go together.

Pamela was so charming about the boys that Helen
readily promised to go down to Eton with her and see
them: to refuse would have been ungracious to a woman
who had been so good to them.   Then they talked about
Henry in the friendliest manner, and Pamela insisted
that she should dine with them when they got back
from Mornington this evening, and go with them to a
play that was being given at the Arts Theatre, a private
performance of course, for the censor had refused to
license it.   The play was by Maurés; it was marvellously
translated, but one couldn't tell how it would sound in

English. The principal characters were two schoolboys and two girls, and the *dénouement,* she believed, was highly unexpected.

Helen, on her side, could give a very contented account of herself. Henry I. had a wonderful circle of friends, English, Italian, French and Russian. They were all women, all tremendously intelligent and as a group wholly self-sufficing. Those absurd jealousies and intrigues and misunderstandings which always arose when a little intimate circle consisted of men and women were expunged from it. Men and women never saw anything with the same eyes from the arrangement of a room to the deepest philosophical questions: there was perpetual discord and fundamental friction between them with short interludes of passion. Whereas when women of a certain type were together, intercourse (though naturally they could have their quarrels and feverishnesses) was founded on a deep-lying harmony, if Pamela understood. Pamela thought she did, and was sure it was lovely.

Both of them had many friends going down to this performance of the Russian ballet, who found it entertaining to see Lady Buryan and Helen Lady Buryan hobnobbing together. How wise they were ! Helen had no time, when they got back to London, to go to Princess Amadeo's house in Chelsea to dress, so Pamela lent her a marvellous tea-gown which she had never yet worn herself, and Helen looked lovely in it. She was delighted to find that the onyx bathroom was unchanged, and so was Henry to see his late wife. They had a brief but chatty dinner together, and went on at once to the theatre, and Henry sat between the two.

The visit to Eton on the fourth of June was equally successful. The two boys were charming: Helen was proud of being the mother of such beautiful young creatures. Dennis, now just turned fifteen, with the sexlessness of youth still clinging to him, was the image of what Helen had been when he was born. They were both a little shy of their mother, and avoided addressing her as such, but they were on the most affectionate terms with Pamela, chattering away to her, as she walked between them, and calling her "Mum": the old married couple followed them down the High Street, as the pavement was too narrow for all to go abreast. There was one moment only of slight embarrassment, when they went to see Henry's tutor, at whose house his boys now were; Henry introduced him to his wife, as his wife and, after a moment's pause, to Helen, as Helen Lady Buryan, for it seemed difficult to describe her otherwise: "my late wife" would hardly have done. His tutor was puzzled, for he would no more have thought of reading the news of the divorce courts than of reading a novel by D. H. Lawrence, and he could not make it out at all. Otherwise, the visit was most satisfactory, and the boys, knowing Helen better than they had done when she came, kissed both their mothers when they said goodbye, and hoped they would meet the two of them again at Lord's.

CHAPTER X

TEMPORIS ACTI

THERE was one member of this otherwise harmonious family who made no attempt even to review, with a possibility of revision, her traditional code, or to see whether there were not clauses in it which the changed world had rendered obsolete. Perhaps old Lady Buryan was wise: she was like the elastic band, before spoken of, that kept the documents of an older code together, and it might have snapped under the strain of including fresh papers in its circlet. She was typical of many women in positions analogous to hers, widowed women already elderly or old, who had once held in their various degrees positions of larger scope than were now theirs, and who had adapted their habits to changed circumstances, but not their minds to a changed world. Probably they could not have done so, but in any case they did not want to: the old, they were convinced, was better, and they disregarded the new, tacitly deploring its exhibitions but not much concerned with them, and prefering to be rather lonely, with many hours to fill rather than to attempt to get out of themselves, if that implied getting in with a world of which they did not

approve.   Of such would be the widow of some small
country squire who, at her husband's death, went to live
in the close of a Cathedral town.   Of such was Mrs.
Thorndyke, widow of the late parson at Hakluyt itself.
She had betaken herself to the neighbouring little town
of Weyford, where she occupied a flat in a semi-
detached house.   There were large signed photographs
of Lord and Lady Buryan on the walls, there was a glass
case containing an albino pheasant, which her husband
had shot at Hakluyt and his lordship had stuffed for
him: there was a bookcase full of theological works, and
Mr. Thorndyke's unfinished manuscript of the "Life of
St. Anthony of Padua."   She was a hoarder of ancient
relics: in her bedroom was a dress-basket full of antiques
belonging to her mother: one was a satin dress which she
had worn only once or twice, and there was a great pad
sewn into its proper place which was called a bustle.
Another property was a strangely mis-shapen lawn
tennis racquet: in those days young ladies used to play in
long skirts.   Her landlady was a pleasant bustling body,
with a great respect for her as being a "real lady," and
she often came in for a chat in the evening, and was
never tired of hearing how Mrs. Thorndyke and her husband invariably dined at the Park on Sunday evening.
Silver plates and the most interesting conversation.   It
was such memories that supplied Mrs. Thorndyke's mind
with it's sole sustenance, and it added a little piquancy
to them to observe how the attendance at Sunday School
had fallen off under the administration of her husband's

successor at Hakluyt. Other such lived in boarding houses and private hotels in the Cromwell Road, South Kensington. It would be easy to expend sentiment over them, but such an emotion would be much out of place, unless we pitied precisely those traits which they cherished with pride.

Of such, and relevant by contrast to this narrative of change, was the Dowager Lady Buryan: she was an archetype of a changelessness that it would be impertinent to commiserate because it was her mode of self-expression, and a demonstration of her duty. She lived, monumentally, in the house in Lowndes Square which she had occupied all the years of her married life, and which her husband had left her at his death. She had brought up from Hakluyt many of her own belongings, a few pieces of big furniture, to which pious memories were attached, such as the mahogany double-bed in which her children had been born, and quantities of china, Chelsea and Worcester and Dresden, which she had inherited from her father, and dozens of signed photographs, given her by eminent and royal personages, which stood, thick as the stars at night, in their ornamental silver frames, fluted and flowered, on the grand piano which was never opened: there too lay the famous visitors' book, so full of amusing sketches. She had reminded Henry of its existence when that auction of which she could not bear to think took place at Hakluyt, and he had withdrawn it from the catalogue, and sent it her, to the great chagrin of a dealer in autographs.

The aged butler, the housekeeper, the cook, her own maid, the first footman, two housemaids and a kitchen-maid all of whom had been in her service at Hakluyt formed her household; and with the help of an "odd man" these eight persons looked after the solitary old lady.

She breakfasted downstairs, for that was her habit, served by the footman.   There were two hot dishes on the sideboard which she seldom touched, but it was right that he should say, "Kedgeree and bacon, my lady," for her cook would have thought it very odd if these were not sent up.   When she had refused them, the footman quenched the spirit-lamp that kept them hot, and left her to herself.   Every morning she saw her housekeeper and her cook, as in the old days, and having read the *Morning Post* and *The Times*, and having written an occasional letter, she was busy with a crossword till lunchtime.   Her husband had left her the landau with the two black horses, in which she had been accustomed to drive in the Park of an afternoon, preferring this slower and more dignified progress, if only air and "carriage exercise" was the object, to whizzing along in a motor; so daily now, unless the weather rendered it utterly impossible, the landau came round at a quarter to three, and the footman asked her if my lady would have it open or shut, and where she would go.   Generally my lady went across Hyde Park, then round the outer circle of Regent's Park and, coming home, she usually went along the road to the north of the Serpentine.   Occasionally this section of the journey was omitted; there might have been an unusual press of traffic in Baker Street or long waits somewhere, and then my lady was afraid that she would not get back to Lowndes Square "in time" if she went round by the Serpentine, though what she wanted to be "in time" for who could tell? Once a week one of her married daughters lunched and drove with her. She got back to Lowndes Square about half-past four: sometimes it was only a quarter past, and then she was pleased to have accomplished her carriage exercise so speedily, for she had "saved" a quarter of an hour: indeed, the time-table of her day really interested her more than any of the occupations that filled it. In the winter lunch was half an hour earlier, and the drive was curtailed. She sat resting till the butler and footman brought in tea at five, and then she got to work on her jigsaw-puzzle or her needlework till it was time to dress for dinner. She dined alone, waited on by butler and footman, and afterwards listened to the wireless. At ten o'clock, whatever was in progress, she turned it off, rang the bell and went up to bed. She seldom read a book, for nowadays one so often came across something that was not quite nice. On Sunday her daughters and their husbands, if they were in town, came to lunch, but there was no drive on Sunday afternoon, for the landau had already been out twice to convey her to and from church.

After the first year of her widowhood this extreme seclusion was relaxed; she dined out occasionally with those who had been week-end guests at Hakluyt, and

gave an occasional dinner party conducted on the old
lines.   But in all her circle there was none who could be
considered a friend.   Never in her life had she formed
a real intimacy: reserve and high-bred tranquillity had
frozen her up.   When she was young it must be supposed that there was something molten and malleable in
her, but she had been poured entire into a mould, and
now it was cold and, in its quiet way, extremely hard.
The very changes that for years had gone on round her
rendered it the more so.   With no set determination,
but with an instinct even more stubborn, she had refused to adapt herself in any degree to a new order of
things or embody in her habits and thoughts any modi-
fication of the old courses.

She had never seen Helen since she divorced Henry,
nor Pamela since she had married him.   She had written
to Helen when she knew the divorce was impending,
urging her not to take so extreme a step. She and Henry
might still make something of their lives together; above
all, there were the boys to consider; it would be terrible,
terrible for them to start life under this stigma.   She
begged Helen to remember the Christian's duty of forgiveness.   A strange confusion of thought lurked under
that admonition, for Helen, eager to be quit of matri-
mony, had quite forgiven Henry, whereas old Lady
Buryan herself had never done so, and she only wanted
Helen to patch it up with him for the sake of appear-
ances.   Helen wrote, quite charmingly, from Venice,
saying that she could not reconsider her decision, and

that she was convinced the boys would be very happy
with their father and stepmother: no doubt their grandmother would often see them. After the divorce Helen,
on a visit to London, proposed to come and see her, but
Lady Buryan declined. Pamela also was more than willing to be friendly with her mother-in-law, but there old
Lady Buryan was adamant: Pamela simply did not exist
for her. She felt no active antagonism towards her; she
was just one of the women one did not think about, and
she had no sort of doubt in her own mind that this was
the right attitude.

The case of Henry was different. Sometimes she was
afraid that she was stretching a point in principle about
him, but in spite of all, including that letter to his father
which, Lady Buryan was convinced, was the direct cause
of his death, and the sale of Hakluyt, she was still his
mother and he her son. Naturally she could not go to
his house any more than she could admit Pamela to hers,
but her doors were always open to him, and he was often
at the family luncheon-parties on Sunday, and acted
as host for his mother at the greater gatherings, for she
liked her guests to know that she had not permitted the
painful past to come between them. There was once an
awkward moment, for Henry's sisters were friends with
his wife and, in slack water of conversation, one of them
said how lovely she looked at Mrs. Bedders's cabaret last
night: but Lady Buryan remained stone deaf till safer
ground was reached. Pamela laughed over this incident
when Henry told her about it, and was perfectly good-

natured about her rigid exclusion. Indeed, she encouraged the boys to go to their grandmother's: they found it exceedingly dull but Pamela told them they mustn't mind. "Poor old Grannie" (her only reprisal) would like to see them, and she would take them to the movies afterwards.

In these domestic estrangements and in her set rigidity, Lady Buryan was entirely to blame. Yet, from another point of view, she was not to blame at all, for she was like that, and the Ethiopian cannot change his skin. The code in which she had been brought up and her pathetic fidelity to it bound her as by the coils of some constrictor snake. But her absolute refusal (perhaps inability) to adapt herself to new values and to a changed world resulted in her becoming not only a very lonely but a very useless and selfish old woman. She was like one who had been shut into a cave, or rather had immured herself there, where water heavily charged with lime dripped slowly but incessantly from the roof, and in process of years had covered her with a hard stalagmite formation: she was a woman encased in a mineral rigidity, from which she never wished to free herself, for this integument was a garment of righteousness and tradition. Her life ticked away in an inviolable routine of nothingness; not one atom of personal service to anybody interrupted, like the striking of an hour, the procession of her days. Her drives, her crossword puzzles, her solitary evenings, her staff of retainers were the proper and dignified thing for a dowager who

had seen great days.   She had been left very well off, her
jointure was paid her free of income-tax, and she subscribed to various charities; but charity began at home,
and her bestowals were made from the surplus that remained after every conceivable expense of her own, and
a small fund, steadily accumulating, for a "rainy day,"
had been budgetted for.   She was not exactly a Pharisee,
for she never thanked God that she was not as other
women are, but she was well aware of the difference between her and them.   But still less was she a friend of
publicans and sinners, for she never could make a friend
of people with whom association brought you into touch
with all sorts of looseness in thought and conduct.

Perhaps it is a mistake to call her lonely, for loneliness
implies the ache of being alone, and no such ache was
hers. Pamela, goodnatured Pamela who, about this
time found the Bright Young People extremely amusing
(though she was a little old for them) and was the life
and soul of many cocktail parties, would have willingly
given up an amusing evening now and then if "poor old
Grannie" had asked her to share her solitude, for Pamela
was incapable of resentments of any sort, and never bore
a grudge. But nothing was further from Lady Buryan's
mind, and she could much more easily have imagined
herself asking her housekeeper to dine with her than her
daughter-in-law. Both belonged to different worlds
from hers, but an evening spent with her cook was far
more thinkable than one with a moral outcast.

As she grew older, she began to suffer from rheumatism, and went every year to Harrogate, living in comfortable lodgings kept by a couple who had once been butler and housekeeper in a nobleman's family. They understood her; they had the deferential ways she was accustomed to, and she was as comfortable as at home. From year to year she occupied the same rooms for the same period and from the same date, and spoke of these three weeks as her holiday. Then followed a visit or two to houses where tradition survived, but with her increasing lameness she was glad to get back home, even when, according to the phrase of a bygone day, "there was not a soul in town." She had drifted far into that saddest of all the infirmities of old age, and had ceased to feel any need or desire for human intercourse. Her eyes were a little troublesome, needlework must be curtailed and patience took its place. But she never played patience on Sunday; it was as if there was something definitely unsabbatarian about cards, for whatever purpose they were used, and Sunday began to be rather an idle day. One summer she gave up driving along the north side of the Serpentine altogether, for bathing sheds with mixed bathing were put up on the opposite bank, and the sight of so many arms and legs (her spectacles, No. 1, for ordinary use suited her wonderfully) combined with the knowledge that they belonged to both sexes was far from pleasant. True, she need not have looked in that direction, but there were gleeful cries and splashings to be heard. But the house in Lowndes Square was still a stronghold: nothing modern or subversive of the right decencies of life could penetrate there, and though a daily drive in the Park was still a duty she owed to her health, it was a relief to hear her front door shut behind her, and know that for the next twenty-two hours she would be safe from any intrusion.

For the last fifty years Lady Buryan had kept an engagement book; the fresh volume arrived for her, on a standing order, in the last week of every December. They were tall books, all uniform, with only three days to each page, so that there was plenty of room to record not only her actual engagements, but notes about the weather, the names of those who had dined with her or stayed at Hakluyt, or whom she had met at other houses, and the series formed a fairly full diary. Since her husband's death, now ten years ago, engagements had been few, but the volumes held all that was of real interest in her life. The Sunday luncheons appeared there, the occasional dinner parties, the drives, the preacher at church, thunderstorms, spectacles, visits to Harrogate. When, as usual, on the last New Year's night she added the volume 1930 to the shelf in her bedroom, it occurred to her to look at some of the earlier books. How astonishingly full life had once been! She was amazed at the number of things she had crammed into one brief day. On a certain twenty-third of June, she had taken the two girls out for a drive round the Park in the morning, she had entertained a dozen distinguished folk to lunch, she had attended a garden party at Marlborough House, she had dined out and gone on to a gala performance at the Opera at which Melba sang.   Reading those entries, her memory glowed with the warmth and effulgence of such wonderful days: she could exactly recall making her curtsey to the Princess of Wales who asked after her little girls; how the Prince had said he gr-reatly looked forward to a day's pheasant shooting at Hakluyt in the autumn, how Melba sang the Jewel Song in "Faust."   (What a drama: Goethe surely intended it to be a warning to thoughtless girls !)   Then there was the Prince's visit to Hakluyt in November: there had been thirty guests in the house: sport had been excellent, and he had given the head-keeper a pair of enamelled links with his monogram on them.   Page by page she skimmed the leaves for the rich cream that lay so thick on the surface: how splendid, how truly memorable such years had been in a fashion long forgotten except by the privileged few.   Surely she could make a most interesting journal out of these jottings, putting it in the form of a plain connected narrative, and describing, day by day and year after year, where she had stayed, who had stayed at Hakluyt and in Scotland with them, with notes about their families and great snowfalls and her garden.   Not much about political affairs or the war, but a stately domestic chronicle, a document recording what the vanished life fragrant with sumptuous memories had been.

She soon became absorbed in her task, for it was her form of self-expression, now that the present had no real existence for her, to live herself into the past again.

Crosswords and puzzles and patience became but a secondary interest in her life, and she was pleased to find that such literary composition as was needful was quite easy of accomplishment, for there was as yet no question of selection or arrangement; she simply amplified the notes in her diaries in due chronological order and found herself steeped in the secure and golden days. Material was abundant, even super-abundant, and she saw that, in her account of some of those seasons in London in the nineties, selection was necessary, for at the innumerable and stately dinner parties of the day the same names occurred again and again, and the balls of one year and the Royal entertainments were repeated in another. . .

Then somewhat more ambitious designs outlined themselves. The young, her grandchildren, for instance, and doubtless many others, would be all the better for knowing what London was like when their parents were children, and she wondered whether she could not privately print for a favoured few these vanished scenes. The Park was a very different place in the days when the roads therein were reserved for those who had horses and carriages of their own. Hired vehicles, such as cabs and hansoms, were not allowed to traverse them: such common conveyances must go outside the preserved area by the public streets, and not profane the highways that were sacred to the leisurely and decorative use of "carriage-folk." How smart and beautiful it was, how stimulating to know that every landau or victoria coming towards you might contain somebody to be

bowed to as an equal or even a superior ! What a difference, too, in the Row when it was full of gentlemen
in top-hats with trousers strapped under their boots, and
ladies in top-hats and flowing riding habits ! Now
many of the latter rode astride wearing breeches, and
the men looked like their own grooms in mufti, only
they did not ride so well. Then motors came in, but
for some time even privately-owned cars were not allowed in the Park, for they were inharmonious with the
stately leisure of those who took the air there, and a
Royal lady much objected to them for, in the decadence
of manners that was even then coming in, ill-bred occu-
pants would come alongside her landau, and then slow
down in order to get a good look at her. No one was
allowed to bathe in the Serpentine after eight in the
morning, and you could walk or drive where you liked
without being obliged to avert your eyes from the de-
plorable mixed exposures of limbs. Even more sacred
was Constitution Hill down which now taxis plied, just
as if it belonged to them. Then, none but the vehicles
of the Royal Family and those who had the *entrée* to
Courts, representatives of foreign powers, Cabinet Ministers and such like were permitted passage there. Lady
Buryan had never resented not being able to drive there
herself, for it was a privilege reserved for her superiors
in rank and office and she was content with her assigned
place in the hierarchy. Those were golden days, and as
she contemplated recording them, the glamour of them
stole round her, and she longed for one of those after-

noons to come back, just one, to feel it all again. She must try, for the benefit of her grandchildren, to write a little essay called "The Park as I remember it."

The idea of writing a "real book" had now begun to take root in her mind, and she realized that, while explicit about the loss of privileges that her class had sustained, she must preserve the proper reticences of her class as well. She could not, for instance, explain that the cause of Buryan and herself and the two little girls leaving London at the beginning of July one year instead of remaining till the end of the month, was that she was expecting a baby, and that the doctor had advised the quiet and fresh air of Hakluyt. That was not a thing to be printed, but any intelligent reader could infer it because she would subsequently say that the bells of Hakluyt Church were pealed on the morning of July 23rd, and that it was a great joy that a male heir had been born. Later, even larger discretions must be exercised: she was determined not to make any mention of Pamela's divorce or of Henry's, or of their subsequent marriage, for that was washing dirty (and clean) linen in public. She would of course refer to Henry's first marriage, but after that the phrase "my daughter-in-law," which would in any case occur but seldom, must cover the identities of them both.

At one of the family Sunday luncheon parties Lady Buryan told her daughters of the great project, and they thought it a very nice occupation for her, and promised to see if they had got any letters from her that might be

of use.   Through the winter and the spring of 1931 she
worked busily and, as each artless chapter was finished,
it was typed by a very nice woman who came to the
house for that purpose, as the author did not like the idea
of her manuscript going to an office to be typed by some
unknown person.   By degrees she became quite friends
with Miss Stevenson who, she ascertained, was of very
good parentage (almost "one of us"), for her mother
had been the daughter of an Irish peer.   Sometimes she
dictated to Miss Stevenson, when the engagement book
consisted mainly of lists of names, and Miss Stevenson
was very useful in turning up the pages of Debrett if, by
a lapse of memory, Lady Buryan could not remember
who somebody's mother had been: sometimes Miss
Stevenson sat in Buryan's study with her typing machine, for the clacking noise was disturbing to literary
composition.   She often lunched with Lady Buryan,
and drove with her afterwards, returning to tea, after
which, on days of extreme industry, they both resumed
their labours.   She took the greatest interest in the work,
she loved the accounts of the princely doings at Hakluyt,
of the visit to Sandringham, and the funeral of Queen
Victoria, and conversation with her awoke in Lady
Buryan more memories yet.   So sympathetic a com-
panion made the memory of the golden days shine again,
and the spring was a very happy one for the old lady,
though she often felt terribly overworked.   But she
knew that it was well worth while to tire herself like this
and scarcely have a moment's leisure for patience, for she

had an object, a cause to serve.   She had, years ago, read Lady de Grebe's *Memories of a Marchioness*, and had been horrified to think that the public would form their picture of aristocratic life on that appalling volume.   Her own would be a counter-blast to its falsity: people would learn how the true aristocracy behaved, would get a real idea of that dignified existence, of their devotion to duty, of their high-bred reticence, of their splendour and simplicity.

At last the book was done, and Lady Buryan wrote a preface saying that her children had insisted on her writing it, and she dedicated it to Dennis and Francis.   No longer was there any thought of its being only privately printed, but under Miss Stevenson's encouragement negotiations were on foot for its being published in the regular manner, and that made her feel very modern. So her wise provision of a little fund for "a rainy day" was now justified for it would have to be beautifully printed with quantities of photographs, and the publisher asked for a sum down to cover the bare expenses of production, and when these were paid he and the author would go shares in the profits.   The agreement would be drawn up when Lady Buryan had selected the photographs, and this would take a week or two more, for there were many albums to be explored; and perhaps a page or two out of the visitors' book, certainly the one on which the Crown Princess of Germany had written her poem, would be produced in facsimile.

And then the end came.   Miss Stevenson bringing

into Lady Buryan's sitting-room an album which had been overlooked and contained some interesting groups, found her sitting at the table where she worked, with her head fallen forward over the visitors' book, unable to move and writhing in pain. A severe operation was immediately necessary, and she died without recovering consciousness.

The typed manuscript therefore came into Henry's possession, a huge pile of paper with the selected photographs. He glanced through it and gave it to Pamela to look at. She brought it back between tears and laughter. "Darling, I don't think you can have it published," she said. "It's nothing: it's a catalogue of dukes. I had no idea she was such a crashing snob. Poor old dear: but it made her very happy doing it, I expect. And that chapter about how lovely Hyde Park used to be. Everyone would scream."

PAMELA's verdict, I think, was incontestably just. Age had not given to Lady Buryan's narrative that patina which renders interesting the small details of social life in a past era, nor were they anything but the exceedingly narrow observations of a very respectable woman. No intimate revelations enlightened them, for it was her creed to maintain in public an inviolable reticence about anything that concerned more than the surface. The golden days which she tried to render and which were so brilliant to her could not fail to produce an impression of a dull and pompous and incredibly snobbish mind.   Pamela was wise.

Lady Buryan was buried at Hakluyt by the side of her husband, and as the procession went to the grave-side, an unobservant golfer portentously pulling his ball from the eighteenth tee, saw it swerving towards the churchyard and shouted "Fore."   Very few of the villagers attended the funeral, for ten years had passed since she had left the great house, and she was scarcely even a name to them, and what she had stood for was vanished utterly.

CHAPTER XI

EMINENT MEN

THERE were two men of the highest ability, who had risen to the most eminent positions in Church and State in the years before the war, and retained all their mental activity for ten years afterwards, who perhaps might have been more eminent still if they had adopted different professions. This may seem a paradoxical statement when we consider that one held for many years high posts in the Cabinet, including that of Prime Minister, and the other occupied the See of Canterbury for five and twenty years, but it is quite conceivable that they might have rendered even greater services to their generation and beyond, if the politician had devoted himself to philosophy and Archbishop Davidson to politics.

The true bent of Arthur Balfour's mind was towards philosophy; it was more at home, with a fireside sense of comfort, among abstractions than in more practical arenas, and during his undergraduate years at Cambridge, when he came much under the influence of Henry Sidgwick, then a young don at Trinity, the balance inclined to his adopting, as a career, the academic

life: if he had taken a distinguished degree he would
almost certainly have done so. The decisive factor that
now intervened was an adventitious one, and had he not
been the nephew of Lord Salisbury, his career most likely
would have been run at Cambridge instead of at Westminster, and who shall say whether he would not have
done more in the wider spheres of abstract thought than
he did as a director of the polemics of a political party ?
There was nothing polemical in his nature, though he
could make the most subtle and deadly play with that
rapier of a mind, and he was never one of those whose
self-expression is primarily controversial or assertive.
His genius lay not in the construction and defence of
measures which, if passed, would be graven on the stone
tables of the law of the land, but in the formation and
criticism of vaster theories, which could never be
proved, but which after due examination might be accounted highly probable or most improbable. In any
case they would have no bearing on the practical eco-
nomics or policies of government, but might enlarge
our conceptions of first causes and final consummations.
His instinctive interests, the subjects on which thought
could be most profitably expended, were to him the
cosmic verities. All had to be weighed, the claims of
the probable, and the handicap of the objections to it:
all sides of these questions must be examined in order to
arrive not at ultimate and absolute truth, for that was
for ever outside human conceptions, but at conclusions
(tentative and by no means certain, and to be thought

out further in the greater leisure of a future life, if there was one) that contained no intellectual inconsistency.

A temper and temperament less adapted to the restless rough and tumble of party politics cannot be imagined. The very qualities which made his mind so fine a percipient when dealing with the abstract were exactly those which militated against his power for political leadership. He brought no passion to it: he was literally unable to bang the drum or thump the tub or inspire enthusiasm in others by being carried away by his own, nor could he mock and execrate the convictions of those with whom (on the whole) he did not agree: indeed his incapacity for rancour was one of his high-minded disqualifications. He was too subtle for such rough work and also too fair-minded, and while fair-mindedness is essential to a philosopher, it is a handicap to the militant politician who, convinced of the general rightness of his measure, pours unlimited scorn on perfectly valid objections to it in the cause of "party."

As was his mind so were the weapons which it forged for him. He was admirable in debate, quick and ready and with a rapier swift in thrust and gleaming with a suave and withering irony which, unfortunately, was too much like sheet lightning, brilliant but practically innocuous. He had no bludgeon wherewith, when in power, to deal knock-out blows, and gladden his party with the sight of the antagonist bleeding, prone and counted out. His delicate and precise rapier work was mainly a critical asset, and he was thus far more telling when leading the opposition than when in power. Nobody was further from being a dilettante, as is sometimes urged against him, than he: all the energies of his mind were concentrated on his work, but his weapons were not half so effective as those of other minds which had not half his intellectual grasp. But he was as far removed from the amateurishness of Lord Rosebery, as he was from the calibre of Mr. Gladstone. Gladstone was a consuming and a ruthless fire, he burned up all that came within reach of his flame, he was a great battleship with broadsides of devastating guns, and the chill of years and the octogenarian frosts never cooled his ardour. "God intended Ireland to have Home-rule," was one of the latest of his thunderings, "and God intended me to be the humble instrument in procuring it." He was not actually right about that, but there was the inspiring temper. Arthur Balfour had none of that colossal certainty: he would never have saddled Providence with the responsibility for his own convictions, nor would he have thought it probable that Providence took so intense an interest in a change of constitution in a part of a very small island in a second-rate planet in a third-rate solar system.

After the war, though he never held the highest office again, his personal ascendancy in the House increased rather than diminished: this was due not to his strength but to his charm, and probably no politician of whatever epoch has been regarded with such personal affection on both sides of the House. His reputation for being dilettante was really due to the fact that a very large number of questions such as rouse most politicians to strong feelings strongly expressed seemed to him in his own phrase "not to signify very much." He was of the same temper in private affairs. For instance, the wife of a member of the Labour party whose husband had been raised to the peerage, came to consult him as to whether she should adopt the style of a peeress or not. She had made a great name for herself as a social reformer, she was connected in the minds of people with the admirable work she had done and, very naturally, she thought that it might mean a loss of prestige or even of public identity if she took another name. It is easy to see how important this question seemed to her, but "I don't think it signifies very much" was his answer. It was not that he wished to snub her, or that he did not look at the thing from her point of view, but on reflection he could not see that it was of much consequence. One thing alone he exempted from his comparative aloofness, and that was the pursuit of philosophic truth. Nothing mattered so much as that, and his own assertion that he took more pride (not quite the right word) in having been Gifford lecturer than in having been Prime Minister, may be taken as his own authentic valuation of the career which he adopted not to the exclusion of the other, but to the relegation of it to the second place in his life's work, and of the career which might otherwise have been his.

THIS immense personal charm, which won him such affection in the dusty arenas, was equally potent in private life. He used it (it would be more accurate to say that it used him) for the banishing of all contacts that irritated him or bored him, and for the provision of those pursuits and companionships which pleased him. He was surrounded by a crowd of charming and cultivated adorers, male and female, who suited his particular temperament, to whom his wish was law, and whose joy it was to strew his delicate path with primroses: never was Sultan or Sultana more sedulously pleasured. He took a boyish pleasure in games, chiefly lawn tennis and golf, and players of international eminence were proud to be his partners. He had musical tastes of an odd kind, with a fanatical devotion to Handel, and his adoring circle was enraptured with his idea of forming a quartet of concertinas, with a piano to assist, and rendering the works of the Master on those excruciating instruments. The great fugal choruses could be performed, and four concertinas blared out "For unto us a Child is born." It amused him: that was enough, and the moment it ceased to amuse him, the concertinas were wrapped up again in their green baize. He liked brisk and mildly intellectual conversation in leisure hours, he liked discussion, not too serious, controlled and conducted by himself, and the cluster of bright spirits known as "The Souls," who afforded the eighties and early nineties so much innocent fun, swarmed round him as bees round their queen. He called them into being, they fanned him with their wings and, though never taking a nuptial flight, he was their effortless leader in graceful intellectual revels. It was made impossible for him ever to sacrifice his own convenience to that of others, even if he had felt the least desire to do so, because others so much preferred giving up their own, in order that everything should proceed precisely as he wished. In the social give and take of life it was he invariably who took, and his most adoring friends could not have acquitted him of selfishness. But it was no unamiable selfishness: he merely took, with a winning cordiality, what they were so ready to bestow.

People in general made only the faintest impression on him: his interest in them as human beings was very mild. He would make himself utterly delightful to a woman he sat next at lunch, and the poor thing thought she had made a brilliant success, for surely no one could have been so charming unless he had thoroughly enjoyed her "style" and her conversation, but next time he met her, even if it was that very evening, he would not have the slightest idea who she was. Perhaps this large indifference was partly responsible for his abnormally bad memory: he never registered sharp impressions about things that "did not signify very much."

One of his gifts to which scant justice has been done, and which would have served him well had he chosen his career otherwise, was that of writing extremely fine prose, classical indeed, at its best, in dignity and weight. The nature of its subject precluded it from being popu-

lar even among those who were capable of appreciating
the beauty of the vehicle, for he dealt chiefly with matters "not understanded of the people," and it was only
those of philosophical predispositions who cared to read
his work.   But the following extract from his *Foundations of Belief*, the substance of which is easy of comprehension, seems worthy to rank among the noblest
specimens of English prose of its particular kind; it is
indeed a perfect piece of prose in balance, in rhythm, in
the entire suitableness of its solemn cadences to the
theme.   The substance moreover is highly characteristic
of the way he looked at the life that animates our
planet, and at its inevitable extinction, without any sort
of cynicism, nor with any touch of regret at its brevity,
but with an unquestioning acquiescence in the ultimate
end, which no concerted endeavour of human sublimity
could conceivably modify.   He wrote:

It is enough that from such beginnings, famine, disease and
mutual slaughter, fit nurses of the future lords of creation,
have gradually evolved, after infinite travail, a race with conscience enough to know it is vile, and intelligent enough to
know it is insignificant.   We survey the past, and see that
its history is of blood and tears, of helpless blundering, of
wild revolt, of stupid acquiescence, of empty aspirations.   We
sound the future, and learn that after a period, long compared with the individual life, but short indeed compared
with the divisions of time open to our investigation, the
energies of our system will decay, the glory of the sun will be
dimmed, and the earth, tideless and inert, will no longer
tolerate the race which has for a moment disturbed its solitude.   Man will go down into the pit, and all his thoughts
will perish.   The uneasy consciousness, which in this obscure
corner has for a brief space broken the contented silence of

the universe, will be at rest. Matter will know itself no longer. "Imperishable monuments" and immortal deeds, death itself, and love stronger than death, will be as though they had never been. Nor will anything that *is* be better or be worse for all that the labour, genius, devotion, and suffering of man have striven through countless ages to effect.

THE second of these great men who, though he attained to the highest eminence in his profession, might possibly have been of a more world-wide value if he had adopted another, was Randall Davidson, Archbishop of Canterbury for twenty-five years, who on his resignation at the age of eighty was raised to the peerage in order that his wisdom and influence might still be available in Parliament. Though, from the point of view of success, no career could have been more complete, it may well be questioned whether his abilities, his tact, his superb sensibleness, his immense personal influence with all varieties of minds might not have found a fuller scope in the secular world. At the age of thirty-four, having been chaplain to two Archbishops, he was appointed, practically by command of Queen Victoria to her Prime Minister, to be Dean of Windsor, because she wanted someone, young though he was, in close touch with her, on whose judgment she could rely. She was not, as a rule, apt to value very highly any opinion which went counter to her own, but for the remaining seventeen years of her life she asked his counsel not on Church matters only, but on other affairs of State, and on private and personal decisions, and, even if at first she strongly disagreed with him, in the end, stubborn though she was and convinced that she knew better than anybody, she invariably took his advice. He became almost the Keeper of the Royal Conscience, and from the first she relied on his judgment and constantly sought it: within a few weeks of her first seeing him she established a private cypher with him. No one since the death of the Prince Consort twenty-four years before, not even Lord Beaconsfield and certainly not any of her subsequent Prime Ministers, had anything like his influence with her. Lord Beaconsfield rarely if ever gave her unsolicited advice or advice which he knew would be unpalatable, unless by dexterous presentation of it he could make her fancy that she had thought of it herself, in which case "with humble duty" he would confess himself convinced, but her new young Dean employed no such artifice if he thought she was contemplating something unwise or injudicious or compromising to her dignity: he preferred to tell her so, and trust to her common-sense, of which, rightly, he held the highest opinion. Perhaps the most remarkable instance of his justified audacity (for indeed she was not accustomed to that sort of thing) was one that occurred when he had been at Windsor less than a year.

The causes that led to this crisis must be briefly indicated. The Queen had published in the year 1868 an artless little volume called *Leaves from the Journal of a Life in the Highlands,* describing the manner of her days at Balmoral with the Prince Consort. It was the kind of book which is usually privately printed by the

author, and given "to a few friends" who thereupon
write to say how it brings back the old days, and instantly relegate it to an obscure bookshelf in a bedroom.
But the Queen was easily persuaded by Sir Arthur Helps
to let these "Leaves" be published, not for a few friends
alone, but for all her subjects. They had always been
deeply in sympathy with the joys and sorrows of their
Sovereign, and it would indeed be a privilege to them to
know "how her rare moments of leisure were passed in
her Highland home when every joy was heightened, and
every care and sorrow diminished by the loving companionship of the Prince Consort." The Queen yielded to
these arguments, and appointed Sir Arthur Helps as
editor. Lord Beaconsfield received a copy, and subsequently wrote, referring to her and himself as "we
authors," and told her that her book and the Bible were
his bedside volumes. Others gave her to understand
that all her subjects regarded it as an almost sacred disclosure. . . Encouraged by this reception, the Queen
followed up "Leaves" early in 1884 with another volume called *More Leaves from the Journal of a Life in
the Highlands,* a very similar chronicle of later days
there after the Prince Consort's death.   In both she described her picnics and her ponies, the cloud of midges
that bit her dreadfully, the blueness of skies, the purple-
ness of the heather, the toothache of one daughter, the
sitting down on a wasp's nest of another, the amusement
of seeing the crowds on the banks of the Clyde, who had

assembled to see the *Victoria and Albert* go by, caught
by the backwash of her yacht, the christenings and
funerals she had attended, the devotion of John Brown
and the present of a plated biscuit tin which she made
him. In fact, in the second volume there was a good
deal about John Brown, and she dedicated it to his memory, for he had died the year before.

Now there had been a good deal of quiet amusement
(of which of course the Queen knew nothing) about
the books generally, for they were of the most trivial
sort; all mention of politics and international interest
was excluded altogether; they were unlit from beginning to end by any spark of humour or of shrewd ob-
servation, and this dedication to John Brown had in particular been the source of innocent merriment. He had
been the Prince Consort's gillie and, starting from that
sacred association, the Queen had allowed him to adopt
towards her a tone of familiarity and a brusqueness in
his demeanour which she would certainly not have stood
from any of her subjects or from her family. The thing
was grotesque: ministers at Balmoral were liable to be
patronized and patted on the shoulder by this ill-bred
and boozy Highlander, whose struttings and swagger-
ings were no longer confined to Balmoral, for he was
with her now at Windsor and Osborne as well. Long
before his death he had become quite intolerable, but
nobody had one tithe of the courage necessary to speak
to the Queen about it: they knew perfectly well how

such a complaint would be received. After his death she put up an effigy of him at Balmoral and, as we have seen, dedicated her second volume to his memory.

She sent this book, as soon as it was out, to Dean Davidson, and told him that she meant to write even more "Leaves," which would certainly contain more, much more, about John Brown.   Davidson instantly saw that this would never do.   More about John Brown was unthinkable: there had been far too much about him already, and she would make herself ridiculous.   His personal admiration of her character was unbounded, he knew that she discharged her great office with noble conscientiousness and wisdom, and he hated the thought that those who did not know her should find excuse for belittling her supreme qualities.   At whatever risk to his career, he was determined if possible to save her from this mistake, and he did what nobody else, especially those who knew her best, would have dared to do. In a letter of great tact and respectfulness he told her that her previous publications, though valued and treasured by all right-minded people, had provoked very unappreciative criticism from those of the baser sort, who had thus proved themselves quite unworthy of the privilege Her Majesty had granted them in making them partakers of her private joys and sorrows; he felt most strongly that they did not deserve any further confidences.

The Queen received this letter with the most signal

mark of her displeasure, namely dead silence, devastating and prolonged silence. She had not asked for advice, but advice of the most unpalatable sort had been given her: nobody had ever dared to write to her like that before. But, all the time, as he hoped she would do, she had been taking counsel with her own superb gift (that almost equalled his) of common-sense, and when next after a portentous pause she sent for him again to learn his opinion on some other matter, no allusion was made to the past. The fresh literary adventure was never heard of again, and she treated her Dean with an added intimacy and a confidence such as she gave to no one else.

Now a young clergyman who had the nerve to tackle that most formidable personage in a manner so wholly unprecedented was no ordinary character. The awful silence of her displeasure had not in the least disintegrated him: he knew he was right, and he believed that on reflection she would come to agree with him. If she did not, he had still done his duty by one who had honoured him hitherto with her confidence, and the event shewed how right he was in his outspokenness. Nobody else would have dared to do what he had done, and probably they were quite right in not so venturing, for their attempt would have been a disastrous failure. But he had judged her correctly, trusting that, unaccustomed as she was to criticism of any sort, she would get over her resentment at this unasked-for frankness, and weigh his advice.   Besides she ought to know (and how could she know unless somebody told her?) that she was contemplating a very unwise thing.

It was not once only or twice, but invariably, when she consulted him, that he gave her the frankness which, at heart, she wanted.   There were moments when on offering her unpalatable suggestions, he was aware of her deadly silence, and knew that those prominent blue eyes, before which her nearest and dearest trembled in their shoes, were fixed on his audacious face, and he wondered if, this time, he had gone too far.   But his courage never failed him; never did he refrain from giving her the counsel that he would have given to any other old lady who, in the matter of friends, was lonely, and who knew it.

The criticism then that, in the high position in the church that he was presently to hold and in his twenty-five years' occupancy of the highest, he showed timidity when boldness would have been better is completely answered by his policy when dealing with the Queen. His courage was unimpeachable, but like all people of an exceedingly subtle mind he coupled with it the gift of caution.   He preferred to win his point through the exercise of persuasion and counsel and even minor compromise, if he thought that he risked more than he might gain by a *coup-de-main*.   This subtlety was not intellectual, but consisted, in the main, of his power in awakening the reasonableness of those who disagreed with him.   He was not in any way a commanding personality, rousing blind enthusiasm and equally violent antagonism, but one whose good sense amounted to genius, and whose diplomacy in dealing with people was unrivalled. An Archbishop of Canterbury is not a Crusader leading his forces out to wage Holy Wars, but an administrator among whose duties it is to avoid them: and he is fettered by tradition and by the control of Convocation and by Parliamentary procedure. Moreover there can be little doubt that, eagerly conscientious though he was in the discharge of his duties, many if not the majority of the questions that incessantly occupied him had not in themselves any very great interest for him, nor the obsessing, haunting quality of dreams that must be realized. The rules and ordinances of the church should certainly be observed, and he was prepared to go to extremes, when persuasion failed, with those who broke them, but he did not personally care a jot whether a recalcitrant incumbent had lighted candles on the Communion Table, or ceremonially mixed the Chalice, or recited prayers for the dead, and at heart he thought it waste of time to be occupied overmuch in such matters. And, as the irony of fate would have it, during the whole period of his archiepiscopate the revision of the Prayer Book demanded his close and constant attention and, at the end, all his diligence and finesse were lost labour, the weaving of ropes of sand. Certainly that was a tragedy in his eyes, but it was not primarily tragic because a cause which he had passionately at heart was unachieved, or because he thought that its rejection by the House of Commons had deprived the realm of some great spiritual benefit. A vast amount of time and trouble had been spent over a few additions and omissions to which, spiritually, like most other people, he was indifferent: he could worship God quite as well according to the rubrics of the old Prayer Book as of the new, and the only object of these interminable committees extending over twenty years had been to define a little more accurately what the laws and bye-laws of the Church were, and how much latitude was allowed to its ministers. It had been a very painstaking drafting of rules, and at the end when all the labour was done the whole went into the waste-paper basket.

By no legitimate use of language could he be called a passionate churchman in that he clung to outward forms because they were traditional, nor was he a theological scholar to whom restorations of correct readings in the original Greek of the New Testament, or their meticulously accurate rendering into English seemed matters of supreme importance. Nor again was he of that burning faith which inspires men to become missionaries. He was a very humble and devout Christian, but his religion was a matter of quiet though unquestioned conviction to him, and did not blaze into ecstasies or enthusiasms. He had no paramount exclusive desire to bring individual souls to Christ, and in a monastic age he would never have become a monk or a great preacher. Missionising work of the direct personal sort was not his *métier*; besides his time was fully and over-fully oc-

cupied with the administrative work inseparable from
his position.   He served the Church with single-minded
devotion, but not with religious passion, and a great
part of his work did not seem to him personally of very
great significance.

It may be questioned therefore whether this work,
vast though it was, gave him scope for all that his superb
gifts of insight and of diplomatic dealing with questions
of wider import fitted him for.   He was at his best
when he was adviser and counsellor, and men in the
highest positions in the political world trusted his wisdom and his farsighted judgment in matters that
had nothing to do with ecclesiastical questions, more
than they trusted that of anyone living, exactly as, for
seventeen years, Queen Victoria had done.   An instance
of this occurred just before the war when there was a
threat of imminent insurrection in Ireland.   On one
particular Sunday morning he was due to hold a confirmation in his diocese, but there arrived at Lambeth
two urgent summonses for his presence elsewhere.
Two leading politicians independently sent for him to
seek his counsel in the crisis.   His first task was to find
another bishop who could confirm just as efficiently as
he, and off he went to render services which no one
could do (such was the feeling of his petitioners) as
well.   There lay his true gift, and he brought to such
functions as secret adviser to men in high public office
abilities that did not attain their full fruition in ecclesiastical presidency.   Immensely, too, did he enjoy

being in touch with great affairs, and pleasure in such
cases is always a whetstone to wisdom: he was at his best
in such dealings.   It may seem strange to suggest that a
man who for twenty-five years had admirably discharged the duties of the first subject in the realm could
have done better yet for his country and used with
greater effect his individual gifts, but such I believe to
be the case, for that man at the age of thirty-four effectively advised Queen Victoria for her good on a
matter concerning authorship, and at the age of sixty-
five was sent for by those who sought his advice on a
matter of national importance concerning Ireland.

So each of these two most successful and highly gifted
men who attained to the greatest distinction that their
careers offered them, might have won an even higher
eminence if they had chosen careers for which they were
more fitted, in that their greatest gifts would there have
found an ampler exercise.   Both of them, as far as
heredity counts at all, followed an ancestral bent, for
Lord Balfour, on both sides, came of political stock,
Lord Davidson of ecclesiastical.   Their minds, each in
its way of the finest, were curiously unlike, the one
aloof and functioning most freely in the air of abstractions, the other intensely practical and boundlessly sa-
gacious in its dealings with men.   They did not become
really acquainted with each other till the years 1902–
1905 when Balfour was Prime Minister and Davidson
Bishop of Winchester, but instantly there sprang up between them strong friendship with that best of founda-

tions, mutual comprehension, each recognizing in the other the value of the equipment in which himself was lacking, practical grip on the one side, and on the other the power of abstract thought. Both throughout their lives were of delicate physical constitution, and both lived to over the age of eighty in unimpaired vigour of intellect.

A THIRD extremely able man, poles apart in the actual scope of his career from the other two, for he did not deal directly with the affairs of State nor, however remotely with those of Church was Ernest Cassel. But his gifts perhaps partook of the quality of both, for the financier frames his projects by the aid of the imaginative vision, though it expresses itself in concrete terms, and his operations in making loans for the construction of railways or of lines of maritime communication or for the building of reservoirs clearly affect the commercial prosperity of his country. He was, in point of age, their close contemporary, but, unlike them, the outbreak of the war brought the active career of his life to a close, though he lived well into the succeeding decade. His vocation, at any rate, could never be called in question, for though, as a young boy, he had dreams of becoming a professional violinist, the thoughts of youth in his case were short, short thoughts, and to be Cassel rather than Kreisler was his indisputable destiny. He came to England from his home in Cologne at the age of fifteen, as clerk in the house of Bischoffsheim, his compatriot both by German and Jewish blood. He at once demonstrated his talent for finance and, while scarcely out of his teens, was lent by his employer to look into and, if possible, straighten out, the affairs of a Jewish firm in Constantinople which had fallen on difficult days: the job, if compassable at all, would take, it was thought, a year's hard work. Young Cassel made a brilliantly successful job of it in three months, and laid the foundations of his own fortunes. After that he set up on his own: he was too clever, thought Bischoffsheim, to be in the employ of anybody, and never, in the making of his very large fortune, did he have a partner, or trust any brain except his own.

HE married an Englishwoman of the Roman Catholic faith, and had by her one daughter, Maud, who married Mr. Wilfred Ashley. When his wife lay a-dying, her irreparable misery was that, according to the tenets of her faith, she would never see her adored husband again in the eternal life on the threshold of which she now stood, for he had no religious beliefs of any sort, and was therefore a lost soul. Ernest Cassel appealed to the priest who was attending her, and begged him to baptize him then and there, and thus he would become a redeemed member of Holy Church. He promised, if this was done, to make a serious study of the faith and a conscientious endeavour to accept it. The priest to his everlasting credit thereupon baptized him, and his wife died happy in the belief that she would be united to him again, when he too was done with the times of probation. For a period of six months following her death, Cassel studied theological matters under the instruction of a priest. But the attempt at spiritual enlightenment was fruitless, and after this honest and thorough trial he gave it up as unprofitable, for he found himself unable to believe a word of orthodox dogma. However, having been received into Holy Church, and baptized into the communion of true believers, he was technically, though he believed nothing, a Catholic, and, after his death, a Requiem Mass was said for him at Farm Street to the astonishment of all but the few who were aware of this strange story.

At first, in his independent business life, he had no success. Never, so he once told me, did he work harder, but nothing went right for his enrichment. All forms of speculation and gambling were abhorrent to him: you did not make your fortune by making guesses, but by intelligence and constructive foresight, but in spite of all his indomitable industry and his genius for finance, money would not come his way. He worked on undiscouraged, for he never doubted his own abilities, and suddenly the wheel of Fortune, hitherto unkindly immobile, began to turn, and his touch became that of Midas: whatever he put his hand to gleamed with gold. Then dawned his great days: he became the most intimate of the friends of the Prince of Wales who subsequently became King Edward, and whom, physically, he oddly resembled, and the King's cronies clustered and swarmed about him. No doubt it was his wealth that gave him his first opportunity there: had he not been immensely rich, he would probably not have come in contact with the Prince at all, but when once that opportunity was his, the friendship that resulted was based on a strong mutual affection and esteem, and throughout his reign there was no man in whom the King more trusted and confided.

Cassel enjoyed it immensely, but this friendship was the only piece of real pleasure, amounting almost to happiness, that his wealth ever brought him. He was both magnificently lavish of his money and also careful of it, he entertained largely, he took the King's friends on *tours de luxe* abroad, paying for the whole regal progress ; he bought the long lease of Brook House, he bought " Moulton Paddocks " at Newmarket, where he owned a racing-stud and had first-rate partridge shooting, he had a flat in Paris, always in commission for the visits of himself or his friends, and later, he bought another big house at Bournemouth, where his sister lived, after her health made it impossible for her to preside for him in London. He bought splendid pictures, the finest examples of great masters: his was the Vandyck of the two young Stuarts, and he had noble Raeburns and a Botticelli, but he did not care for pictures. He bought the rarest books, but he was no bibliophile, and very fine early English silver. His collections of Italian bronzes and particularly of Dresden china were remarkable, but he did not really know a bronze from a piece of porcelain. He bought anything that was sufficiently expensive and of testified excellence, but all such were only the trappings suitable for a very wealthy man, and not the hard-won and intelligent acquisitions of the true collector who does not have his treasures driven to him, but stalks them himself. Neither picture, nor book, nor horse, nor bronze gave him any keen intrinsic pleasure, for he had no instinctive tastes for art or sport or literature. In the same way his constant and magnificent liberality towards hospitals and worthy charities did not primarily spring from any innate sense of sympathy with the suffering: it was the recognised duty of a man of great wealth to give largely to good objects. Nothing, I am aware, can be more false and cynical than to say that a rich man is not generous because he does not feel the loss of what he gives, nor cuts down the gratification of his own luxuries in order to give more liberally yet: but, though kindly, there was about Cassel something of that strange and barren inhumanity which is not rare among those whose abilities have long and exclusively been devoted to the acquisition of wealth. Often they lose the power of all other enjoyments, and when the keenness for money begins to be blunted, there is no other savour for them in life, and this curious impotence to experience pleasure results. What should have been a means only of giving and receiving enjoyment has become an end, and the process of acquisition has produced some sort of poison-gas in the fumes of which all other enjoyments have wilted. The pursuit of wealth for its own sake would seem to be a bar not only to entering the Kingdom of Heaven, but also the Kingdom of Earth: *obstant Divitiæ*.

His income during the days of his great harvestings must have been very large, though not comparable to the far vaster American fortunes, but never was there a hint of sharp practice or of unscrupulousness about his methods. With that deluge of money pouring in upon him, and being instantly sent out to irrigate fresh fields of honourable fertility, it must have been difficult to estimate it. When the Budget of 1915 came out, and the wail of the wealthy who declared they were completely ruined, went up to Heaven, his riches were sufficient to enable him to refrain from these pathetic lamentations. He shut himself up with his pass-books in his study at Bournemouth for the whole morning, instead of going for his usual two-hour walk, and emerged at lunch-time with the consoling reflection, "It is not so bad after all." On another occasion he enquired what was the "incomm" of a certain large London landowner, the late Sir Richard Sutton, who was supposed to be a wealthy man, and on being told that it was about £200,000 a year, he replied, "I do not call that rich."

At the same time, like many men, whom even he would have called rich, and who spent largely and gave nobly, he retained, probably owing to some remote complex formed in childhood, when he came to England as a junior clerk at the bottom of the ladder, strange and minute economies. During the war, for instance, when starch was expensive, and the wages in laundries high, he gave up wearing his invariable white waistcoat at dinner, since it cost eighteen-pence to wash. It was not worth it: he had something better to do with his money. Or again, one night at Bournemouth we had had partridges for dinner. His servants were on board-wages, and Sir Ernest must have observed that one bird went away uneaten. At lunch next day he said sharply to his butler: "What has become of that other partridge ?" A very relevant question: if he had been on board-wages he would not have dreamed of filching a partridge, and he wanted to know that he was being served as honestly as he would have served himself. Luckily it was among the cold dishes on the sideboard. . . Conversely, the fact that coffee, which he liked very strong, and drank four times a day, had not gone up much in price afforded him satisfaction: this was something to be thankful for when provisions were getting so ruinously dear. Such reflections can only gratify very rich men: the person of moderate wealth would continue to wear his white waistcoats, and not be particularly pleased that coffee was still fairly cheap. Possibly some streak of conscious not unconscious humour lay at the bottom of these economies, but I scarcely think he would have liked his friends to be amused when he gave his reasons for abandoning the use of white waistcoats, or enquired after the missing partridge.

But neither money, nor his benefactions, nor purchase nor prudent economies brought Sir Ernest any real enjoyment: money could only procure for him rarities for which he had no hunger, enable him to make endowments for objects with which he had no active sympathy, and view with equanimity the rise in supertax; and when there came to him a need in comparison with which he held his millions cheap, they were powerless to help. His daughter and only child who had grown up and married, was stricken with consumption, and his wealth availed nothing. She was the woman in the world to whom he was most devoted, and her death early in 1911 followed on that of King Edward, the man to whom he was most genuinely attached. With no other of his subjects did the King so completely escape from the fierce light, or in whose house did he more freely enjoy the unguarded diversions of a private life. Of all alien nationalities it was with Jews and with the French that he felt himself most thoroughly at home, and of all Jews Sir Ernest suited him best. He enjoyed his company, he trusted his cosmopolitan sagacity and he knew that in tastes and ties alike Sir Ernest had completely identified himself with the country of his adoption.

And now Cassel's daughter and his best friend had gone, and in his career as a financier there came hitches of the most humiliating kind. Already he had been officially, though privately, asked by the Government to start in Constantinople an English bank in rivalry and opposition to the Deutsche Bank. He had consented to do this, and all his acumen and power of organization had been enlisted in the project, when the Government changed its mind, and no longer required his services. Unbacked by England he had, naturally, no inclination to risk his capital in an unstable state. That was the first instance of the English Government's entire want of comprehension about what was going on in Turkey: had the scheme which they had asked Sir Ernest to promote been carried through, Germany would never got that complete control over Turkish finance, which enabled her, as soon as the War broke out, to use her in the way she did. There would have been always a solid focus of English interests in Turkey, resisting the German peaceful penetration which by 1914 had invaded every vein and artery of her system. We should have had also a reliable source of information as to what was really going on, have realized that the party of Union and Progress was completely under German domination, that Turkish troops were being trained under German supervision, that artillery was being brought in from Essen, and Turkish credits pledged for payment thereof; and that Germany was going to bring Turkey into the war at the precise moment it suited her best. As it was, the Foreign Office was repeatedly informed by our Embassy there, that all was going well, and a little patience alone was required to bring Turkey in on our side, or at any rate assure its neutrality.   A sad disappointment.

Then again, also before the war, Sir Ernest, working this time independently, had schemed and adjusted and combined, until one day he was in a position to offer the option of purchase of the Constantinople-Baghdad railway to the British Government. "You can have it," he told them, "at this price:" and the price was quite moderate.   They refused that also: what did they want with the control of the Constantinople-Baghdad railway ?   From that time forward, after this double rebuff he never embarked in any further large financial operation.   He had made a very big fortune, and money had been the ruling paramount interest of his life.   Now, when his adopted country had withdrawn from the project of establishing a check on Germany's domination of Turkey, which they had asked him to put through, and had turned down a *coup* of his which would soon have proved of illimitable value, he was sickened of it all, and became, like so many others whose business is their life, a tired and disillusioned man.

War broke out three years after King Edward's death. By blood Cassel was entirely German, but he had long ago been naturalised as English, he had received honours and a high Order and was a Privy Councillor, and his loyalty to the country of his adoption was as firm as that of the Royal House of Hanover itself, who by blood were actually nearly as German as he.   But now many, indeed most of those who had battened on his hospitalities, who had travelled and been treated at his expense, who had made large money on his advice, who had sat bright-eyed with expectation in the hope that he would ask them to be his guests when the King dined at Brook House, or to stay with him at the Paddocks when the King was there, turned cold and elegant shoulders towards him. He was a Hun, they said, but surely they had known that before. He was a Jew, they said, but that had not prevented those of Norman blood from refreshing themselves with his excellent champagne. Much allowance must be made for them, for the country of his birth was at war with theirs, and racial antagonism in such circumstances is a matter of instinct that overscores reason. These purists, anyhow, quietly disentangled themselves, say, for the period of the war: forgetting, it is to be feared, that people like him, who, though of German birth, had lived for half a century in England, completely identifying themselves with her, were precisely those who, in such a crisis, needed friends most, and most needed sympathy. Possibly Sir Ernest had already rated at their correct value such friends as his wealth and his intimacy with King Edward had brought him: possibly he did not care. But had the King been alive, it is impossible to imagine that he would have taken part himself in so shabby an exhibition.

Sir Ernest behaved with the utmost discretion and dignity. He went on living his restricted life without any indication of resentment, neither asserting his absolute loyalty to England, nor aware that it could possibly be called in question, but he never attempted when the war was over to resume the social position he had held in King Edward's lifetime. It would have been impossible, and he no longer coveted it: he was disillusioned, he had seen through it, and he was quit of it. He had amassed a great fortune, but he no longer cared to add to it by further industry: where was the good ? It was easier to let the days go by, not disagreeably, but he would certainly never have chosen to live any single one of those days over again. He took long daily walks every morning for the sake of his health, and to combat a growing obesity, tramping four miles round the Park if he was in London, or along the sands at Bournemouth, with the adoring Pekinese dog that he had given to his daughter and resumed possession of after her death. He took it abroad once, forgetting that it would be quarantined on his return, and the little animal broke its heart with pining for him and died. . . Then after lunch, he read the papers, glancing to see if any of his horses had won a race, and he played Bridge for a couple of hours before dinner, and a couple more afterwards. He had no artistic tastes, the papers supplied him with sufficient literary sustenance, and so the days passed, according to his own devising, but without joy. Then one afternoon, after his morning's walk and his lunch, he went as usual into his study to read the paper, and a servant coming in two hours afterwards with his cup of black coffee, found him sitting with his head dropped forward. He had died without a struggle; for there was nothing that cost a pang to relinquish.

OTHER victims, besides Sir Ernest Cassel, of a grotesque race-antagonism during the earlier months of the war were Sir Edgar Speyer and his wife. He, too, was German-Jew by birth, but had been long naturalized, and was a Privy Councillor and Baronet of the United Kingdom. His wife, Leonora von Stosch, was half German, half American by birth, and previous to her second marriage to Speyer had been a professional violinist, not of the first rank, but an extremely sound and competent artist. Socially, up to the outbreak of the war, she had been a very hospitable and successful hostess in London on the up-grade; music was her platform, and during the summer before the war she was sailing bravely before a steady wind of prosperity, and had given at their house in Grosvenor Street concerts attended by Royalty, at which Debussy and Strauss had conducted their own works. Sir Edgar was Chairman of the Queen's Hall Concert Board: year by year he had been making good the deficit on the Promenade Concerts, paying upwards of £2000 annually in order that the less opulent class of English music-lovers could hear the best music, under the conductorship of Sir Henry Wood, at a ludicrously small sum: fourpence a night was the figure at which a season ticket worked out. He was also Chairman of several Hospitals, to which, like Cassel, he gave munificently, and of the amalagamated Company of London tubes and busses. He was thus intimately wrapped up in English interests.

But as soon as the war broke out he and his wife (perhaps it would be a shade more accurate to say his wife and he) were subjected to a persecution far more stupid and aggressive than any which had been directed against Sir Ernest Cassel. We have seen how he was credited with an incredible system of signalling from his house on the coast of Norfolk to German submarines in the North Sea, but that was negligible, the generic rubbish of lunatics which nobody really heeded, compared with far more serious attacks. It is true that his position in the world of international finance was a very unfortunate one, for, unlike Cassel, who had neither partners nor any connection with other financial houses, Speyer was a member of the firm of Speyer Brothers who were bankers in Frankfort and in New York. Sir Edgar was head of the London branch; his brother James Speyer in New York was notoriously anti-English, while the house at Frankfort was, of course, purely German in location and sympathy and everything else. Instantly the surmise and then the statement that Sir Edgar was in treasonable communication with his brother in America, and was supplying funds and information to the enemies of his adopted country was put forward, and obtained credence not only in the lunatic-submarine school of thought, but among level-headed and sensible people.

Previous to the war, of course, correspondence and transactions between the American and English houses

were part of the routine of business, but as soon as the
war broke out, Sir Edgar severed all connection with the
American firm, and had no further dealings with it as
long as he remained in England. This was duly and
prominently announced in the public press, but it had
no effect whatever in stopping the accusations of disloyalty and treasonable dealings that were flying about,
and even after his death in February 1932, the obituary
notices in the English press made no mention of this
severance. But until he and his family were practically
forced to leave the country within a year of the outbreak of war, there was no more ground for any suspi-
cions against his correct behaviour, than against the most
loyal of the King's subjects.

Meantime the persecution was intolerable. He and
his wife were cut, pointedly and deliberately, by friends
who in the summer had been staying with them and
enjoying their hospitality. Edgar Speyer was requested
to resign from the Chairmanship of a certain hospital,
because of the threats of substantial withdrawals of
subscribers if he remained on the Board. His wife was
asked to remove her young daughters from the school
they attended in London, for otherwise the parents of
English girls would take their daughters away, and she
was told that her presence at societies and associations
for women's war-work was not desired. A ring of
groundless suspicion was formed round them, and it was
also intimated to them that it would be wiser for them
not to go down to their house at Overstrand. Possibly,

had they carried on quietly, this monstrous hostility might have worn itself out, but unfortunately Lady Speyer lost her head a little, and spoke bitterly and unwisely about the ingratitude and perfidy of the English when the only possible course was to be silent: but indeed, it is difficult to see how the nerves of a highly-strung woman could possibly have stood the brutal treatment they were undergoing.

In the spring of 1915 Sir Edgar wrote to Mr. Asquith, then Prime Minister, intimating that he desired to resign his membership of the Privy Council. Mr. Asquith referred this request to the King; and, in answer to Sir Edgar's application replied that the King did not wish him to do so, and in strong and unmistakable terms he stated that he had the firmest belief in Sir Edgar's unimpeachable loyalty to His Majesty. Language could not go further, but it had no effect at all on this unreasonable hostility, and in May 1915, he and his family left England for America. From that time (and it is really difficult to blame him) he associated with the pro-German party in New York, to which his brother belonged, and indentified himself with them in utterance and in deed. This naturally became known, and eventually in 1922 he was deprived of his membership of the Privy Council, which seven years before he had desired to give up, for disloyalty, and no doubt the sentence was just. But it must be remembered that before this wholly intolerable persecution had driven him out of England, he had voluntarily dissociated himself from the pro-German interests of the firm to which he belonged, and that the Prime Minister, after investigation had pronounced himself fully satisfied as to his loyalty.

CHAPTER XII

GRUB STREET

I

JUST as it had been generally expected by an optimistic public that, the war once over, a period of dazzling prosperity in trade and industry would dawn on the nation, so those who were interested in the pleasant fields of art and of literature, expected that there would be a great flowering therein such as had blossomed at Athens after she had triumphed over Persia at Marathon and Salamis, or such as had been manifest in England in Elizabethan days after the galleons of the Armada had become jetsam on her coasts, and the might of Spain was broken. But these optimistic views were disappointed, for the analogies on which they were based were quite unsound. Neither Athens nor Elizabethan England were in any sense exhausted by their wars, but stimulated. In Greece the loss of life had been negligible, the war was won in two battles each of which lasted less than a day, and Athens was actually the richer for the war by reason of her capture of Persian spoils. Similarly in Elizabethan England the decisive naval battle that broke Spain was over in ten days, instead of lasting for more than four years, and instead of its having been won at frightful cost, not a single English ship had been lost: moreover the piratical expeditions of Drake and others to the Spanish Main had brought into the country very considerable treasure. In both these cases victory had been a strong stimulant to adventure and expansion, and a tonic to the imagination. "Where men will not give a doit to relieve a live beggar, they will give ten to see a dead Indian."

But now the case was utterly different: the nation collectively and individually was exhausted and impoverished by years of colossal sacrifice and expenditure; and of those who now, as artists and writers, should have been entering on the years of keenest vision and liveliest inspiration, for whom the time of the singing bird had come and the dream of "beautiful things made new" only a remnant was left, and they were not drunk with the heady joy of battle nor lyrical with the songs of victory, but sick of the foul horrors of the last four years, and cynical and tired and drained. Their imaginations had not been quickened, but were gravid with ghastly memories that must be digested or disgorged before they could regain their lucidity and sanity. No artist or writer can create except out of the stuff with which his mind is a-flame, and it was exactly that which they turned from with loathing. They should have been the morning stars of the new day, but of what were they to sing together? Of all that they longed to forget, and of all that nobody wanted to hear about ?

Fiction, it was soon evident, was to be the predominant form in post-war literature, and critics and readers waited for the appearance of some fresh mode, some new point of vision and method in the handling of the endless store of human experience, which the emotional stress and travail of the war had brought to birth. There were many competent novelists and story-tellers of an older day still at work, but it was not to be expected that they would now refashion their minds to newer forms. Rudyard Kipling, Galsworthy, and Wells were among these, stars of considerable magnitude, swinging serenely along on their ascertained orbits, and there were many other cheerful, established little luminaries as well. But the world knew about these more or less: what it wanted was the rising of the morning stars born of the long black night.

And then it began to be whispered that one such had risen: an entirely fresh method, an entirely fresh sort of presentation had been discovered. This star was James Joyce, and his method, in rough definition, was to describe in the utmost detail all that passed during a certain period through the mind of one person in his book, with collateral excursions. There was little or no selection employed; all that passed through his mind was relevant, and the sum was the exhibition or reflection of his stream of consciousness during that period. *Ulysses* was Joyce's masterpiece, an immensely long book, to be described by the thoughtful blurb-writer as the diary of Leopold Bloom's mind for one day. Then a second star, clearly belonging to the same constellation appeared: this was Mrs. Virginia Woolf, and the most notable example of the same method in her shining was *Mrs. Dalloway*. As in *Ulysses*, a mind and the impressions it received (again for a day) was the medium through which, with collateral excursions, all events and happenings were seen, and it was the consciousness of that mind, drifting along as if encapsulated in a transparent bubble, that surveyed the external world. What it registered constituted the entire record.

Now some quite intelligent and literary folk regarded these books as works of supreme genius initiating a new form of literary conception and construction: others not less intelligent regarded them as a record of unreadable trivialities, a catalogue, without any effort at selection, of the thoughts that passed through a human mind, the quality of that mind, whether subtle or commonplace, being apparently of no account. Instead of being presented with a story of some sort, with the reactions of mind upon mind, and with the developments in conduct and incident that result therefrom, they protested that all the mental sustenance they derived from these diaries was the uncohering reflections of some isolated and insulated consciousness that droned on, seemingly for ever, about the uncensored film-picture that passed before it. They asked if they understood the work in question correctly, and if that was all.

The fervent explained that that was all, and that it was infinitely more than had ever been put into a book before. What constituted the unique quality of these works was that they were no second-hand narrative, told from outside, of what befell, but the picture of these befallings in the mind of the watchers (Bloom or Dalloway), and thus they gave not only the befallings, but the stream of consciousness which carried them along. As for the want of selection complained of, the crowning glory of them was that there was no selection: positively not a trace of it. You were given the whole: for an hour or a day you were Bloom or Dalloway, instead of being told bits about them. The human document, so often proclaimed, and so invariably found to be full of omissions and interruptions, had arrived at last, entire and unexpurgated. Gloria in Excelsis !

Then James Joyce went further into regions where even the fervent lost sight of him sometimes: it was an Ascension, and clouds intervened. The English language was not flexible enough nor comprehensive enough to convey the complete stream of consciousness, and in his later works (such as *Anna Livia Plurabelle* and *Haveth Childers Everywhere*, episodes, complete in themselves, from his *Work in Progress*) he not only goes in largely for misspelling of English words, no doubt to convey the impression of dialect, but invents quantities of others. Sometimes it is quite easy to guess what they mean: when Anna talks of a "box of biscums," or an "amnibush," the signification is plain, and those who are accustomed to solve Torquemada's cross-words will no doubt think of the derivation of "galligo shimmey," and "porcupig's draff." But often conjecture as to meaning is vain, and "puertos mugnum" and "flaxa-floyds" and "mahat flumming" and such ejaculations as "Sachs eleathury ! Bam ! I deplore over him ruely. Mongrieff ! O Hone !" do not convey anything to most readers' minds. The orthodox view about such is, I believe, that they are expressive of Anna's mood. She felt like that, and since the English language (which Anna speaks of as "Angleslachen") did not provide her with words that adequately expressed what that mood was, she had to put it in her own way. "And why," asked one of the fervents to whom I had come seeking explanations, "why be so pedantic and ask what *precisely* Anna means ? Have you not also moods and vague stirrings of emotion which you could not accurately set down in words ? So had Anna Livia Plurabelle" . . . We left it at that.

In somewhat similar fashion (so the unconvinced reflected) did Humpty Dumpty remark to Alice: "Impenetrability: that's what I say." He could explain what he meant by it, and no doubt Anna could explain flaxafloyds bam. He would have got on admirably with Anna, and they would both have talked a language completely unintelligible to each other and everybody else.

But apart from the verbal felicities, with which these

episodes teem, and apart from the question of James Joyce's genius, the astounding thing is that the method (stream of consciousness) of this development of post-war fiction was ever thought to be new. As a method, it is precisely the same as that on which Henry James deliberately founded his whole scheme of the writing of novels. It was not invented by him, for Richardson, Gautier and, in particular, early Victorian novelists in that once-favourite device of the letter-writing hero and heroine, employed it to some extent, the letters recording the impression made on a mind by external events, but Henry James was the first great writer of fiction who deliberately and intentionally based his entire method on it. In his prefaces to the revised and definitive edition of his novels, he explains this method, and gives his reasons for adopting it to the exclusion of all others. In each book he took one character and made his mind or hers the mirror into which the reader looks in order to follow the story. Rowland Mallet, for instance, is the mirror for *Roderick Hudson;* Morton Densher for *The Wings of the Dove,* Strether for *The Ambassadors,* Maisie for *What Maisie Knew.* As author, he, of course, fashioned the mirror in each case, but when it is set up in its place, it is not the author who tells the story, but the story is reflected in that mirror: the mirror's stream of consciousness conveys the story. This method, it need hardly be said, is an extremely difficult one, for the author no longer tells his story directly (a comparatively simple matter) but presents it as it presented itself to a person in the story itself, the whole of which is seen through his eyes; but the advantages of it, if it can be successfully carried through, are enormous. The reader is no longer being informed by the author of what takes place, but is in the middle of it all himself, and vividness and intensity, the sense of being wrapped round and incorporated in the story, are vastly increased by this focus.

The method therefore, which was hailed as a new discovery in the art of fiction was not new at all, but had already been analysed and documented. Not only had Henry James consistently practised it, realizing its beauty and efficaciousness, but in these prefaces, which are his last will and testament regarding his novels, had written a complete primer as to how it was done. Whether James Joyce and Mrs. Virginia Woolf had studied them, or whether, being persons of admirably artistic perceptions they had inferred the method from his novels, or whether they had independently evolved it for themselves, it remains that for fully forty years Henry James had been working on these lines. The later practitioners, it need hardly be added, were not in any sense plagiarists, any more than is a pictorial artist who adopts a lately-discovered medium. Giotto worked in tempera, but when oil-paint was discovered it was open to anyone to use it: there is no patent in methods.

But Henry James's application of the method, which, as a defined and documented technique, he invented, was far more strict than that of those who subsequently adopted it, and, in its use, he employed that economy which distinguishes the great artist. The mirror he set up for the visualization of his story was permitted to reflect nothing but the matter in hand. It was securely fixed: it could not stray from its objective, nor did he permit it to wobble or swivel round to reflect anything, however enticing, that was not immediately concerned with it. There were no collateral excursions: also the mirror itself had qualities of its own, a magician, a Klingsor had fashioned it. By the end of the book therefore we are in possession of the uninterrupted impressions of what we have seen in the mirror, and of what the mirror itself was like, for the character of its series of reflections have characterized it. In *Roderick Hudson*, for instance, though Rowland Mallet (mirror) has shewn us nothing that has not been directly concerned with the tragic history of his brilliant and brittle friend, the unselfish and devoted part which he has played in that history has given us a portrait of him that is as vivid as what he has been reflecting. But a far greater diffusion marked the work of those who followed the technique of Henry James: diffusion indeed, a straying of focus, so far from being rigidly excluded, is an essential part of it, the idea being that anything, even the most extraneous and least significant that enters the stream of consciousness, tinges it, and is therefore worth recording. But the method is the same, and in both there is the same high seriousness of aim.

A FEATURE in post-war fiction was the flood of novels which were wholly concerned with sex, and which treated it with a frankness and wealth of physical detail hitherto unknown. It cannot be denied that the relations between men and women have been and will certainly always be of perennial and paramount interest as topics for fiction, and that novelists and playwrights will continue to dip into that ever-bubbling stock-pot to furnish the basis for their soup, but now we witnessed an epidemic among these gifted writers of serving up the stock-pot without other ingredients and flavourings, and floating on the top of many of these bowls was a layer of rancid fat. Often the soup was of the most tepid temperature, and one wearied of the plethora of joyless adulteries, bloodlessly committed in order to fill in a half-hour in which there was nothing particular to do. The contracting parties did not seem even to enjoy their lusts, which is the only thing that makes fornication and other allied pursuits interesting to read about, far less did they bring to their self-imposed task anything approaching passion. It was in vain that the late Mr. Arnold Bennett in his weekly manifestoes in the *Evening Standard*, (of which more presently), urged his colleagues to explore some other fields of human enterprise. The Stock Exchange, the Church, the management of an industrial business, chemical experiments, all these, he assured them, contained stuff out of which most nourishing and palatable soups could be concocted, and he practised his preachings when, not long before his lamented death, he wrote a prodigious treatise about the running of an hotel, in which, it must willingly be conceded, the whole staff from the general manager down to the junior boot-boy showed a far greater zest in their respective departments than the weary adulterers and their yawning mistresses in each other.

Now this greater freedom and frankness concerning sex in post-war literature was no doubt to some extent the result of the war: it reflected in the written word the greater liberty now accorded to the spoken word, for there was practically no taboo any longer on anything that might be discussed between boys and girls or men and women. On the other hand this Priapic license in the treatment of such subjects in books was, in the main, part of a continuous process that had been going on for decades before the war, and was wholly independent of it. There had been, for instance, about the year 1890 an animated debate in the Union Society at Cambridge, as to the propriety of removing the novels of Mr. George Moore from the shelves of the Library there, on the grounds of their indecency, and of the evil effect they were likely to exercise on the scrupulous morals of undergraduates. But long before the war these dangerously lascivious volumes were regarded as classics. Similarly Thomas Hardy's *Tess of the D'Urbervilles* had been regarded in the nineties, even in houses not ultra-puritanical, as the sort of book that should not be left about, lest a pure-minded girl might pick it up and suffer instant corruption. But long before the war it too had passed into the rank of classics. Similarly, Miss Rhoda Broughton once told me that for fifty years she had been writing exactly the same type of book, but whereas, when she began to write, no nice mother would let her girls read her stories, fifty years later no nice girl would care to read such mild stuff herself, but would not the least object to her mother doing so.

The flood of erotic fiction then that succeeded the war must not be taken to be anything like exclusively the result of it, but of a process that was continually at work. Certainly books are now constantly published which once upon a time would never have found a publisher, or, on their appearance, would instantly have been proceeded against, but to say that the war was responsible for the increased freedom with which such subjects were treated, is to disregard a process that had been going on in fiction since the polite world was shocked and startled first by Charlotte Brontë's *Jane Eyre*, then by George Eliot's *Adam Bede*, and then by George Moore and Thomas Hardy.

But this branch of post-war fiction certainly exhibited one new feature, namely that sexual perversion became a legitimate though for the present an incidental topic. Though all normal folk naturally regarded it with disgust, it had come to be recognized as a pathological deformity of mind rather than a mark of unspeakable moral obliquity, and fiction now included anything pathological as a legitimate subject. Book after book appeared in which it was introduced without disguise or reprehension, and it formed the main motif in the wittiest and most amusing farce of the decade, Mr. Compton Mackenzie's *Extraordinary Women*.   In the same year the topic appeared, no longer *pour rire*, but as the basis of a serious study, in Miss Radclyffe Hall's *The Well of Loneliness*.   The book had the respectful reception that it deserved as an able and sincere piece of work, it was spoken of with high commendation in so responsible a journal as *The Times Literary Supplement*, and it was in its second edition when a certain journalist (the time of the year being the "silly season" of early August) started a crusading campaign against it.   We must, of course, credit him with being absolutely honest and conscientious in his intentions; the subject of the book genuinely shocked him, and he assured his readers that he would prefer to put a phial of prussic acid into a girl's hands than let her read it.   It seemed to him most dangerous in tendency, and likely to corrupt the soul of a normal girl.   Better the prussic acid which would only kill her body.   So violent was the agitation that he raised that the Home Secretary intervened and, after a trial before a police-magistrate, in which witnesses who wished to speak on behalf of the book were not given a hearing, the order was made that it should be withdrawn from circulation, and the appeal against this decision failed.

But never was there so profound a psychological blunder as that which inspired the crusade which led to its suppression.   It is an admitted fact that many, if not most young girls and boys alike are first physically attracted by those of their own sex: the *schwärms* between girls, the school-friendships of boys are the awakenings of their uncomprehended passions, and must be regarded as normal not abnormal. Then with the maturity of their adolescence, the enormous percentage of these develop on normal, hetero-sexual lines, but there is a time when the emotional sex of both is in the balance: a girl may under a very strong stimulus, which puts homosexuality before her in an alluring and attractive light, be inclined over to that side, and her balance be permanently upset. But never was there a book which could give a girl whose emotions were still unstable a more terrible warning against abnormality. It presented a picture of the natural pervert who, not by her own fault in any way, nor from a lust for vicious experiment, found herself from birth tragically alien to her own sex, and deprived when she grew up of normal fulfilment of a woman in marriage and motherhood. It is one of the saddest books in the world, painting, as it does, in the most convincing colours the misery and loneliness, the sense of being a pariah that awaits the unfortunate women of this type. It would be far more likely to make any girl who had wavering inclinations, to turn with a mixture of horror and, it is to be hoped, pity, from the curse of such a predisposition. The book is its own antidote against the poison it was supposed to contain: it is impossible to imagine a stronger deterrent. Indeed, if the journalist mentioned above wanted to save any girl from what he thought might be the effect of its perusal, there was no need for his fatherly prussic acid: the perusal of the book itself would produce the desired effect.

IT is perhaps worth while examining a pronouncement recently made by one of our most authoritative and vocal author-critics which bears on the consideration of post-war fiction, because it sets down with admirable definiteness his conclusions as to the effect of the war on contemporary English literature: its precision makes it useful as a text for comment. Our critic says that it gave rise to a "period," which lasted for about ten years and is now (1932) dead. There were five authors who created this period (he tells us) and the most notable of the five whom he thus selects are James Joyce, Lytton Strachey, and D. H. Lawrence. The typical work of D. H. Lawrence (who after James Joyce next concerns us) was *Sons and Lovers*. The spirit that bound these five together was "their special brand of pessimistic negation," and the sentiments that inspired them were as follows: "This monstrous and absurd catastrophe (the war), through which we have just passed makes the soul of man a joke. Our heads are bloody, but we have at least the grim satisfaction of honesty. And we can still grin through our collars. . ."

Now passing over the unthinkable image of Lawrence ever grinning through his collar and the unfortunately stubborn fact that he wrote *Sons and Lovers* before,

not after the war, the notion that the bent and quality
of that tragic genius, perhaps the most original of any
fiction writer of this century, was in the smallest degree
affected by the war, is surely incomparably fantastic.
It would be every whit as reasonable to suggest that the
Greek War of Independence in 1820 inspired Gautier
to write *Mademoiselle de Maupin*, that the Crimean
War sowed in the adolescent Swinburne the seeds of
Poems and Ballads, or that the Franco-German War
of 1870 had anything to do with the development of
the genius of George Moore. Lawrence, as we all know
from *Kangeroo*, hated and loathed the war, but what
was there that he did not hate? And how could the
war be supposed to determine the mould of a mind that
had already completely declared itself in *Sons and
Lovers*?

Lawrence was an enigma, not by any means an unan-
swerable one, but one to which no single solution com-
prises the complete answer: the complete answer in-
cludes mutually contradictory solutions. In one aspect
he belonged to those to whom the seen world, com-
pounded of beauty and tragic hideousness, of torture and
rapture fortuitously distributed is the only reality, and
exists self-contained and final and inexplicable. Now
and then some genius of golden speech or song arises,
who celebrates the joys and bitterness thereof: Swinburne was one of these, and he, it is interesting to notice,
had like Lawrence strong masochistic tendencies: to both
pain was as fascinating as rapture, to Swinburne physical

pain, to Lawrence spiritual self-torture.   Chiefly, in this aspect (but in it alone), Lawrence was in revolt against the idealism that sees in spiritual yearnings and aspirations the highest emotion of which the consciousness of man is capable.   That puritanical gospel looked upon human beauty and the desire thereof as a devil-laid snare to entrap the soul: it even regarded the passionless beauty of Nature as only worthy of admiration if it led the soul to deduce therefrom the infinite loveliness of its celestial archetype, of which the semblance of things seen is only the faintest reflection.   To Lawrence the highest conceivable beauty was the visible: the swelling breasts of girlhood, the lithe muscles of a boy's shoulder, the sumptuous curves of a woman's body and the vigorous flanks of a young man were more to be desired than the glories of a remote heaven. Like *Mimnermus in Church* "the kind warm world was all he knew" and the kind warm world was his torture-chamber.   Asceticism or continence, the starving or the reasonable discipline of the flesh was to him not a virtue but a crime, yet not perhaps a crime so much as a stupidity, a thing not to be punished but to be pitied.   Sheer naked sensualism was an obsession with him: he stripped everything to the skin, and even the skin must go too, if such was the sentence of Lyre-bearing Apollo.   He ranked intensity of physical sensation higher than any consummated aspiration of the spirit, or the illumination of the intellect.   From it he drew his inspiration, and because, as we shall see, it tortured him, he loathed it.

This unbridled carnality is the chief theme of *Lady Chatterley's Lover* in the unexpurgated edition, as he wrote it; it and the counterpoint he weaves with it and the lyrical loveliness which accompanies it, are strangely disconcerting to its readers: but this was Lawrence. They feel as if, when wandering in some rose-garden of unearthly beauty, their nostrils were suddenly challenged by a pungent and abominable stink, and next moment they find themselves immersed in a cesspool. But it is that cesspool that fertilized his roses, and the more abundantly he fed them with it, the more matchless were the petals and the perfume of their flowering. The book contains the most exquisite of his writing: there is no height of crystalline ether to which he does not soar just because there is no well of deliberate animalism in which he is not simultaneously wallowing.

And yet behind the ecstasy and the pageant of physical passion, there is the sense of a gnawing emptiness; in spite of the enraptured indecency of it, it reminds us of the habits of an elderly man who, with the chill of old age freezing his veins, tries to warm his blood by exquisitely drawing improper pictures. The gamekeeper Mellor, Lady Chatterley's lover, stands for what Lawrence desired to be, a stallion-man in physical prowess, thereby fulfilling himself and reaping in purely physical acts the harvest that his nature needs. But Mellor fulfils himself only as a hungry man satiates the gnawings of his appetite by a smoking and half-raw beefsteak, and here, as in all the other stories in which

Lawrence deals with this theme, it is the woman not he who has the ecstasies, and who finds behind the physical fulfilment something of which the man has no idea. Precisely here, for Lawrence, the torture began: even while he wrote, thinking how content he would be, if he could gobble up such menu of graduated physical consummations as he devised for Mellor, he knew that such satiety was murderous of a higher ecstasy, for he longed to be merged in the soul as well as the body of the woman he loved, and he was incapable of being merged in either. Here then is the second answer (part of the whole) to the general enigma, and it is flatly contradictory of the first. In consequence of these simultaneous antagonisms, he viewed with hatred, as an enemy of his soul, the beauty that roused desire, he got to hate as an enemy of fruitless bodily desire, the yearnings of his soul, and he got to hate with a frenzied jealousy all normal men and women who found in sexual intercourse the peace that the satisfaction of it gives. He exempted neither woman nor man from this elemental hate, and most of all he hated himself, because he loved them, and because his love for them caused him this unspeakable anguish. And yet that very anguish (a third answer) afforded him a satisfaction that he got neither from hate or love in itself, because it was self-torture, and gratified his masochistic instincts. He sought for peace and found impotent nightmare: he sought for that complete mutual comprehension which alone would satisfy him, and the deeper he dug for it, the more the soil of his soul writhed

with the undying worm, and there was rapture in that.
And he feared all men and women alike, whom he hated
and loved, and most of all himself, for they and he were
his torturers.   He fled from them, though he never out-
distanced himself; he sought for peace in loneliness with
none to wake desire, and in mindlessness, so that thought
itself might be stilled, and with it hate.   Sometimes he
seemed to have attained that, at least he could imagine
himself to have done so, and he wrote:

> I am washed quite clean.
> Quite clean of it all.
> But e'en
> So cold, so cold and clean
> Now the hate is gone !
> It is all no good
> I am chilled to the bone
> Now the hate is gone !
> There is nothing left:
> I am pure like bone
> Of all feeling bereft.

No doubt he hated the war, for there was nothing to
which he refused that distinction, but beyond a couple
of medical examinations that proved his unfitness for
any sort of service, he never came remotely in contact
even with the fact that it was going on.   He lived, for
the greater part of its duration on the remotest coast
of Cornwall where, his wife being a German, he was
subject to a certain local hostility.   But he cherished this,
partly because it gave him something to resent, partly
because it was uncomfortable for his wife, and he refused
to move inland.   There he remained grilling over the

fires of his own stoking, unable not to hate and to love anyone who came within the range of his consciousness, and he devised (was it for his wife's express humiliation ?) a homo-sexual attachment to a young Cornish farmer who, instead of responding to his advances, laughed over his letters with his friends, and here was a further cause for self-torture.

This quarrel with life, and this hopeless desire to love was life-long: the first to incur his hatred was his own mother, when he was a boy, because by "seeking to make him nobler than he could be, she destroyed him." And yet this verdict was compatible, in the judgment of his tortured soul, with a deep tenderness for her. Anything in which moral codes had interfered, became to him anathema: his ideal, as indicated in all he wrote, which formed the entire subject of his *Apocalypse* was to get back to something completely pagan, a state in which neither virtue nor vice had any existence, nor law, nor obligation, to start afresh with the unregulated savagery of primeval instincts, and remain on that basis. The fact that civilization had been evolved out of them, did not concern him, nor the fact that the human race, however often he started them at the beginning, would evolve on precisely the same lines again. Desperately unhappy, hating the torture of love, and loving the torture of hate, his intelligence protested against the value of intelligence, and he reasoned in favour of a wholly irrational existence. Long before the war his *via dolorosa* that led nowhere was determined, and the war, at the most, furnished him with a further handful of sharp flints eagerly to lay thereon, so that he might traverse them with bleeding feet, but it had not the remotest effect on the development of his genius.

REFERRING briefly once more to the pronouncement above we find Lytton Strachey classed with Lawrence as a creator of a post-war period of "pessimistic negation": his typical book being *Eminent Victorians*. But that was published, not after the war but during it, and Strachey in his two other important books, *The Life of Queen Victoria* and *Elizabeth and Essex* employs precisely the mode and the technique which he had adopted before the war had had any chance of affecting either. Nor was his method new when he published *Eminent Victorians*: the method was really originated by Edmund Gosse, who, in his masterpiece, *Father and Son*, brilliantly and successfully revolted against the traditional method of Victorian biography, of which Mrs. Gaskell's *Life of Charlotte Brontë* is a typical example. That method was one of judicious suppression of anything that could detract from the mental and spiritual perfections of the subject: the biographer, fired by his own admiration, produced an idealized portrait, he omitted, he toned down, he exaggerated. If his hero was actually possessed of a foul temper, he wrote that he was quick to resent injustice: if he was a coward, he wrote that he was cautious: if he was of an ill-favoured countenance, he wrote that his face wore a winning or an intellectual expression, and the result was wholly false as the representation of an individual, and, generically, scarcely human.

It was Gosse who broke through that tradition of pious unreality: he held that truth was not the same thing as malice in dealing with the dead, and that a faithful portrait did their memories a better honour than a blue-eyed wax-figure of faultless features. There Lytton Strachey undoubtedly followed him, though without sacrificing one whit of his own originality. Both, moreover, in their actual technique, were masters of a suave and delicate irony, and employed in their drawing those fine etching strokes from the multiplicity of which, almost before the beholder can quite see what is emerging, there leaps from the page a cruelly faithful little sketch of their sitter, with just a touch, for more memorable vividness, of caricature. But in no sense whatever were Strachey's talents or that brilliant detached perception of his moulded or marred by the war.

II

THOUGH, until a certain vogue for books about the war started, the war itself gave birth to no "period" in English fiction, nor was responsible for any new mode, the years succeeding it saw the recrudescence of novels of colossal size; but, unless we conjecture that because the war had lasted longer than anyone had expected, books did the same, we can scarcely consider this as a result of it. At various times in the history of English fiction, the most distinguished novelists have habitually produced very long books: Dickens, Thackeray, George Eliot, all did so. But their length was determined by their contents, whereas in this new breed of elephants the contents were determined by their length. Length in fact seemed to be considered a merit in itself, and forthcoming books by these masters were advertised as consisting, say, of 720 pages: it was as if quantity was a guarantee of quality. To plan, to conceive on a large scale is no doubt a supreme, perhaps the most supreme gift in the writer of fiction, but the mere fact of length does not, unfortunately, imply large conception: a gigantic canvas may be filled with the pettiest images, and a small one vastly exceed it in essential size. A family history, for instance, covering many generations, and running to many hundreds of pages need not in any sense be a big book, nor need a detailed life of Methuselah through all his nine hundred years be anything but the most trivial of chronicles.

The fashion of very long books was practically obsolete before the war, though in the first decade of the century there had been two very remarkable specimens of this *genre*, one French, one English, both ranking from the moment of their appearance as obvious classics. *Jean Christophe* and *Old Wives' Tale* were truly big: their authors, both men of very high talent saw largely, and could not without curtailment of their sweep of vision and of the due perspective of a homogeneous picture have condensed what their subject demanded into a smaller compass. They were not beating their material thin, nor bolstering it up with parenthetical generations: the texture throughout is rich and solid, and the strength of the structure amply supports its weight. It rises, massive as a cliff. But with one noticeable exception, those who have since tried their hands at epical narration, seem to have suffered from the delusion that there is something big in mere length. On and on the weary chronicle proceeds, fresh characters people its pages, in the manner in which the same irrelevant crowd passes in various costumes across the stage of a moving picture; and just as the advertisement of a new cinema show entices us by the sumptuous announcement of how many people appear on the stage, so the author of one of these majestic tomes informed us in a typically advertising foreword how many "speaking" characters would be met with in the ensuing pages, and their number was certainly prodigious. But when it comes to construction then the weakness appears, and, as the architect adds fresh floors to his monstrous erection, rafters sag, ominous cracks open in the walls, extraneous fowls hoot in the chimneys, and their unfledged nestlings tumble down on to fireless hearths; vaultings crumble, and before the roof is on the whole crazy structure collapses, and the reader drags himself dustily from out the débris. And then, as like as not, he is told that the ruin is but the first instalment of a trilogy, and the architect is plotting out the site already. The next instalment will be founded on the ruins of the last, it will crash in its turn, and a third, vast and highly perishable, will take its place, and presently be merged in the underlying mausoleum. Such books when the author has not the power to plan largely or build firmly, but only to continue interminably now litter the fields of fiction. They do not, as Henry James once said, "come within measurable distance of being readable." Arnold Bennett succeeded once in epical fiction, when he wrote *Old Wives' Tale,* and since then, J. B. Priestley has succeeded once in *Angel Pavement,* in producing a long book of that rare quality. But Arnold Bennett failed dismally when he made his final attempt to write a big book, and only succeeded, like the rest, in producing a long one. In *Imperial Palace* he mistakes size for significance: it is a balloon-book, dismally collapsing when the gas is let out. The number of napkins that must daily be washed, the number of spoons and forks that must daily be provided for diners, the shelves of tablecloths in the linen cupboards, the saddles of mutton in the meat-safes amazed him, and he thought that the quantity of all the paraphernalia gave size to his book. He hoped to impress his readers with it: whereas the running of a small lodging-house where the landlady is not sure that the hash will go round, and the forks used for fish must be hastily washed and used again for pudding, and where the pensioners must put their labelled napkin-rings round their napkins, in order to ensure that they may

have their own "soilings" at the next meal, is really a
much bigger theme. But a large hotel was an obsession
with Arnold Bennett, just as sexual relations were with
Lawrence: he could not get over the fact he might walk
into those majestic portals, find a table reserved for
him, and set the vast machinery in motion for his solitary
meal. It was a fairyland, and he never quite understood
that others could enter its enchanted acres without ex-
periencing similar ecstasies.

But besides writing *Old Wives' Tale,* the book which
he himself claimed as causing the revival of long novels,
Arnold Bennett was chiefly responsible for another nov-
elty in the world of letters which has now attained monstrous proportions, namely that of novelists of a certain standing setting up as professional critics and
enthusiastically reviewing each others' productions.
The first objection to the system is that, as a rule, authors
are not good critics of their own art; and Arnold Bennett was no exception. For some years he wrote weekly
articles in the *Evening Standard,* on *Men and Books.*
They were chiefly about books, but when they were
about men they were entirely about himself. They were
pontifical pronouncements, curtly delivered like the sentence of a judge in a court of final appeal, and this habit
of peremptory judgments entirely ruined his style in
English: it is hardly possible to realize that the dignified
periods of *Old Wives' Tale* came from the same pen
as the jerky squirting ejaculations of *Imperial Palace.*
Apart from that, the habit of infallibility caused him to

become incredibly pompous in all matters of literary judgment. A friend of mine, for instance, once recommended to him a book I had just published; he glanced at it a moment, and assumed the official robes. "The worst of him," he said, with long pauses, "is that . . . He can't . . . Write." The sentence was duly conveyed to me, and so I sent back a message by the same mouth. I told him that I had duly received his pronouncement: naturally it was a blow, but though much cast down, I knew that when he had spoken the matter was finished. So, as I couldn't write, I thought I had better read, and I sent for one of his books. Then, to my despair, I found I could not read. . . The message had to be delivered twice, before he could take it in.

This practice, initiated by Arnold Bennett, of authors doubling with their own work that of regular and professional critics, has become a very general institution. Some, like him, having attained eminence as novelists, brought their prestige to bear on their new function; others sought to overscore their failure in the creative line by critical acidity; others, by a continual diet of novels, hoped to build themselves up into writers. Between them there came into being a ring of critics, all of whom are fairly prominent authors (or at least have tried to be), who can hardly help looking with a favourable eye on each other's works, aware that when their new book comes out, favourable eyes will be turned on them, and that they will be certain of a "good press." No doubt they all admire each other's work enormously, and since they have doubled the profession of authorship with that of criticism, why should they not say so ?   No doubt also they are all persons of strict integrity, and as critics would not dream of praising a fellow author-critic's work, unless they were genuinely convinced of its outstanding merit, but to know that if you praise your fellow-craftsman's work, he will certainly praise yours, is to lead integrity into temptation.

The principle does not commend itself, and if applied to other arts the undesirableness of it becomes manifest. Imagine the criticisms on a new play by Mr. Ivor Novello being written by Mr. Somerset Maugham, Sir Arthur Pinero and Mr. Noel Coward; or Messrs. Rubinstein and Cortot giving their views on a pianoforte recital by Mr. Mark Hambourg; or a Committee of Royal Academicians pronouncing on the merits of each other's pictures in the summer exhibition at Burlington House !   Whistler, it is true, asserted that nobody had any right to criticize a picture except a practising artist, but he screamed with rage when fellow-craftsmen failed to appreciate his symphonies, and called them dunces and ignoramuses.   But author-critics of today do not commit these gaffes.

Out of this willingness, even eagerness, of authors to extol each other's works, arose the philanthropic and literary venture called the Book Society.   Four persons, all of some standing in the literary world as critics or authors or both, with an Oxford Don, making five in all, were moved to do something for the book-loving public which, as one of the encyclicals in their monthly pamphlet so justly pointed out, felt itself bewildered by the immense mass of publications, mostly fiction, which offered itself for their perusal. They were shepherdless, and so these five shepherds, twitching their stockings blue, arose to guide them to the richest pastures. The sheep could enter the fold of the Book Society without money and without price, and having entered it there was an end to their bewilderment, for the five shepherds would every month select for them the best book that had appeared during that period, and recommend six others. Their recommendations with highly appreciative reviews signed by the eminent shepherds were sent forth free, gratis and for nothing to the sheep in a chaste little pamphlet, accompanied by a book-plate of a female Centaur carrying a torch. The only obligation on the sheep was to buy one of these books at the price he would have paid for it, if he had got it from the publisher, and if he did not like it he could change it for another, and put the Book Society's book-plate in that. *O bonum commercium!*

Of course it was not to be expected that the shepherds should be spending so much of their valuable time in helping the public not to lose theirs in the perusal of rubbish, for nothing. They received, as one of their pamphlets disclosed a year or two later, a small salary for their services, but, as the chairman of the literary committee lucidly pointed out, "not so high a wage that we could not earn more if we did something else instead."

What really repaid them for so much trouble, was that their office gave them "influence and power." It enabled them to help towards the wider reading of good books, and more especially they could call attention to new and young writers of high merit, who might otherwise have been long in coming into their own. This led sometimes to the exchange of very pretty and proper compliments.

But in spite of the grand work of helping the ignorant public to choose worthy books for their reading, and the noble service rendered to young and rising authors, the Committee was faced with certain recurring difficulties. Every month they were pledged to point out to their flock a book of great merit, such as anyone would be eager to possess, and it was not always that they succeeded in discovering one. In that case they had to select something which their fine taste must have told them was of very second-rate quality, and then the flock was disappointed and demanded something else. But these rare dearths did not deter them, and they went on punctually proclaiming masterpieces and recommending with hardly less fervour half-a-dozen other books. Just occasionally the hands that held the guiding crooks faltered, and once with regard to a selected book, the reviewing shepherd confessed: "Let me say at once that in my opinion ———— is not in the first class as a work of art." But that would never do, so he added: "I don't know what the first class is. There are no classes in literature." Then he gained confidence, and said that —————— was a book "that refuses not to be read," and ended on that firm note of unqualified praise. For very just reasons of delicacy the committee could not recommend each other's works, or all would have been easy, and they equally refrained from selecting the works of well-established authors, for the sheep knew about them already; it was therefore all the more to their credit that they found such an astonishing number of fine books. And every month of the year they took all this trouble for quite a small salary because of the power and influence it brought them in educating the taste of the public and in helping young authors.

The Book Society had, of course, its business aspect as well as its high literary aims: it was a private limited Company, consisting of some thirty shareholders, and its business was that of a bookseller. The literary Committee made its selection for the month and then the business manager or directors of the Company placed their order with the publisher of the selected volume. With their large membership they required thousands of copies, and thus obtained an exceptional discount, for the publisher could naturally execute so substantial an order at much lower rates than he could offer to the bookseller in a smaller way of business who only ordered a few dozen copies. Moreover the high opinion that the distinguished literary shepherds held of the book in question was a very good advertisement for them, and they were pleased to announce that it was the choice of the Book Society for the month. The shepherds were thus

not only educating public taste and helping to bring
young and meritorious authors into notice, but were
doing invaluable work by their recommendations for
the publisher and for the Book Society itself which
earned its dividends by buying at a discount which
could not be granted to smaller booksellers, and selling
to its members at the published price. For some reason
the shepherds were harshly criticised by certain folk
who professed to have at heart the dignity of English
letters, but how could a band of distinguished authors
(when they were not writing their own books) use
their powers more generously or serve the cause of good
literature better than by this sedulous search for masterpieces, and by these eloquent proclamations of their discoveries ? May they have more power yet, more sheep
to shepherd and much bigger salaries !

I have briefly alluded to the activities of this benev-
olent Society, because they were symptomatic of that
pleasant friendliness which during this decade from
about 1920 to 1930 prevailed among author-critics.
Never have authors generally spent so much of their
valuable time in praising the works of their brothers,
and in discovering for the benefit of all concerned so
many masterpieces. Nor was the Book Society alone
in its monthly good fortune: week by week critics in
the literary columns of the press discovered supplementary works of genius. Some of these were readers for
publishers as well, and then, of course, since they had
recommended their firms to publish a book, believing in

its merits, they were quite right to endorse their opinion of it as critics of the same to the *nth* power of superlatives. The belief that some great outbreak of literary splendour was about to dawn after the night of war or at least that one great master would presently arise, was in part perhaps at the bottom of these high expectancies: some young Messiah must soon be coming along, and it was wiser to salute with extravagant eulogy a hundred books by new authors rather than miss the chance of being John the Baptist. There might, too, be a whole group of Messiahs to be discovered among the sex-specialists, (and how humiliating to miss a whole group), or, among the great herd of elephant-books, a bevy of white elephants. It was far safer to hail every new writer, especially of the female sex as the long-expected, and not in a hundred years of literary history have critics discovered so many works of genius as they did in this decade.

Yet in spite of all these optimistic Chaldeans continually scanning the face of the literary heavens and hailing every new meteor which shimmered for a moment like a scratched match on the darkness, as the great epiphany, these bright little Lucifers never burst into flame, and the weekly crop of geniuses never showed signs of ripening. The number of sound competent writers enormously increased, and experimentalists in unheard-of frankness were as the sand of the sea, but, apart from books already mentioned, nothing of the slightest real importance appeared during this decade.

But *Angel Pavement*, big in conception, evidenced a certain detached ruthlessness, which may possibly be taken as a post-war note, and a propter-war note. A Dickensian quality superficially attributed to the author amounts to nothing at all: like Dickens he is a first-rate story-teller, but there is nothing further in common between the two. Of the established and recognized authors of the older sort, some rested from their labours, and Thomas Hardy, who died during this period, may safely be regarded as having joined the immortals of English fiction, but no other produced anything of such novel conception or treatment as to make us think that the war had awakened in him this fresh quality: they went on, some still briskly, some a little wearily, doing what they had done before. Of James Joyce, D. H. Lawrence and Lytton Strachey, I have already spoken. Highly significant work of theirs appeared during these ten years, but none of them were in any sense a product of the war, nor would they have written otherwise if it had never occurred.

CHAPTER XIII

STOCK-TAKING

WE HAVE glanced under the guise of parable or in direct review at certain aspects of life, in order at the end to sum up what effect those four and a half years of war had produced on the social, the economic, the religious, and the artistic conditions of the nation: to notice how collectively we differed, after the blessings of peace were restored, from what we had been before they had been withdrawn in August 1914, and what developments in the years that followed had resulted from that difference. In every respect, except with regard to the enfranchisement of women, the change had been destructive, and not a single constructive betterment or illumination had resulted. The nation had been hopelessly impoverished with providing on the largest possible scale the engines and apparatus of death, whereby its enemies also should be brought to the brink of ruin: taxes had soared, trade was irretrievably lost, and above all, colossally outweighing these colossal detriments, millions of its young manhood, in whose brains and blood had been stored the treasures of the rising generation, with all its prospective credits and potentialities, had been maimed and massacred. All that was sheer loss without compensation of any kind.

How the nation had rallied when the call came ! Men had dropped their wranglings and discontents like the unheeded toys of an idle hour of childhood. They had been knit together then in so imperishable a bond that never, surely, if in after years internal dissensions should arise, could the coherence of their essential unity be dissolved. All ranks and classes had fought side by side, and they must have been enlightened with the comprehension of each other which is the root of love. But all such visionary idealism proved to be as the idlest of dreams when the night is over and awakening comes. The war had not brought nearer to any that realization of the brotherhood of man which had been so confidently predicted, and the class-antagonism which had been seething before the war was now fed with fresh fuel in the furnaces that had been temporarily allowed to smoulder down, by the eager stokers of the Labour Party in and outside Parliament. Strikes broke out again, and were waged with a more bitter animosity than ever before, and this brotherhood distilled from comradeship in a common peril was indeed none other than the brotherhood of Jacob and Esau, who, ere birth, had wrestled together pre-natally in their mother's womb.

The Fatherhood of God fared no better than the brotherhood of man, for the war which, according to the message preached from a thousand pulpits, was to have brought near and made living to the indifferent and

the faithless, His protective paternity had proved that
these privileges must be heavily paid for and in advance.
Or perhaps he was a God like the God of Abraham, who
demanded the blood-sacrifice of his son for the due test-
ing of his faith and, this time, had insisted on its consum-
mation.   Already, before the war, the national indifference to matters of religion had been on the increase,
and the Church had been losing hold, and these four
years had vastly accelerated the process.   Some, those
chiefly who had seen service, rejected it with scorn and
bitterness, but apart from them, the attitude of the mass
of the nation was to turn from it as from some topic
that lacked interest and reality.   There was no slogan
or crusade against it; it was merely a bundle of discarded
and obsolete pieties, rubbish that lay littered in the house
of life, and had perhaps better be cleared away, lest the
microbes that bred in those mediæval rags should again
infect the spirit of man with fevers of childish supersti-
tion.   The house must be cleaned and set in order, made
habitable for a race that now looked on the world with
a more enlightened eye.   Perhaps if religion had been
actively attacked, the jellied indifference to it would not
have been so wide-spread, for those who still held to their
faith and their churchmanship might have put up a
fight; no cause is lost while there are enemies to be
fought, and while there is the will to fight them.   But
there were no enemies, for the mass of the nation was not
hostile to religion at all, and it did no harm in their opinion.   By all means let anyone who felt like that go to

church, and say his prayers, and believe that a Power, immanent and eternal and transcendental and accessible to human petitions, took an omnipotent interest in the flux and flow of temporal affairs in one of the smallest of the stars that he had idly peppered over the sky, and that he regarded with fatherly concern the needs of the queer little insects that crawled about there for a day and were gone.   They shrugged and smiled, not unkindly, and since Church and State (the former an odd survival of a superstitious code) still formed the constitution, the Censor saw to it that religious topics should not be treated with irreverence on the stage, and the police saw to it that ribald orators should not be blasphemous in the public Parks.   That was just a matter of good taste, and had no radical significance.   And the Church itself, as an organized body, lagged behind instead of leading: it behaved much in the way that the old people had done at Hakluyt, in refusing to stir out of the traditional ways, or examine into new ideas that were certainly cognate to its work.   Science had advanced, and psychical investigations had opened up a whole new field somewhere on the borderland that lies between what is called the natural world and the supernatural.   There was evidence that — possibly — communication was being established between the quick and the dead: the Church considered that the whole subject was so mixed up with fraud (as was indeed the case) that it had better be disregarded: there was evidence that certain men had the power of miraculous healing, and though such power was recognized in the early Church, the later thought such things had better be left alone. It did not recognize that our knowledge of God may increase as our knowledge of the powers that He has planted in Nature and in man increases, but preferred to remain incognisant, and dozed in its pulpits. Once the Church had been like ivy, firmly gripping and clothing the stone and brick of the structure of the nation, but now, owing to the growing indifference of its flock, which it did not attempt effectively to combat, and owing to the disillusionment of the war, it was as if some, at any rate, of its branches had been severed at the root, the sap nourished its growth no longer, and the withered tendrils, losing the vitality of their grip, peeled off and were rubbish to be swept away.

Nor, economically, so far from a new era of prosperity dawning, was there any sign, or indeed possibility, of a return to the secure solvency of pre-war days. Unemployment increased by leaps and bounds, with disastrous effects on trade, and the landslide that was bearing the nation to bankruptcy, spread over ever widening areas. Already the war had torn an immense chasm in the seeming-solid world, but now, when that huge rending was over, it began to be clear that not only could no concentration of human effort ever fill it up again, but that the edges of it along all its crumbling circumference were in a condition of the most perilous instability. Fresh falls from the sides of the chasm slid away into the unplumbed abyss, new fissures opened right and left, for the very foundations of the hills had been removed, and

the torrents of hidden springs poured from the frac-
tured walls, bearing with them the mud and sand of insecure strata.   None could tell what further disintegration might result, or what gigantic work of shorings and
proppings might not be necessary to avert further catastrophe.   The whole structure of Russia once thought
to be an impregnable bulwark against the enemy had
crashed, its granite cliffs had tottered and fallen, and in
their place was now a prodigious area of quicksands,
threatening to swallow up neighbouring kingdoms, and
of molten lava for their excoriation.   None dared to
guess how far that disruption might spread or what civilization it might not engulf.   France had her devastated
areas to repair, and in England successive Governments
shewed how completely blind they were to the growing
danger of national bankruptcy, by vieing with each
other in orgies of expenditure.   Or if they were not
blind, they shut their eyes to it.

And the nation was tired, the nation was bored, bored
with rationed offal and death and darkened streets and
Dora.   It wanted to forget and to amuse itself, to have
its cup-ties and league-matches, its race-meetings and
boxing contests and county-cricket to look at.   A little
relaxation after all this abstinence, and such amusements
as had been its year-long pastime before, must take prec-
edence of all other occupation.   Most of this interest in
sport was merely spectatorial: the vast crowds that began to flock again to the Oval and to Stamford Bridge
had no more intention of playing cricket or football

themselves than the Romans who thronged the Coliseum of entering the arena as gladiators, and just as the government of those imperial days thought that the best way of counteracting revolutionary tendencies was to amuse the people, to give them "panem et circenses," food and shows, so the successive post-war governments in England thought that the best way of dealing with industrial distress and unemployment was that the workers should have their unrationed food and their diversions. For the unemployed there was the dole.

England had always been particularly proud of her athletic supremacy, considering herself the birthplace and breeder of runners and fighters, and the home of all manly sports, and now she must re-establish herself again after this long interregnum. But during this decade a series of the most unexpected disillusionments awaited her. Other nations besides ours were taking up games with much greater keenness than before, and it soon became clear that our previous supremacy was due to the fact that no one had ever seriously challenged it. Now, one by one, all the laurels which we had imagined were ear-marked for English brows were snatched from us: there was not a single branch of sport in which, when challenged by others, we did not succumb to their superior prowess. Here and there, where foreigners did not compete, our laurels only passed to other races within the British Empire: nobody else, for instance, played cricket, except Australia and South Africa, so that remnant of birthright remained in the family, and nobody else for some years yet played our national forms of football. "Team-work," cried the patriot, "the real essence of sport is unselfish Anglo-Saxon team-work, and there no one can touch us." But when polo afforded a criterion of team-work, the results were not so reassuring. . . Far less reassuring were those of individual championships both in professional and amateur events. Georges Carpentier had already debonairly dethroned all English heavy-weight boxers, and then was beaten by Jack Dempsey of America, who surrendered the title to his compatriot Tunney, and in golf Walter Hagen took across the Atlantic the English professional trophy, and Bobby Jones presently annexed both it and the amateur cup. In tennis Jay Gould, an amateur, beat the English professional champion, and Etchebaster, Basque-French, is world-champion now; while at lawn-tennis, male and female, successive Wimbledons repeated the melancholy story. In international skating, not a single Englishman could be considered in the same class as the amateurs of Norway, Sweden, Austria and other countries. Though it may seem absurd to take so unessential an affair as games as a test of national fitness, it must be remembered that we ourselves had always done so for about a century before other nations began to play them, and had pointed to our unchallenged skill in them as a proof of our physical superiority to the rest of the world.

As might have been expected, we found a ready reason for our now demonstrated inferiority, and said that whereas we had always treated games merely as games

and nothing more, our rivals took them seriously.
There was a lack of ingenuousness about this, for no
country had ever treated games more seriously than we,
nor spent so much time and energy on them, and while
we were accounting for our *débâcle* in this manner,
school-masters were complaining of the fanatical worship of athleticism. The battle of Waterloo, according
to the dictum of the Duke of Wellington, which we
loved to quote in defence of games, had been won on the
playing-fields of Eton, but it was now impossible to believe that the great war had been won there as well.
The true explanation of our decline was that the young
men of every other nation were naturally just as keen of
eye and as swift of limb, and when they began to take
games about as seriously as we did, and were less hap-
hazard and more intelligent in their methods of training,
down we went. American universities, it is true, have
developed the teaching of athleticism to an extent unknown in any other country, but they concentrate
chiefly on base-ball and a peculiarly savage form of football, in neither of which branches of games does any
other nation compete.

Our decline in this particular province of activity, un-
important though it may be in itself, was symptomatic
of what was happening to us in every other. We were
slipping downhill, our tide was on the ebb, and never, it
may be safely asserted, in the whole history of England,
were ten crucial years, those from 1920 to 1930, allowed

to go so utterly to waste. It was as if the war with its ruinous expense in life and capital had brought back the golden age, and there was no attempt on the part of the Government to dispel this fatal fallacy, or to bring home to the people the need of industry and economy. The Liberal party, in a manner that has never been quite satisfactorily explained, was fast disappearing as a force in politics, and the remnant of it, by some sort of devolutionary process became like a malevolent ape, gibbering and chattering from its denuded tree: if it could not do anything itself it could at least prove a hindrance to others by pelting them with Welsh leeks. Nor were the gradually increasing forces of Labour nor the diminishing vigour of the Conservative leaders occupied to much better purpose: both were wholly taken up with party-interests, and either did not see or, seeing, wholly disregarded the paramount national needs. There was not one inspiring word, nor hint of warning from either of them, and though Rome was already smouldering and ready to burst into conflagration, no fire-alarm interrupted the incessant fiddling. Unemployment mounted and mounted, and money was borrowed to discharge the dole: exports dwindled, for the ruinous burden of taxation loaded on to capitalists and the rise in wages caused hundreds of factories to be closed, and the whole energies of the two parties, Labour and Conservative, were devoted to the capture of votes, and when they captured them, to fritter away time, which was already running short, and money which was running even shorter. In 1924 a Labour Government came in to power for the first time, and spent its few months of office in spending money. The same year the Conservatives got in by an overwhelming majority: their period of office was marked by an extension of female suffrage, as a bid for more votes, by muddled finance, by the absence of any attempt at economy, and by the amazing conjuring-trick which caused its majority to disappear like the vanishing lady: none could tell where it had gone. Five years later the Labour Government came in once more, and like a merry party going to the Derby Day, drove the poor ricketty old coach ever faster towards the crash that now seemed inevitable. The two parties in the House approximated so closely in voting-power, that they might be considered rival coachmen, each of whom held a rein. So the monkey dropped down from its tree on to the box, and said: "The true view of the situation is that I hold both reins. If one of you pulls the right, I shall pull the left, and vice-versa."

A degrading affair; so frank a prostitution of party-politics had never before been witnessed. Never had successive governments shewed less trust in the voters who had returned them to power; never had there been such a concealment of facts which it was criminal not to face and to publish. It was known to the first Labour Government, to the Conservative Government that followed and to the second Labour Government that there could only be one end, namely the sheer precipice, of this road along which they were driving loose-reined; they were in touch with financial experts who solemnly warned them that strict economy, and firm handling of the problem of unemployment could alone avert catastrophe. But neither dared sacrifice the votes which they thought economy would have lost them, nor, though the cost of living was now falling, made a corresponding diminution in the rate of the dole, nor investigated the patent abuses of its distribution. It was perfectly well known that hundreds of thousands of men and women took casual jobs for three or four days in the week and avoided regular employment, because thus they earned wages and were entitled to the dole as well. Any action with regard to this would have been unpopular and have led to loss of votes, and that was the one thing unthinkable. Every leader of a political party is naturally averse from doing what can injure his party, but none seemed to realize that a party is entrusted with power in order that it may act in the best interests of the nation, of which its party is but a fraction. As it was the nation became the paying-guest at extortionate prices of a bankrupt landlady, who still had sufficient credit to provide board and lodging without paying her rent or catering bills which, as she knew, were piling up year after year, and which she could not meet. At all costs she must keep a good table in order to avoid her guests' grumbling. As for the growing pile of bills, she would hand them over to her successor with a pretty curtsey. And did.

Meanwhile, with a view to preventing the recurrence
of any such conflagration as had lately burned up half
the world, the League of Nations was pursuing its academic activities at Geneva.   Five powers constituted its
permanent board, England, France, Germany, Italy and
Japan: other states were affiliated *pro tempore*.   The in-
clusion of Germany was obviously necessary if only for
the fact that she was now (leagued by blood and late
alliance with Austria) the buffer state between Western
civilization and the menace of Bolshevism.   The League
was also designed to be a Court of Appeal: it would ar-
bitrate in quarrels that arose between various states and,
with the five powers to back it, no fire could henceforth
be kindled, which would not have this magnificent hose
turned on to it before it could be dangerous.   But
neither America nor Russia belonged to the League, they
made no contribution to its debates, nor did they recognize the force of its decisions as being in any way binding on them.   America, having won the war for the Allies, * retired again beyond the Isles of Sunset.   Like the
nymph Danaë she had been wooed and won by a deluge
of gold, and now with a smile and her I.O.U. in her
pocket, she left her denuded lovers to puzzle out the
problems that were frankly insoluble without her aid.

And all the time, while the streets of Geneva were
a-flutter with olive-branches and resonant with cooing
doves and four times a year the delegates of the Powers
met to frame the regulations which should make war

* Page 84.

impossible and to adjudicate in minor disputes, the
chemists and mechanicians of the world, with their wits
sharpened by the thorough tests of four years, were in
unceasing session to render war, just in case it did occur,
a thousand times more ghastly than it had ever been.
Aerial warfare hitherto had been mere child's play with
toys, amateurish and productive of only the most trivial
destructions: a bomb dropped on an undefended town
might wreck a few houses and kill a score of civilians.
But there were attractive developments within sight:
there must be fleets of aeroplanes instead of small squad-
rons, and they must convey not only explosive bombs,
which were so disappointingly limited in their range of
devastation, but bombs charged at high pressure with the
deadly gases on which chemists were now fruitfully
busy. These experts in mortality had discovered some
most interesting new mixtures, the effects of which were
quite as satisfactory as the highest explosives, and of incomparably larger range. An aeroplane could carry far
more of these, for their casing need be but light, and the
buzzing queen-bee that led the flight of death and loosed
them from her womb could lay a whole comb of these
eggs as she passed. The gas they contained would be
heavy, it would creep along the ground and, as it spread,
lay a royal drugget of death over a vastly increased area.
Possibly also something useful might be done with bombs
filled with the bacteria of deadly diseases, and plague and
pestilence would rank among the artilleries of the future.
With the extension in the range of flight of the newer

planes, there was no camp or town in an enemy's country which would be out of reach. On the more circumscribed areas of military lines great developments might be made in the use of monster tanks: mine-fields would be multiplied in the seas, and submarine warfare was yet in its infancy.

By the spring of 1931, over twelve years after the end of the war, the League of Nations recognized that these new engines of frightfulness were in course of development, and in their debates over the limitation of armaments began to consider qualitative as well as quantitative limitations. There would be little use in limiting the tonnage of fleets on the sea or of battalions on land (quantitative) if these far more powerful engines of death (qualitative) were not prohibited altogether. If the League makes good progress in their debates on this subject, they may within a few years decide that poison-gas, plague (black death and other varieties), monstrous tanks and submarines are not legitimate weapons of war. What result that will have, we will presently consider.

Now it is beyond question that for a decade before the war the ever-increasing armaments of the great powers had been the true provocative of its outbreak: its immediate cause was merely incidental, and anything would have served for that. Germany's new and formidable fleet provoked an increase in England's naval strength, and the huge works of Krupp at Essen demanded a corresponding activity at Vickers' and Armstrong's: again

Germany's new military railways towards the Russian
and French frontiers automatically produced similar
construction on the part of her neighbours. Germany
meant war as soon as she was ready, and when she was
ready she took advantage of the murder of the Arch-
duke Franz Ferdinand, at Serajevo. But anything else
would have done, and this was merely an opportunity
which, adroitly handled, (and her handling was mas-
terly), would serve her purpose. And today, while the
nations are still suffering from exhaustion and disorganization, and while their representatives at Geneva are
trying to render war impossible, precisely the same provocative causes are at work again, making it every day
more possible and in the long run as inevitable as it was
in 1914. The olive-sprigged senators at Geneva may
succeed in imposing a limit on standing armies or on
battle-fleets, granting to each country adequate armaments for their reasonable protection, but by what sort
of ordinance can they prevent them building fresh fleets
of aeroplanes for express passenger or postal service, and
constructing convenient cradles which will hold and re-
lease the bombs for more effective destruction? Even
if the senators should some day succeed in agreeing that
poison-gas is *not* to be used in warfare, it is idle to suppose that if any of the nations, though signatories to such
a convention, found themselves involved in a war, they
would not instantly violate such an obligation in antici-
pation of an adversary who was sure to do the same.

Large armies and huge battleships are already growing
obsolete as the deciding factors of war in the future,
even as the strongest forts, thought to be impregnable,
were proved to be obsolete during the last war, and presently it will be as useless to impose a limit on armies and
ships as on cross-bows and culverins. The value of man-
power decreases as the efficiency of lethal contrivances
increases, and it is a Utopian dream to imagine that in
the future any nation determined to go to war, will submit to arbitration (as has already been proved in the
Orient), or refrain from using the deadliest weapons
that its laboratories can supply.

For all these Councils and Congresses are based on the
fallacy that man is at all times a reasonable animal. He
knows perfectly well, when he reflects, that war is bound
to entail incalculable loss and suffering on his country: he
knows, in his reasonable moments, that the various nations of the world, though they may preserve a racial individuality, are dependent, for their own welfare, on the
welfare of others, and that the world, like a hive of bees,
can only prosper when it realizes that the well-being of
every other nation affects his own, but never yet when
the stress has come and his blood boils with the sense of
injustice or the lust of conquest, has he remembered that.
Nor does he remember it to any purpose even when the
whole world, as is the case today, is impoverished and mu-
tilated by the effects of war, but uses the subtlest of his
brains to devise engines of more damnable efficiency.

A FURTHER extension of the financial shoals on which the world now has long been aground, was caused by the hoarding of gold by America, France and Belgium. Two things, gold and the brains which fecundate it and cause it to breed make the wealth of the world, and to store gold, as was now being done on a gigantic scale is to rob the world of its productive qualities. Gold packed in boxes and hoarded in vaults is not fulfilling its proper functions, which is to pay wages and to buy the materials for the advancement of wealth-producing industries, and as long as it remains out of circulation it is worth no more than boxes of earth. In reality, gold is concentrated industry: when fertilized by brains it will breed production, and production in turn will breed wealth. It is the distillation, in marketable symbol, of work, and yet we have the illogical spectacle of America, gorged with gold, suffering more from unemployment, from actual want and from stagnation in trade than any other nation of this disorganized world.

Such in brief were a few of the disastrous results of the war, and for years England drifted on under successive governments which aggravated instead of attempting to cure or at least to palliate them. The situation grew steadily worse, and by the year 1931 our hopeless insolvency was patent to all the world, and there was a rush on the part of foreign depositors to withdraw their credits from English keeping, since they regarded London, quite rightly, as being an exceedingly insecure harbourage for their capital. The pillars of the house were

quaking, there was not the slightest chance of balancing
the budget, and bankruptcy stared us in the face.   Not
till then, when a more imminent danger from within,
than had ever threatened England from without, was actually established in the house of her heritage, did the
Labour Government, then in power, officially acknowl-
edge to what a pass years of inaction, of fiddling and of
waste had brought us.   Pilot after pilot had steered for
the rocks, charted straight ahead, without altering the
course by a degree, while the passengers played quoits on
deck.   In spite of the derided warnings given two years
before by Lord Rothermere that insolvency was weekly
and monthly getting nearer, the nation, never consulted,
had never grasped the imminence of the peril, and now
they were up against it.

The events of the autumn of 1931 are too recent to
need any but the briefest allusion.   An election was held
and a National Coalition Government was formed, in
which Labour, Conservative and Liberal ministers of the
past and present all held office, the Conservatives, by a
natural reaction from the latest exhibition of irresponsi-
bility, forming once more the vast majority in the new
House of Commons.

The balancing of the budget, economy instead of extravagance and tariff reform were the three immediate
objectives.   Mr. Lloyd George was prevented by illness
from taking any active part in the campaign, but on his
return in the spring of 1932, he showed that his powers
of indiscriminate invective, when all other power had

gone, were quite unimpaired. Never has a man who had been Prime Minister of England, one, too, who in the darkest days of the war was steadfast and illuminating as a light-house beacon over a stormy sea given tongue to such a paroxysm of gutter-snipe abuse. Himself a master of political manœuvre and sleight of hand, he failed to recognize that "party" was for the present extinct, and choked with indignation that the country had been fooled and tricked by the Conservatives whom Liberals had always regarded as the Stupid Party: there was a humiliation! Showers of Welsh leeks were aimed at his late colleagues as well as at political opponents, for they were renegade. Sir John Simon, as usual, was sitting on the fence: Mr. Runciman was a self-centred Stylites on a pillar of his own building: Sir Donald Maclean, Sir Archibald Sinclair and Sir Herbert Samuel, who had been Shadrach, Meshech and Abednego, willing to be cast into the burning fiery furnace rather than bow down before the Golden Idol of Protection, had apostatized: Mr. Ramsay Macdonald was like a deranged motor-car that moves backwards with greater ease than forwards: Mr. Baldwin, not a man of volcanic energy, only resembled a volcano because he was so incessant a smoker, and the whole Government, though representing seven-eighths of the electorate was a naked sham. Then, perhaps unwittingly, he let slip the emotion that really inspired this scarcely sane tirade, and he told his audience that unless something was done, the Liberal Party would disappear altogether. Such were the spicy breezes that "blew soft from Ceylon's Isle," whence he had just returned, and his speech, otherwise better forgotten, is worth putting on record as a perfect and complete exposition of the policy which had so nearly wrecked England, namely that of putting the interests of Party before national needs.

But the mischief (so we must suppose that Mr. Lloyd George would call it) had already been done. Party had been shelved, exactly as had happened on the outbreak of the war, and for the present it counted for nothing as a motive force: to bring back buoyancy to a water-logged ship was a task that needed all hands at the pumps. For England during the wasted years that had elapsed since the war had become a second-rate Power, and she was on the verge of insolvency. To think of her thus was very difficult, but the sooner we managed to do so, the better. The question was if, nationally, we could ever learn that exceedingly bitter lesson, and, having assimilated it — for that was the first necessity — if we could behave in such a way as to accept our humiliation without bitterness, and to recover the respect of others and our own. It looks as if there is a chance.

May 11, 1932